Early Learning Theories Made Visible

Other Redleaf Press Books by Miriam Beloglovsky and Lisa Daly

Loose Parts: Inspiring Play in Young Children

Early Learning Theories Made Visible

Miriam Beloglovsky
Lisa Daly

Redleaf Press®
www.redleafpress.org
800-423-8309

Published by Redleaf Press
10 Yorkton Court
St. Paul, MN 55117
www.redleafpress.org

First edition 2015
Cover and interior design by Ryan Scheife, Mayfly Design
Cover artwork composed from images: (white background visible through the blue paper wrapped) © inxti/iStockphoto; (Green vintage background texture) © Maly Designer/ iStockphoto; (photo of child) by Crystal Devlin and Jason Devlin
Typeset in the Quadraat OT and Whitney typefaces
Interior photos by Crystal Devlin and Jason Devlin
Printed in the United States of America

21 20 19 18 17 16 15 14   1 2 3 4 5 6 7 8

Library of Congress Cataloging-in-Publication Data

Beloglovsky, Miriam.
  Early learning theories made visible / Miriam Beloglovsky, Lisa Daly.
     pages cm
  Summary: "Go beyond reading about early learning theories and see what they look like in action in modern programs and teacher practices. Each theory is defined—through engaging stories and rich visuals—in relation to cognitive, social-emotional, and physical developmental domains"— Provided by publisher.
  Includes bibliographical references and index.
  ISBN 978-1-60554-236-2 (pbk.)
1. Early childhood education. 2. Child development. 3. Education—Philosophy I. Daly, Lisa. II. Title.
   LB1139.23.B45 2015
   372.21—dc23
                        2014023961

Printed on acid-free paper

To our mentors for your guidance and wisdom.

To our students for inspiring us and reinforcing our commitment to the field.

To our colleagues for sharing the journey of preparing early childhood educators.

To our families for your support and encouragement.

Contents

Acknowledgments

Writing this book has been an incredible learning process. I am thankful to have embarked on this journey with my friend and writing partner Lisa Daly. Her integrity, creativity, and knowledge are a source of inspiration. This process was enriched by the incredible support from Alexis Baran, Arielle Baran, Alex Rudnicki, and Max Jaffee. Their encouragement, wisdom, ideas, designs, and editing made my own writing stronger. I want to thank my parents, sister, niece, and nephew for being there. And my friend Chris Marks who gave me the freedom to work the long hours. To my Niqui and Diego for their enthusiasm and love. —Miriam Beloglovsky

This book could not have been written without the support and encouragement of many family members, friends, colleagues, students, and editors. I treasure my writing collaboration with my dear friend Miriam Beloglovsky. I value our friendship and her reflective and academic abilities. For generous encouragement and countless listening hours during the writing process, I thank my California and Colorado families. They have always believed in me, supported me, and encouraged me to pursue my dreams. To my husband, Dan, I am forever grateful for his constant love, support, and patience. I would like to give sincere appreciation to my children, Ted and Jenna, who are a blessing and an inspiration. My colleagues Janis Jones, Debora Larry-Kearney, and Eunyoung Hwang provided continual encouragement and important insight over numerous lunch engagements. My 6:00 a.m. workout partners at Curves and my friend Kathie Congdon, who walks the trails of Folsom Lake with me every morning, helped to relieve stress. —Lisa Daly

We express our thankfulness to Crystal and Jason Devlin and all the children and families at Crystal's Creative Kids who provided the real-life stories. We want to thank David Heath, Kyra Ostendorf, and Redleaf Press for believing in this book. Our gratitude also goes to Elena Fultz for her thoughtful editing and guidance. —Miriam and Lisa

Introduction

Many students in our college early childhood education (ECE) courses teach in community early care and education centers. Some of these students enroll in our college classes to fulfill employer- or state-mandated licensing requirements. A smaller percentage of students have never worked in the ECE field but plan to in the future. Often many of our students have received their teaching positions prior to meeting all of the state regulations.

What is common to all students, regardless of why they are in classes, is their experience with the ideals of in-class theory versus the realities of real-life practice. They see a huge discrepancy between what is happening at their work sites or during field observations and the developmentally appropriate practices that are taught in their ECE classes. During classes students often share their frustration with inappropriate practices in the field and having to follow a standardized curriculum that is overwhelming for them and the children they teach. They comment on how they desire to work in the early learning classrooms described during our class meetings but question if such programs really exist. They marvel at our presentations that depict inspiring programs—the ones that show intriguing environments, meaningful activities, and children who are joyful in their explorations and experimentations. Frequently our students ask how they can approach their supervisors about making changes. They know what is best for children based on what they are learning in classes, and it resonates with them. Yet they find that they are unable to articulate their position about what they know is best for children.

Challenges Educators Face

If you have experienced these feelings, you are not alone. Many teachers today experience frustration in expectations to implement inappropriate practices, are overwhelmed by content standards, and are unable to articulate a philosophy of education and advocate for the right of children to learn through direct, active, hands-on experiences—that is, through play. These are serious challenges that face the field of ECE today.

Leaving Play-Based Curriculum for Prepared Curriculum

Early childhood professionals understand that children learn through play-based experiences, and yet many teachers find it a challenge to implement teaching strategies that support children's learning through play. It is increasingly difficult for teachers to provide experiences for children that are active, child-centered, intellectually engaging, and constructive. There is pressure from well-intentioned groups, such as policy makers and administrators, to push academics for young children, and many teachers are required to teach using a prepared curriculum. Families, too, are worried that their children will not be prepared for kindergarten without what they consider to be academic rigor.

And yet prepared curriculum often has little interest to children, in part because it often contains activities that are inappropriate and involves meaningless tasks. It typically does not take into consideration how children learn. The rationale to use such curriculum is to improve standardized test scores and prepare children academically for kindergarten, not to support their growth and development. Prepared curriculum also limits teachers' critical thinking, creativity, and active engagement in curriculum development based on the needs and interests of the children they teach.

Narrowing In on Standards and Accountability

All states have adopted standards or guidelines for preschoolers that outline skills, abilities, and knowledge that children should achieve in key learning areas of development. Many of these standards are based on elementary school content areas such as math and literacy and do not recognize that how young children learn is different than how school-age children learn. Learning is profoundly integrated in young children. Early childhood educators are required to teach so children can meet the standards, and some states are beginning to hold educators accountable for making sure that children have mastered required outcomes. This means that some teachers are mandated to measure outcomes and provide evidence that children have mastered required measures.

It is a challenge to balance the standards' emphasis on academic rigor with research findings that value play and young children's developmental needs. The standards may be designed for teachers to plan curriculum or for use as a framework for general planning, but they can also lead to narrowly focused teaching and inappropriate expectations. Too often, a teacher's time is dominated by completing assessments and required forms and conducting teacher-directed activities rather than spending high-quality time with children engaged in meaningful investigations.

Learning to Articulate a Philosophy of Education

A third challenge facing teachers is their need for a deep understanding of how children learn. In order to teach children effectively, teachers need to have a philosophical foundation for their work; however, many early childhood educators face a challenge when it comes to clearly articulating their field's practices and principles. Even if they instinctively understand it, many teachers struggle to explain their rationale for specific actions, environmental design, and other choices in the learning environment.

As professors of current and future early childhood educators, we have seen our students record good observations of children's behavior. However, many of the same students have difficulty connecting their theoretical knowledge with the observations they witness in a classroom. It seems that many early childhood teachers have difficulty bringing a critical-thinking perspective into their work with young children—and this is not for their lack of good intentions!

Today more than ever, professionals in ECE need to be the voice of children and speak up on behalf of children's rights. They must be able to make critical decisions based on strong knowledge of theory and research-based practices, and they need a solid foundation that allows them to do so. As ECE professionals, we see the need for teachers to practice intentionally connecting theories with real-life stories and real children. In our experience, ECE students' ability to understand and respond to children's needs and interests, and thus support their learning, is based on a strong theoretical foundation and reflective practice.

Moving from Theory to Practice

Many of our ECE students report that they have a good grasp of how children grow and learn. However, when they begin student teaching, many also admit that their theoretical foundation is not enough to facilitate children's growth in a significant or comprehensive way. It is not easy to thoroughly understand a theory that was introduced during ECE Child Development 101 along with multiple new and unfamiliar concepts. It is difficult to remember these theories without relevant review, even when students know they are important. And the theories are often introduced in a dry, isolated manner without concrete examples of real children. This approach makes it hard to transition from a theoretical to a practical application. It is problematic to try to comprehend, internalize, and apply theories if teachers have not clearly *seen* them first. We need to move toward a deep understanding and thoughtful analysis of theories. Then teachers can begin to make decisions that support children's learning based upon solid theoretical foundations.

When we teach ECE classes, our goal is to address these challenges by helping future teachers gain a solid understanding of child development theory. More importantly, we want teachers to be able to observe, reflect on their observations, use their knowledge of theories to support children's learning, and confidently articulate the *reasons* behind their practice.

How to Use This Book

This book is a blueprint for learning to understand and implement child development theories. It is written in a way that will help you practice learning, observing, and reflecting on theories based on children's behavior. Knowing child development theory contributes to understanding children's social-emotional, cognitive, and physical development, which then leads to real, supported practices. This book shows the connection between theories and real life, and invites you to practice doing the same.

Teachers of young children need to understand how young children learn. The theorists who researched and created these child development theories hoped to learn exactly the same thing. As you learn more about the theoretical models, you will find that you gain an immensely practical knowledge as well. Learning about child development theories helps you trace young children's social-emotional, cognitive, and physical development; however, theory needs to be seen in real life multiple times so that it is embedded in your consciousness. A teacher's knowledge is not about memorization; it's about application and practice.

This book focuses on making child development theories visible in an exciting and concrete way, but it should never be used apart from real experience with real children. Whether a first-time ECE student or a veteran teacher of twenty years, every teacher needs personal stories and experiences to move their knowledge from theory to practice. The chapters in this book guide you in really getting to know children, engaging with them, and responding to their interests in meaningful ways based on theory. As a group, early childhood educators are charged to verbalize what we know is "best" for children. This book presents a new framework for connecting theories to promote effective practices and develop strong philosophical arguments to support them.

Our Model: Looking for Everyday Examples

In our ECE classes, we often take time to visit our respective campus early learning programs to observe, reflect, and identify different practices. In one particularly significant visit, Miriam was at her college's center with students. Upon entering the classroom, the students noticed skin-colored art materials attractively displayed on a small table. Miriam told the students the classroom teachers set up the materials as a provocation. The term *provocation* is used by teachers working in Reggio Emilia, Italy, who place intriguing, challenging, or surprising materials in the environment as a way to provoke or stretch children's thinking. Provocations are not organized activities; they are materials simply—but intentionally—placed in the environment. Once in place, the teachers wait expectantly to observe how the children respond to them.

Miriam continued to facilitate the class discussion about the provocations. The students observed the children sorting and classifying the skin-colored materials on the table, and they discussed how this related to Jean Piaget's cognitive development theory. Piaget's theory reveals how children understand differences and similarities as they accommodate new information—in this case, by sorting and classifying skin-colored materials. Miriam clarified that this is Piaget's concept of how children connect new information to previous knowledge.

During the observation, one child commented, "Dark skin comes from mud" while exploring the materials. Miriam explained that children have preconceived ideas based on encounters with previous information. The students were able to connect the child's comment with Piaget's theory—their observation illustrated how a provocation can build upon children's thinking and increase the children's knowledge about skin colors. Miriam also brought up how Lev Vygotsky emphasizes the importance of language and conversations in promoting learning. A student asked if children discriminate at a young age. This question prompted Miriam to introduce the work of Louise Derman-Sparks and anti-bias education (ABE), which supports children's identity development and promotes justice, equality, and inclusion.

As the discussion continued, Miriam invited students to think further about the theories by introducing a variety of inquiry questions: "What theory do you think the teachers used as they selected the art materials in the demonstration environment? What other selections can be added to promote Maslow's concept of self-actualization through creativity? How is Gardner's theory of multiple intelligences (MI theory) integrated into the different spaces?" These kinds of inquiry questions challenge students to practically apply the theories learned in class.

After this observation, students shared with Miriam that the theories were starting to make sense. Their comments revealed a new appreciation for having a deep knowledge of the science of child development. The combination of a strong basis of child development, real-life experiences, and reflective thinking helped students connect theory and practice.

This same model of learning is used in this book as a strategy for you to acquire a solid theoretical foundation and implement the inquiry process to support children's learning. Going forward, we encourage you to deepen your understanding of early learning theories, develop a strong educational philosophy based on theory, and apply teaching strategies that support children's growth and development through play.

What's in This Book

The Learning or Developmental Theorists

Many excellent researchers have developed theories about how children develop and learn. For this book, we chose to focus on the work—the theory—of child development theorists who provide the foundation for the field's current early childhood practices. Each theory offers a particular viewpoint that supports different aspects of the development of young children. These varying perspectives provide a diverse, comprehensive view of the whole child. Throughout the book, we use the terms *child development theories* and *early learning theories* interchangeably. It should be noted that even though some of the theories offer specific developmental "ages and stages," these divisions are not static; children move at their own individual paces and are also influenced by the culture in which they live.

Part 1: The Theorists and Their Models

Part 1 contains an explanation of the theoretical model and its use in everyday life. It introduces the seven theorists we cover—Jean Piaget, Erik Erikson, Lev Vygotsky, Abraham Maslow, John Dewey, Howard Gardner, and Louise Derman-Sparks—and provides a summary of each of their theories and focuses. This overview offers the foundation needed to understand each theoretical framework. To help you understand the basic theory, a story showing children at play is set alongside each theorist, followed by an explanation that connects the children's behavior and development to that specific theorist's ideas.

Parts 2, 3, and 4: Theorists and the Developmental Domains

Parts 2, 3, and 4 look at the social-emotional, cognitive, and physical developmental domains through the eyes of seven child development theorists. Presenting the content by children's development through these three domains provides definition and clarity. The social-emotional domain involves social, emotional, and personality development. The cognitive domain involves all the mental processes that are used for thinking, language, and acquiring knowledge. The physical domain involves a child's physical growth and motor skills. The theorists did not necessarily divide their work into these categories, yet each theorist addressed specific components of value for each developmental domain. Looking at the domains in a holistic way offers a broader understanding of child development: every aspect of a child's development is related to all three domains as they interact with and influence one another.

Parts 2, 3, and 4 each begin with an overview of the developmental domain (social-emotional, cognitive, and physical). The overview establishes the fundamental basics of the domain and its critical role in children's development. The discussion of each theory follows a specific order: first we define the developmental specifics of the theory being discussed, which is followed by a story of real child development, then an analysis of that story through the theorist's lens. The children in the stories attend Crystal's Creative Kids, a home-based program owned and operated by Crystal and Jason Devlin. These stories and the photographs share their experiences of friendship, conflict, negotiation, and learning in their relationships with the children in their thoughtful and responsive program. We wrote the stories based on conversations with Crystal and her observational notes and photographs.

The discussion of each theory concludes with action pages that provide helpful ideas to guide you in your work with children and put the theories into practice.

Parts 2, 3, and 4 each end with a conclusion of the developmental domain and an example story to further your analytical skills. The example stories are designed to help you practice analyzing children's play based on theory. Throughout each part of the text, the foundation has been laid for you about theory and developmental domain, and the connection between story and theory has been made visible. The concluding exercise is an opportunity to reflect and further your thinking by putting theory into practice and articulating the connection between the two.

Part 5: A Professional Learning Story

The final chapter chronicles Crystal's growth as an early childhood educator. Crystal began her educational journey while in college, working full-time and embracing her roles as a mother and wife. As she gained a deep understanding about child development theoretical foundations, Crystal was able to facilitate children's growth in a significant way. We find her journey inspiring and empowering, as she transformed her teaching practices, environment, and curriculum based upon her research and knowledge of child development theories. Today Crystal is able to clearly articulate her foundational philosophy of education. Her journey provides inspiration for educators who desire to be a force of change in ECE.

Our Hopes for You

We hope this book helps you to develop a solid understanding of early learning theories. Knowing the theories is essential since they offer teachers a reflective perspective and a way to respond to children's thinking and ideas. Early learning theories strengthen the decisions teachers make about how to support children's learning within a theoretical framework. While knowing theory is one component of being an effective teacher, educators also need to be able to apply their knowledge of theory to real-life situations. Throughout this book, we hope the theories will help you gain understanding of how children learn and grow and guide you in supporting children's development.

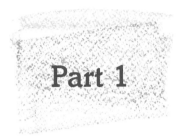

Part 1

The Theories as a Framework to Support Children

hild development theory gives educators a foundation of how children grow and develop socially, emotionally, cognitively, and physically. Theories help explain how children think and learn, develop motor skills, make friends and work with others, and gain self-esteem and a sense of identity. Each theory highlights specific behaviors and abilities that help early childhood educators know what to look for as they work with children. These aspects help teachers identify what is happening with a child and determine ways to support children's learning and development.

Teachers of young children must have the knowledge, skills, and dispositions that inform their practices about how children grow, develop, and learn. Many individuals enter the field with the idea that loving to work with children is all that is necessary to be a good teacher. But to fully understand and make informed decisions about children, teachers need to have a strong understanding of child development theories. Why are theories so necessary?

- Theories provide ideas, principles, and strategies that apply to working with children.
- Theories offer context to analyze and interpret children's behavior coherently and bring together different facts in a way that is meaningful and makes sense.
- Knowing the theories is having power to make informed decisions that influence children's lives.
- Theories provide a comprehensive way to organize and reflect on observations of children.

- Theories allow relationships to be established and implications to be explored between collected facts.
- Theories increase curiosity and move educators to further reflect, question, and research their own practices.

Think of the theories as a woven tapestry that creates a solid base to inform the work you perform with children. Each theory serves a function and offers a different view of how children grow and develop. Theory inspires the use of research-based teaching strategies and the creation of new and innovative perspectives. To better understand the theories, it is crucial to take a closer look at how each theory demonstrates and supports development.

Exploring Multiple Theories

Even though many of the theories include specific developmental stages, it is important to point out that these stages are not static and should not be used to assess deficits. They instead offer a view of multiple possibilities into the way children grow and develop. For instance, recognizing that trust is something that is built throughout the life span and not just a stage in the first year of life opens further possibilities and applications of Erikson's theory.

Theories do not function in isolation. The theories in this book share commonalities and challenge the discrepancies in each theorist's thoughts and principles. Each one offers an important contribution to your work with young children, and thus the theories need to be fully integrated as a framework for the decisions you make in your work with children.

Jean Piaget (1896–1980)

In Plain View: Piaget's Theory Defined

Piaget is regarded as an influential researcher and theorist in the field of developmental psychology and in the study of human intelligence. Piaget focused his research on how children's minds work and develop. He spent much of his professional life listening to and observing children and then analyzing his resulting data. Piaget's cognitive development theory reveals that children spend time making sense of the world around them through active involvement in meaningful activities. This theory emphasizes how children construct an understanding of the world around them and adapt their thinking based on what they know and through active engagement with the environment.

Piaget's theory is based on his understanding that children's minds process new information as children move from one stage of thinking to the next through relevant play experiences. He proposes four stages of development:

- *Sensorimotor* (birth to two years old): Children use their senses and motor skills (for example, sucking and grasping) to gain information about the world around them.
- *Preoperational* (three to seven years old): The ability to learn through symbols (language and mental representations of thought) is developed. Children use interactions with meaningful experiences to acquire knowledge that can be integrated into previous information. Children are egocentric.
- *Concrete Operational* (seven to eleven or twelve years old): Children have the ability to think logically about direct experiences and perceptions. Their thinking is restricted to what they can personally see, touch, and hear.
- *Formal Operational* (eleven or twelve years old through adulthood): Adolescents and adults have the ability to think abstractly and reason analytically. They can be logical about things they have never experienced.

Piaget suggests that children have their own unique way of thinking that differs from that of an adult. The terms that follow are from Piaget. They explain the cognitive processes that allow children to move from one cognitive stage to the next. They also apply to how adults incorporate new information into existing knowledge.

Adaptation is the process that happens any time new information or a new experience occurs. Adaptation takes two forms, assimilation and accommodation:

- *Assimilation* occurs when a person tries to make new information or a new experience fit into his existing concepts.
- *Accommodation* occurs when a person has to modify or enlarge her usual ways of thinking (or her *schemas*) in order to take in new information.

Equilibrium is the mental balance a person seeks between existing thought structures and new experiences.

Disequilibrium is the lack of balance and confusion experienced when existing thought structures and a new experience do not fit exactly into what a person (previously) knows.

Piaget understood that balance as described in the definition of equilibrium is accomplished through the assimilation and accommodation of conflicting experiences and perceptions. Assimilation, accommodation, and equilibrium occur, for example, when children visit a zoo. Aaron visits the aviary at the zoo and sees what he calls a "rainbow bird." Even though he has not seen a green-cheeked Amazon parrot before, he incorporates or assimilates his observations into his existing knowledge about birds. Aaron knows the animal he sees has feathers, wings, and can fly—so it is a bird. He doesn't know the name of the bird, but he sees the many colors and names it for himself. Samantha sees a koala bear and thinks it is a bear because the word *bear* is part of its name and because it has fur. Samantha is confused, however, as she sees the koala bear in a tree and not on the ground similar to other bears she has seen. She rejects the idea that a koala is a bear. She also rejects the idea that koalas are monkeys, as koalas do not chatter or swing from branch to branch. In doing so, Samantha extends or accommodates her thinking about koala bears. She knows that koalas are animals and has been told that they are bears. She needs to change her thinking to accommodate this new species. She achieves equilibrium when her mental concept of the animal name "koala bear" matches her new knowledge of real koala bears.

Organization is the mental process by which a person organizes experiences and information in relation to each other. This process allows a person to arrange existing ideas and adapt to new experiences in a way that is understandable, connected, and integrated.

Schemas are concepts or mental representations of experiences that help a person adapt and organize his environment. Schemas help people organize knowledge. Children use schemas to think or guide their behavior. For example, infants first learn about their environment through a sucking schema and a grasping schema—their methods for learning about the world affect the type of knowledge they can learn. A preschooler has a schema for a dog, friendship, or zipping her jacket. The schema structures develop and change with age and experience.

Piaget recognizes that children are active makers of meaning and that they construct their own knowledge when engaged in meaningful and authentic problem-based learning. As ECE professors, we validate Piaget's view of children as scientists in search of knowledge. We want early childhood teachers to know and believe that children are indeed the "protagonists" of their own learning, as shown in the following story.

Going on a Treasure Hunt, *Argh*

Constructing Knowledge

The children discover a shiny object in the rock garden. This exciting find leads to a search for more "lost treasure" and a complex treasure hunt dramatization that goes on for days. The teachers offer pirate hats and eye patch props to enhance the children's interest in becoming pirates in search of "the biggest hidden treasure ever found." The children use shovels to bury treasure (small, gold-painted stones), cover them with dirt, and then immediately dig them up. They read picture books about pirates and stories about hidden treasures and compare their own ideas to those presented in the stories. Bella thinks pirates bury treasure to keep it safe while Alex believes they bury it to keep bad guys from finding it. An argument occurs about the best place to bury treasure in the yard to keep it safe. Alex thinks behind the tree is best, but Alina believes inside the playhouse is safer.

Alina: You have to have a map so you know where to find it (the treasure), like in the book.

As the focus turns toward maps, the teachers offer real maps to support the children's thinking and help them create their own treasure maps based on their theories and assumptions. Bella insists on making an "X" to show where to find the treasure.

Alina: It's called "X marks the spot."

The teachers bury a treasure that the children then find in excitement.

Making Piaget's Theory Visible in Play

Throughout the pirate play sequence, the children negotiate, argue, and test new ideas and hypotheses. They learn about mapmaking, giving clues, the various treasures found by treasure hunters, and the tools treasure hunters used to accomplish their discoveries. The children build relationships, solve problems, and make sense of the world around them.

Piaget recognizes the capacity human beings have to gather information from external events and make them fit into previously acquired mental structures. This is seen in the way children manipulate the real maps to create their own treasure maps. Piaget views this process as a fluid one. In other words, new information is constantly adapted into previous knowledge. Knowledge continuously changes based on the information provided by a changing environment. As the teachers respond to children's ideas by adding new materials to make maps, they support the children's abilities to accommodate new information into existing knowledge.

Piaget connects developmental growth to the important interactions children have with peers and other adults. He argues that children construct knowledge as they interact with people, places, and objects in their daily life. The children in the story have a schema about pirates and buried treasure. They accommodate their "pirate schema" to fit the new information they learn about pirates from the books. The children reach a resolution (equilibrium) that treasure is buried to keep it safe from bad guys; however, they experience confusion or disequilibrium about where pirates bury treasure. One thing they discover is that pirates use treasure maps, and there is agreement that a map needs to be used to find the buried treasure. As the children pretend to be pirates, they demonstrate how Piaget's theoretical model maps out their own development—social-emotional, cognitive, and physical.

Erik Erikson (1902–1994)

In Plain View: Erikson's Theory Defined

Erikson was a pioneering psychoanalyst who introduced psychosocial development theory, which addresses the importance of mastering specific tasks in order to achieve success at later stages of development. In this theory, eight stages of development unfold as children and adults go through life (Erikson 1963). At each stage, a major conflict exists. For healthy development to occur, an individual is challenged to successfully negotiate the crisis or achieve a balance between two extremes. Erikson hypothesizes that if a crisis is not positively resolved, later problems will result in life. For example, if an infant does not develop a strong sense of trust, he will have problems trusting others as he moves through future stages. The first four stages are especially important as they describe unique social-emotional developmental tasks that occur in the life of the infant and young child. They are:

- *Trust versus mistrust* (birth to twelve months): During the first year, infants are busy building trusting relationships with the adults that care for them. Infants begin to develop a sense of their identity or who they are as the adult caregivers respond to them.
- *Autonomy versus shame and doubt* (one to three years): As toddlers, children become social beings and productive learners, gain a sense of self, and learn to master skills themselves. During this time, a sense of independence is obtained. Children establish their ability to be independent and express their own free will, ideas, desires, and abilities—against or separate from their elders and leaders.
- *Initiative versus guilt* (three to six years): During the play years, children take initiative through purposeful self-initiated play and gain a strong sense of accomplishment. Children develop a sense of self that allows them to express their ideas and thinking. They begin to take ownership of "who they are" and what they choose to do, both individually and as a member of a group.
- *Industry versus inferiority* (six to eleven years): During the school-age years, children learn to be capable and productive. Children master new skills that help them gain confidence and competence in their own abilities.

The next four stages cover the span between adolescence and late adulthood (old age). These stages are: identity versus role confusion, intimacy versus isolation, generativity versus self-absorption, and integrity versus despair. In this book we focus on the first four stages as the significant stages in young children's development.

Identity is another major aspect of Erikson's theory. Erikson addresses how a child develops a sense of identity, which is the ability to define oneself as a unique person with a sense of self. Erikson defines *identity* as the primary task of adolescence as an individual attempts to develop a moral, religious, and sexual identity separate from others. However, he discusses the beginnings of identity in childhood. A basic sense of ego (which means "self") identity is provided when an infant receives continuity, consistency, and sameness of experience. Erikson stresses that emerging identity bridges the stages of childhood: "Identity gains real strength only from wholehearted and consistent recognition of real accomplishment—i.e., of achievement that has meaning in the culture" (Erikson 1963, 235–236). This means that both culture and genuine acknowledgment from others have a strong influence on a person's identity.

Oh, How the Wind Blows

Mastering Challenges

As the children walk outside near the air conditioning unit they notice air blowing from it. Colter stops and puts his face close. He laughs when his hair blows with the air's force from the unit. Attracted by the sound of his laughter, other children approach him. They start to get close and let the air blow on their faces and hair. Colter picks up a leaf from the ground and releases it in front of the unit. The leaf swirls away from the air's power. Teacher Crystal approaches the children.

Colter: Wind, Crystal, wind.

Crystal smiles at Colter's fascination.

Crystal: What else can the wind blow?

The children begin to bring different items and watch mesmerized as some objects float in the air and others drop to the ground. Colter runs inside and returns with a feather. He tests to make sure that it too floats in the wind. After observing the children's interest in how certain items float with the wind, Crystal researches different opportunities for them to explore. She gives the children various objects to blow on using straws. The children test different ways to make objects move with their blowing.

The children: Which blows farther, a balloon or Ping-Pong ball?

Ryder: Oh, that is how the wind blows.

As the children's interest continues, Crystal sets up a hair dryer to blow Ping-Pong balls.

Making Erikson's Theory Visible in Play

As the children discover how the wind affects different items in the environment, they demonstrate autonomy of thinking. They have developed enough trust in themselves and others that they are free to explore multiple possibilities without the fear of criticism. They demonstrate initiative as they find new objects to both generate wind and to be moved by the wind. As they take the initiative in their play, the children are asserting power and control over the environment that surrounds them. With the support of Crystal and the other teachers, the children are planning experiences that allow them to test their ideas and thinking as they blow on a variety of objects using straws. While they play, they are able to test the limits of their own hypotheses about how different objects move in the wind. In this way, children begin to feel that their self-initiated efforts lead to a sense of purpose and success. The children in this story are gaining trust, becoming autonomous, and demonstrating initiative as defined by Erikson's theory.

Lev Vygotsky (1896–1934)

In Plain View: Vygotsky's Theory Defined

Vygotsky was an educational psychologist who introduced sociocultural theory. This theory asserts that children's cognitive, language, and social development is enhanced by their social-cultural environment. Vygotsky believes everyone has a culture and what and how children learn is determined by their culture. He calls language and symbols "cultural tools" that help people succeed at particular goals just as physical tools do. Tools such as language, signs, symbols, numbers, and pictures serve the purpose of supporting children in expressing their feelings, needs, and ideas as they navigate their social environment. In various cultures, specific words are used in speech and particular symbols are used for written print and numbers—what is the same across cultures is that they all use these cultural tools (words and symbols) to accomplish tasks. Central to Vygotsky's theory are the beliefs that children construct knowledge, that language plays a central role in children's development, and that development cannot be separated from its social, cultural context.

Children construct knowledge through active engagement and social interaction using their cultural tools. This means that children need hands-on experiences in order to construct their own understanding along with teachers who provide support. Consider four-year-old Harold, who finds pinecones on the ground during a nature hike. If his teacher points out the various types of pinecones by tree name, Harold will form a different concept than another child whose teacher points out the sizes of the cones.

Vygotsky emphasizes the social context of learning and development. According to his theory, cognitive development is always socially mediated. This means the construction of a person's thought processes—including remembering, problem solving, and critical thinking—are influenced by social interactions. Two of the main principles of Vygotsky's work that show the social nature of learning include the "more knowledgeable other" and the "zone of proximal development" (ZPD).

The more knowledgeable other is someone who is more skilled or experienced than the learner when it comes to a particular task, process, or concept. This person—who may be an adult or peer—adjusts the amount of guidance needed to support a child's potential level of performance. The more knowledgeable other provides more assistance when the child is challenged and less assistance as the child masters the task. This concept is known as *scaffolding*, although Vygotsky never used the term.

The ZPD is a concept Vygotsky (1978) defines as the distance between the most difficult task a child can accomplish alone and the most difficult task that he can accomplish with help. For example, a preschooler who struggles to put a jigsaw puzzle together alone may be successful with a little guidance from another child or teacher who suggests separating the edge pieces from the inside pieces.

The influence of play on development is an important component of Vygotsky's theory. He thinks play supports the whole child, including children's emotional, social, and cognitive development. According to Vygotsky, real play consists of dramatic or make-believe play and contains three aspects: "children create an imaginary situation, take on and act out roles, and follow a set of rules determined by specific roles" (Bodrova and Leong 2007, 129). There are specific rules of behavior to follow as a child assumes a role in dramatic play. For example, when a child pretends to be a firefighter, there are definite rules about how to behave that differ from pretending to be a dog. Vygotsky maintains that a child gains self-restraint, or the beginning of self-regulation, by taking on these roles in dramatic play. Vygotsky believes that not only does play support the development of self-regulation, but it facilitates a ZPD for cognitive skills and assists children in separating thought from objects and actions (thinking independently from what she perceives).

Vygotsky's theory reveals the importance of play as the main process in which children learn. As ECE professors, we want early childhood teachers to recognize the importance of powerful relationships and to build environments that cherish each voice, including their own.

How We Take Care of Baby

The Social Context of Learning

There are many new baby siblings in the program, and the children are very curious about how various families take care of babies. The children have noticed that when parents drop off the babies, they carry them in their arms or use different slings and "kangaroo" carriers. The children have also been observing how Teacher Crystal feeds the babies every day, and they spend time imitating her. They ask many questions and their curiosity engages them in a small-group investigation about baby carriers as well as the feeding and caring of babies. To respond to the children's interest, the teachers collect a variety of baby carriers and place them in the environment. They make sure to include certain types of carriers used by the families in their program, such as rebozos, *mei tai* wraps, and slings. The teachers also place in the environment photos and books representing families in their program caring for infants. They place baby bottles in the dramatic play area and incorporate more blankets for the children to use. The children feed the dolls and then rock and sing them to sleep. Bella gently pats her doll on its back and is heard saying, "There, there. It's okay. I'll sing you to sleep." She softly sings "Rock-a-Bye, Baby" to comfort her doll. Later the children test the carriers and spend time placing their dolls in them. The children are particularly interested in the rebozos and slings used to wrap babies on an adult's back. The children use the baby carriers to transport their dolls while they paint, build with blocks, and play outdoors. Teacher Monéa helps Bella secure a doll to Bella's back. Alina watches Monéa's instruction and uses a scarf to wrap a doll to her own back without assistance.

Vygotsky

Making Vygotsky's Theory Visible in Play

Vygotsky's sociocultural theory offers a view into the connections between people and the sociocultural context in which they live, using their cultural tools. In this story, the cultural tools of books, pictures, and language are used to support children's caregiving learning. By selecting specific books about caring for babies (which have the cultural tool of print) and incorporating family photos into the environment, the teachers increase the children's curiosity and offer them a way to compare and contrast the families in the program. The children also gain knowledge about caring for babies by talking and listening to others' ideas (using the cultural tool of language). The teachers offer children opportunities to talk about what their families use to carry infants, and they provide experiences for the children to explore the carriers and incorporate dolls in their play. This also helps to strengthen the children's relationships with their own baby siblings.

Through dramatic play, the children create an imaginary scenario of taking on and acting out the role of caregiver. They follow specific caregiver behavior by feeding their dolls with the baby bottles and then rocking and singing to the dolls in an effort to comfort them. The children follow other rules of caregiver behavior, such as keeping their dolls close to them and transporting them in carriers. These caregiver actions highlight Vygotsky's concept of play, which includes acting in specific ways that correspond with the role of caregiver the children are playing.

Vygotsky's ZPD is seen as Alina observes and then copies Monéa's instructions to wrap the doll with a rebozo. In this situation, Alina is learning from Monéa, who is more experienced at wrapping fabric. The children will continue to learn about their world through relevant cultural tools and play, and will gain the ability to accomplish new tasks through the support and guidance of adults and more knowledgeable peers.

Abraham Maslow (1908–1970)

In Plain View: Maslow's Theory Defined

Maslow was a psychologist whose main contribution to psychology was his hierarchy of needs. This is a motivational theory that looks at the needs humans have and how individuals behave to satisfy those needs. In other words, it asks: What motivates people or puts them into action toward trying to fulfill their needs? Maslow focused his work on a humanistic approach to the education of young children. He first introduced the "hierarchy of needs" in 1954 and continued to develop them as a way to explain the importance of the steps required for a person to achieve self-actualization, or reach her fullest potential (Maslow 1971). This hierarchy of needs is often represented in the form of a pyramid, with the largest and most fundamental levels of human needs at the bottom and the need for self-actualization at the top. The bottom two levels, physiological needs and safety needs, are called *basic needs*. These are the physical needs required to sustain life and essential psychological needs for security and safety. The top levels of love and belonging, self-esteem, and self-actualization, are called *growth needs*. As children satisfy the basic needs for food and shelter, they progress to a higher level in the pyramid where love, personal esteem, and acceptance take priority. This is what Maslow labels as gaining "self-actualization" or "self-fulfillment." In other words, self-actualization is the human need to be the best that each of us can be. The following is an overview of the characteristics seen at each level of Maslow's hierarchy of human needs:

- *physiological needs*: air, water, and food for survival, as well as clothing and shelter for protection from the elements
- *safety needs*: being able to trust your environment, including adults and peers; protection, stability, and order
- *love and belonging needs*: family affection, relationships, and peers' friendship
- *esteem needs*: self-esteem, confidence, achievement, responsibility, mastery, independence, respect of others, and respect by others
- *self-actualization needs*: realizing personal potential, creativity, spontaneity, self-fulfillment, lack of prejudice, morality, and acceptance of facts; and seeking personal growth and problem solving

In addition to his basic hierarchy, Maslow also discusses the significance of cognitive and the aesthetic needs.

Cognitive needs are the desires to know and to understand. They initially are seen in late infancy and childhood and include impulses to satisfy curiosity, to know, to explain, and to understand (Maslow 1987). Maslow states that children are naturally curious, fascinated, and absorbed. He believes cognitive needs are closely tied to basic needs since the desire to know and understand is often just as urgent as other "basic" needs. Maslow asserts that children are ready to learn and will learn when their basic needs are met.

Aesthetic needs include a desire for beauty, order, and symmetry. Maslow believes a craving for beauty "is seen almost universally in healthy children"

Maslow

(Maslow 1987, 25). Maslow (1971) is a proponent of education that fosters individuals who are creative, inventive, courageous, and independent, and he sees art education as a way to develop those characteristics. He writes, "If we hope for our children that they will become full human beings, and that they will move toward actualizing the potentialities that they have, then, as nearly as I can make out, the only kind of education in existence today that has any faint inkling of such goals is art education" (Maslow 1971, 55). In fact, he proposes that the concepts of creativeness and a self-actualizing person were much the same thing (Maslow 1971). Maslow believes humans need to think divergently in order to live in a constantly changing world, and art education is a means to develop critical-thinking skills. He emphasizes the importance in creative work of process over a final product.

Maslow provides early childhood teachers with a framework that builds on meeting children's needs to help them gain self-actualization. As ECE professors, we want to validate his work and introduce his contribution of creativity development. Maslow's work supports the creative process as an essential component in gaining self-actualization. We value creativity as another important developmental domain that has to be nurtured and supported. We want teachers of young children to find their own creativity and to create environments that offer hope and respect for every member of the community.

~~~~~~

My Body Is a Canvas

Advancing Creativity

Colter enjoys art and finds opportunities to engage in using a variety of materials and media to create his "masterpieces." He seems most interested in the movement

of the tools he uses and the sensory aspect of feeling various textures as he experiments by painting with his hands and feet. His delight is evident in his smiles and laughter as he makes short, thick, sweeping brushstrokes on cardboard and random scribbles with markers on easel paper. He works on little and large canvases, from a small piece of paper to a large piece of cardboard placed against the fence. Lately Colter has discovered a new canvas: his own body! The blue paint is spread all around his mouth as if he is putting on lipstick. The teachers enjoy watching every new creation and research different possibilities for Colter to experiment and paint with. They anticipate with excitement his daily prize showpiece!

~~~~~~

Making Maslow's Theory Visible in Play

Maslow argues that creativity is developed through the arts. The story illustrates how the teachers support children's creativity at each level of Maslow's hierarchy. When teachers focus their energy on motivating children to be creative and to recognize their own power and abilities, they are encouraging children to achieve self-actualization.

At Crystal's Creative Kids, art is an important part of everyday experiences. Opportunities to engage in art are present throughout the environment. Multiple chances are offered for children to express their ideas and to think through the use of the visual arts. The teachers design the environment, offer art experiences, and provide support for Colter to fulfill fundamental levels of his human needs and move to higher levels of Maslow's hierarchy. Although not stated in the story, Colter's basic needs for food and shelter are provided through the center's physical structure and meals prepared by Crystal. The environment is arranged so that Colter can paint in a safe, protected area without fear of criticism, thus supporting his need for safety. The children trust the environment, but more importantly, they trust themselves. They know they can experiment freely and that their work will be valued. They know they are free to make choices and use their bodies as canvases. Colter's need for love and belonging are supported as the teachers recognize, encourage, and value his creativity. They provide time, space, and materials for creative expression and support the creative process by offering new art opportunities that are free of preconceived messages. Through his smiles and laughter as he paints, it is evident that Colter's esteem needs are being met. These are also signs that he feels competent, confident, and assured in his ability to paint on different surfaces.

Maslow defines *self-actualization* as an ongoing process in which the goal is gaining full conscious awareness and full use of one's own abilities (Maslow 1971). Maslow argues that children benefit from multiple opportunities to engage with meaningful materials and interactions. This is demonstrated in the story "My Body Is a Canvas." Colter engages in exploration with his body, and the teachers offer him support and encouragement. Colter's spontaneous enjoyment demonstrates Maslow's theory that creativity is a process that promotes self-actualization.

Maslow

John Dewey (1859–1952)

In Plain View: Dewey's Theory Defined

John Dewey was an American psychologist, philosopher, and educator. He was a strong proponent of progressive education that included innovative changes in school curriculum and school practice. Significant aspects of his beliefs include the importance of whole-child development, learning by doing, curriculum based on children's interests and needs, and collaboration and problem solving as important components of the curriculum. Dewey asserts children must be invested in what they learn. He advocates for an experimental, rather than authoritarian, approach to learning. By experimental, he means that children learn through being active and pursuing their own interests rather than through drills and recitation. He argues that an environment that offers children meaningful interactions with materials, real tools, and solid relationships is crucial to the acquisition of knowledge (Dewey 1998).

Dewey encourages schools to be more responsive to children's needs. He insists that education involves meeting the needs—physical, social-emotional, and cognitive—of the whole child at each developmental stage. He identifies a wide variety of what he calls children's "instincts" that influence whole-child development, such as children's interests in investigation, artistic expression, communication, construction, attaining knowledge, socialization, and exercise.

In his book *Democracy and Education*, Dewey asks, "Why is it, in spite of the fact that teaching by pouring in, learning by a passive absorption, are universally condemned, that they are still so entrenched in practice?" (2008, 38). He understands knowledge as a product of doing rather than receiving. Dewey believes learning is a process of constructing meaning from direct experiences. He advocates that schools should provide materials and experiences that allow for hands-on doing. For example, if a teacher reads to children about the (literal) process of absorption, the children will probably not understand the process. But if children have opportunity to play with sponges and water or sand and water, they will experience the concept firsthand and will be more likely to understand what *absorption* means.

Dewey criticizes the traditional schooling of his time for its "passivity of attitude, mechanical massing of children, its uniformity of curriculum and methods" (1990, 34). He believes instead that schools should be like a home, in which a child participates in conversations and meaningful work. Children, he says, have four interests that lead them to learn: "the interest in conversation, or communication; in inquiry, or finding out things; in making things, or construction; and in artistic expression" (Dewey 1990, 47). For early childhood educators, this means knowing children, identifying their interests, and offering activities that have value and significance to further their learning.

Dewey wrote prolifically about democracy and education because he believes the two are closely connected. In his view, education is about gaining intellectual knowledge but also about learning how to live—about acquiring skills to be a productive citizen and using learned skills to become socially responsible. He advocates for a democratic classroom where every child's voice is heard and invited to be part of the decision-making process.

Dewey's theory informs educators about the importance of respecting children's interests, listening to their ideas, and responding by creating environments that encourage learning. As ECE professors, we believe in the importance of creating experiences for young children that are meaningful and real. This has inspired us to question our own practices and reflect on the ways we teach and learn. We want teachers to learn how to create meaningful and democratic environments where children can explore the freedom of learning.

Dewey

The Many Colors of the Leaves

A Community of Learners

The teachers observe the children collecting leaves that have recently fallen from the trees. Ryder, Alex, Cruz, and Nick are interested in putting all the leaves together in large piles. Jd is ready to jump in the piles of leaves and wants to help collect them. Sammy comments on the different colors of the leaves on trees.

As the teachers reflect on the children's interest in leaves, they agree that this is an opportunity to extend the children's knowledge about leaves, trees, and the changing of the seasons. They gather the children and invite them to explore the variety of leaves carefully. This curiosity goes on for days. Alex and Ryder continue to make piles of leaves as soon as they arrive at the program. Seeing this interest, the teachers add rakes for the children to build larger piles and practice their physical abilities. The children build a huge leaf pile they all jump into and become buried in the leaves. This challenges them to take risks and use their senses to explore the leaves in depth. The children argue, collaborate, and engage in meaningful conversations.

Other children begin to ask, "How do the colors change?" The teachers engage in research to find answers to the children's questions. In their studies, they dis-

cover that leaves get their color from three pigments: chlorophyll (green), carotenoid (yellow, orange, and brown) and anthocyanin (red). The teachers set up a chromatography experiment for children to investigate how pigments give leaves their colors. This simple scientific experiment helped children gain knowledge on how the leaves change color.

After a few day of testing different possibilities, the children's interest changes and they begin to pick up leaves and classify them as small, medium, and large. The teachers once again reflect on ways to extend learning; they place the leaves in plastic sleeves so the children can measure them. They include a chart for the children to record their findings. As the children do this, they are acquiring mathematical principles of classification, measurement, size, and width.

A strong sense of community is present, and the children once again work together to answer their many questions and research their multiple hypotheses.

Making Dewey's Theory Visible in Play

According to Dewey, children learn by doing. He believes the role of education is to create a community of learners where children can be involved in real and meaningful tasks. In the story, the learning begins with a simple discovery in the yard. The seasons are changing and the trees are shedding their leaves. As the teachers reflect on how to support children's exploration of leaves and how trees change with the seasons, they are learning along with the children about science and the weather's effect on trees and the changing of the leaves color. The teachers integrate mathematical concepts by supporting the children as they sort, measure, and classify the leaves. The children are practicing real tasks as they rake the leaves and gather them into piles. In this story the curriculum is relevant and the children are learning practical tasks, which according to Dewey are crucial to education and learning. In this example of democratic education, the teachers and the children learn together and make decisions that affect their interaction as a community of learners.

Howard Gardner (1943–)

In Plain View: Gardner's Theory Defined

Gardner is the Hobbs Professor of Cognition and Education at the Harvard Graduate School of Education. In 1983, he introduced the MI theory, which reveals that people use many types of intelligences, not just a single, general intelligence that is traditionally measured by an intelligence test. Gardner proposes that intelligence comprises eight different intelligences that can work independently or collectively. The eight identified intelligences are bodily-kinesthetic intelligence, linguistic intelligence, logical-mathematical intelligence, musical intelligence, spatial intelligence, interpersonal intelligence, intrapersonal intelligence, and naturalistic intelligence. Gardner believes each person has varying levels of strengths and weaknesses among these intelligences. He theorizes that intelligence is a combination of heredity and skills that can be developed through meaningful experiences (Gardner 2011b). It is important to note that Gardner does not see multiple intelligences as learning styles. Rather they are different faculties used for solving problems. "An intelligence entails the ability to solve problems or fashion products that are of consequence in a particular cultural setting or community" (Gardner 2006, 6). Gardner's MI theory serves as a framework to support children by revealing that children solve problems based on different intelligences and that all children have the capacity to create and invent in a variety of ways.

- *Bodily-kinesthetic intelligence* encompasses the ability to coordinate one's own bodily movements in specific and differentiated ways, skillfully manipulate objects, and use the body in an expressive way. This type of intelligence is easily identified in athletes, dancers, artists, performers, inventors, and other creative people. Strengths and interests include sports, movement, dance, acting, and motor activities such as running, swimming, biking, and climbing.
- *Linguistic intelligence* is the ability and sensitivity to communicate through spoken and written language. Strengths and interests include speaking, writing, reading, listening, rhyming, creating stories, discussing, learning languages, remembering information, and playing word games.
- *Logical-mathematical intelligence* includes skills needed for logical, analytical, mathematical, and scientific tasks. Strengths and interests include math, reasoning, problem solving, logical and

Gardner

abstract thinking, scientific experiments, pattern recognition, logic games, numbers, and computers.

- *Musical intelligence* involves skills needed in the performance, composition, and appreciation of music. Strengths and interests include singing, dancing, playing a musical instrument, recognizing rhythmic patterns, remembering songs and melodies, and listening to music.

- *Spatial intelligence* is the ability to perceive the visual world and manipulate and portray visual images. Strengths and interests include being observant, having color sense and visual imagination, doing art and 3-D modeling, looking at pictures, drawing, completing jigsaw puzzles, and reading maps and charts.

- *Interpersonal intelligence* has to do with the ability to communicate and work well with others. It builds on a core capacity to notice distinctions among others—in particular, contrasts in their moods, temperaments, motivations, and intentions. Strengths and interests include an ability to listen and empathize with others, making friends, socializing, collaborative work, strong leadership, and conflict resolution skills.

- *Intrapersonal intelligence* is the ability to understand your own needs, strengths, limitations, desires, and dreams. This is someone who is reflective and possesses a strong sense of identity and purpose. Strengths and interests include understanding self, knowing strengths and accepting limits, working alone, pursuing own interests, and reflecting.

- *Naturalistic intelligence* is the ability to understand the natural world. Strengths and interests include an interest in plants, minerals, animals, water, stars, weather, and seasons. People with naturalistic intelligence enjoy nature, being outdoors, hiking, caring for animals, and collecting items such as shells, rocks, or insects.

Gardner's MI theory offers the early childhood field a perspective to inform the way teachers work with young children. Gardner states that intelligence is not static or measured by an IQ test. Instead, intelligence is pluralistic and children have the possibility to use multiple intelligences to solve problems they encounter in real life and to generate new problems to solve. Children can develop the ability to create something new and innovative by using multiple intelligences in their learning. Teachers can support children's learning by being keen observers to identify children's strengths or intelligences and providing multiple ways for children to learn according to their strengths. As ECE professors, we want teachers to value their own learning and to recognize that intelligence is fluid and represented in multiple ways. We want to encourage teachers to use the MI theory as they design early childhood environments and guide children in learning.

~~~~~~

Mirror, Mirror

Supporting Multiple Intelligences

Mirrors are part of the environment at Crystal's Creative Kids. The mirrors are intentionally placed throughout the environment as provocations to support children's multiple intelligences. Children are challenged to make sense of their world through mirrors using their intelligences. Mirrors are mounted on the wall of the dramatic play area and above the work surface in the art area. One day John, Ryder, and Kainoa put on dresses. They sing and dance in front of the mirror in the dramatic play area. The boys laugh as they move their bodies rhythmically and expressively to the music's beat. They watch their reflections in the mirror as their bodies weave around each other at a fast and slow pace.

In the art area, Izzy works on adding texture to her clay cat sculpture. She uses a seashell to make fur marks on the back side of the cat by looking in the mirror as she works rather than rotating the cat to face her.

Izzy: I saw a cat that was so cute. It was only this big (she holds out her hands to show its size). It had little itty-bitty ears and cute little whiskers. Its teeth were sharp and pointy. They really hurt when they bite you. And it had claws, like this (she shows her fingernails in clawlike fashion).

Izzy continues to sculpt as she describes what she knows about cats.

Crystal set up mirror boxes (made from mirror tiles) on the tabletop with pattern blocks for children to explore and use in any way they chose. Sammy places geometric shapes inside the box on the bottom mirror tile. She forms a flower shape with a circle in the center and symmetrical triangles radiating out from it. She smiles as she looks at the flower's reflection in the adjacent mirrors.

Gardner

Sammy: Look, I made four flowers! (She moves the flower to different positions while looking at the mirror images.) I want my flowers to make room for more flowers to grow.

Sammy struggles with the flower's positioning, taking multiple glances from her hands to the reflections.

Mirrors are used in Crystal's environment specifically to support the infants and toddlers in discovering who they are and their relationship with the world. Colter spends his time looking at his image in the mirror. He gazes into his eyes. He touches his ear, mouth, and nose. He places his hand on a mirror lying flat on a table, removes it, and then places it on the mirror again. He presses down his other hand, which sticks slightly to the mirror. He pulls it up and presses both hands down. This game continues for some time. He leans forward and kisses his reflection in the mirror.

Making Gardner's Theory Visible in Play

Mirrors in Crystal's environment offer multiple perspectives, take children's learning in new directions, and provoke wonder and questions. Using mirrors in a variety of ways demonstrates how a teacher can support children's multiple intelligences through the inclusion of a simple material. In the story, the children's capacity for multiple intelligences is visible as they use mirrors in their play. John, Ryder, and Kainoa use bodily-kinesthetic, musical, and spatial intelligences as their bodies move purposefully to the music's rhythm. The children negotiate space as their bodies move in varying speeds and directions. Interpersonal intelligence is visible in their collaborative dancing effort.

Izzy's work with clay illustrates her strong bodily-kinesthetic and spatial intelligence. Her intellectual competence in these areas is seen in her ability to control fine-motor movements, envision a cat, and then sculpt a representation in clay. She is able to use her sense of perception, which is another characteristic of spatial intelligence, as she uses the mirror's reflection to make fur on her cat with the seashell. Izzy's linguistic intelligence is seen as she recalls specific details about a cat she has seen.

Sammy's work with the mirrors and pattern blocks shows her strong bodily-kinesthetic, spatial, and logical-mathematical intelligences. She is fascinated to see how different the flower looks with the mirrors. She uses her bodily-kinesthetic and spatial intelligence to problem solve how to move the flower to the right position. Her logical-mathematical intelligence is visible in the symmetrical flower pattern she makes.

Colter is developing his intrapersonal intelligence as he gains awareness of who he is. As he looks in the mirror, he sees his physical attributes, learns who he is, and how his body functions. Intrapersonal intelligence is visible in all of the children in the story as each one gains understanding of their own body's strengths and limitations, whether it is through dancing, sculpting, or designing. In this story, we see how children use what Gardner defines as *different intellectual capacities*, or mental systems. Also apparent is how children may use one or multiple intelligences and how teachers serve an important role in supporting children's full range of capabilities.

Louise Derman-Sparks (1940–)

In Plain View: Derman-Sparks's Theory Defined

Louise Derman-Sparks is professor emerita at Pacific Oaks College and originator of anti-bias education (ABE), which was originally termed *anti-bias curriculum*. This "theory" offers values-based principles and methodology to develop and support higher critical thinking around issues of justice, equality, and inclusion. Although Derman-Sparks did not develop a formal theory as Piaget or Erikson did, she conducted forty years of extensive research in the areas of race and education and multicultural education. She generated an anti-bias education approach to raise awareness about bias and teach how to reduce it, which has had a profound impact in the field of ECE.

Derman-Sparks and Olsen Edwards (2010) outline four goals of anti-bias education. They serve as a strong framework for early childhood programs to develop anti-bias environments that promote respect, justice, equality, and inclusion, while celebrating human diversity:

- *Goal 1—Knowledgeable and Confident Self-Identity*: "Each child will demonstrate self-awareness, confidence, family pride, and positive social identities." According to Derman-Sparks, this goal involves not only nurturing each child's individual and personal identity, but also includes nurturing social (or group) identities, which is a foundational component of anti-bias education (Derman-Sparks and Olsen Edwards 2010, 4). In an anti-bias

Derman-Sparks

approach, teachers take responsibility to respectfully support and make visible all children and their families to help children develop positive personal and social identities.

- *Goal 2—Empathetic Interactions*: "Each child will express comfort and joy with human diversity; accurate language for human differences; and deep, caring human connections" (Derman-Sparks and Olsen Edwards 2010, 4). This means guiding children's development of the cognitive awareness, emotional disposition, and behavioral skills needed to respectfully and effectively learn about differences, comfortably negotiate and adapt to differences, and cognitively understand and emotionally accept the common humanity that all people share.

- *Goal 3—Critical Thinking about Bias*: "Each child will increasingly recognize unfairness, have language to describe unfairness, and understand that unfairness hurts" (Derman-Sparks and Olsen Edwards 2010, 5). This means having the cognitive skills to identify "unfair" and "untrue" images (stereotypes), comments (teasing, name-calling), and behaviors (discrimination) directed at one's own or another's identify (be it gender, race, ethnicity, disability, class, family lifestyle, age, weight, etc.), as well as having the empathy to know that unfairness causes emotional pain.

- *Goal 4—Ability to Stand Up against Injustice*: "Each child will demonstrate empowerment and the skills to act, with others or alone, against prejudice and/or discriminatory actions" (Derman-Sparks and Olsen Edwards 2010, 5). This "activism" objective includes helping every child learn and practice a variety of ways to act in a variety of situations, such as when (a) "another child behaves in a biased manner toward her or him," (b) "a child behaves in a biased manner toward another child," (c) an adult acts in a biased manner (Derman-Sparks and Olsen Edwards 2010, 5). Goal 4 builds on goals 2 and 3 because critical thinking and empathy are necessary components of acting on behalf of oneself or others in the face of bias.

Individuals do not all experience bias in the same way. As adults, we are often unaware of our biases. Therefore, we unintentionally perpetuate the biases in environments we create. Understanding bias and inequality is a long-term process that can be difficult. It requires a critical analysis of our own personal attitudes around issues of biases. It's important to create an environment for adults as well as children where everyone's participation is sought after and valued and where it's okay to disagree. Derman-Sparks and Olsen Edwards (2010) write about how an anti-bias approach serves as a framework to look at differences without giving biases a value base that can affect children's identities. Anti-bias education offers a philosophy to support teachers and children in confronting prejudicial messages.

Children naturally perceive differences and similarities in people— from a very early age they notice their own and others' physical and cultural characteristics (Derman-Sparks and Olsen Edwards 2010). It's not a problem that children notice differences. The problem is when adults respond to or ignore children's comments and behavior about differences in ways that teach biases, fear, and stereotypical thinking. In other words, children learn prejudice from prejudice. It is important to teach children to celebrate human diversity and find commonalities while respecting differences. An anti-bias early childhood environment encourages teachers, families, and children to grow and learn together. The goal is to create a school community in which all members feel respected, valued, and a sense of belonging.

Derman-Sparks's goal of empowering children and creating communities where there is freedom, justice, and equality for all significantly impacts our work as ECE professors. Her anti-bias theory and perspectives strive to give children the ability to construct knowledge, be confident in their identity, and develop comfortable and empathetic interactions with diversity. We applaud the concept of social justice and desire to give children and teachers the tools and power to stand up for themselves and others in the face of injustice.

The Many Scarves I Wear

Learning about Differences

The children have a strong relationship with Monéa, a student teacher, and they spend a lot of time talking and sharing their ideas with her. She often brings creative experiences for the children to explore and discover new ways of doing things. One day, Monéa wore a scarf on her head.

Izzy (to Monéa): Do you wear a scarf because your hair is different?

This opened a conversation about differences in hairstyles and hair textures. The

Derman-Sparks

teachers took time to gather the children and listen to their ideas about differences and similarities in hair and skin color. They spent time finding specific books that would increase the children's understanding. They wanted to diffuse stereotypical thinking and help children learn respect for each other. They decided to incorporate a basket of colorful scarves into the environment. The children tied the scarves around their heads, wore them around their necks, and used them as capes. Monéa helped the children tie the scarves the way she does.

~~~~~~

Making Derman-Sparks's Theory Visible in Play

Children begin to notice differences and similarities among the people in their lives at a very early age. They also use this awareness to attempt to understand who they are and how they relate to others. In the story above, the children have noticed a difference in Monéa, in the way she dresses and wears her hair. Derman-Sparks notes that it's not a problem that children notice differences. The teachers in the story recognize that in our society, some differences are valued as positive and others as negative, and children absorb and act on these values. Recognizing this problem, the teachers want to empower the children to reflect and respond to prejudicial messages. They decide to engage in conversation with the children to identify the children's perceptions about hair and skin color and address any confusion or negative beliefs. The teachers want the children to gain respect for themselves and others, thus they take the time to listen to the children's views, answer questions, defuse stereotypes, read books, and allow the children to wear the scarves. According to Derman-Sparks, such actions create an environment for adults as well as children where everyone's participation is sought after and valued and where it is okay to disagree.

In Conclusion: Understanding the Theories

Child development theories are based on scientific study and observation. Theorists develop their beliefs from careful observation and analysis of children's behavior. Just as you use the theories to understand children's behavior, you should also practice observation to understand the children you work with. Through a solid understanding of child development theory and their own observations, teachers are able to know if each child's development is on target, recognize each child's needs and interests, plan meaningful curriculum, measure progress, extend each child's learning, and communicate development to families.

Part 2

Social-Emotional Development: Building Relationships to Learn

Social and emotional development are interconnected and typically referred to together as the social-emotional developmental domain. Within this domain, children learn to recognize and regulate feelings and emotions and establish healthy relationships. They acquire the social skills that allow them to focus, self-regulate, collaborate with others, and negotiate healthy arguments with people. The social-emotional domain includes a person's emotions and interpersonal relationships within the social contexts of family, community, cultural background, and larger society.

Social skills involve abilities such as working and playing cooperatively, getting along with others, seeing things from another's point of view, helping, sharing, and taking and waiting for turns. It is the process of becoming aware of oneself and others and gaining competence in initiating, developing, and maintaining social relationships. Friendliness, empathy, altruism, and actions of respect, consistency, and concern for others are all characteristics of social development. Emotional development includes acquisition of skills surrounding a person's emotions, self-esteem, self-regulation, and a sense of belonging, independence, and initiative. It is the ability to recognize emotions in ourselves and others and express feelings verbally, and includes a sense of self-identity.

Educators see social-emotional development happen as children spontaneously engage in dramatic play through the recreation of familiar, frightening, or confusing scenes. A child might be pretending to be a dad cooking, a mom caring for a baby, a police officer chasing bad guys, or a veterinarian taking care of a hurt animal. Social-emotional development can also be seen as children collaborate while constructing a city with blocks or painting a mural of the ocean. Social-emotional development is visible as children observe and imitate positive and negative behaviors of other children and adults. It is influenced by internal and external factors; each theorist's explanation contributes to the understanding of how children develop within this domain.

Jean Piaget

Arguments, Discussions, and Disagreements That Build Relationships

Jean Piaget on Social-Emotional Development of Young Children

Piaget believes that social-emotional knowledge is attained using the same methods as cognitive knowledge—that it is cultivated in the context of meaningful relationships and develops as children see things from another's perspective.

Development of social-emotional knowledge: Children use their developing social cognition—their understanding of other people's perspectives and feelings—to organize information about people and relationships, just as they organize all of their experiences to logically make sense of their world. To understand social relationships, children naturally group people according to children's perspective of identified attributes (for example: girl, sister, friendly, cooperative, or helpful). They also begin to categorize social and emotional behaviors such as "sharing" or "sadness." The concept of *equilibration*—the process of modifying or fitting new information into preexisting ideas—applies to social-emotional development. For instance, Michael likes baseball and may believe Joey is his friend because Joey is wearing a baseball shirt and asks Michael to play ball. Michael fits the new information of Joey's shirt and invitation to play into his preexisting ideas of friendship (that friends like the same things and do things together).

Context of meaningful relationships: Piaget also believed children learn in the context of meaningful relationships. This includes relationships with parents, family members, friends, and teachers. He believed social life is a necessary condition for the construction of logical thinking. According to Piaget (1965), peer interactions are critical to a child's development of social and moral feelings, values, and social and intellectual competence. He believed that when activities are emotionally and intellectually satisfying, they lead to prolonged effort or perseverance (Piaget 1981). This means that when a child enjoys interacting with someone, he will stay engaged for long periods of time.

Obtaining knowledge through another's perspective: Piaget found that young children are egocentric, which means that they think only about themselves and see things from their own points of view. As children's thinking develops, they become less self-centered and more aware of another person's feelings and thoughts. This ability to see things from another's perspective advances social development through empathy, moral development, and collaboration. The motive for cooperation emerges from feelings of mutual affection and mutual trust, which develop into feelings of sympathy and consciousness of the intentions of the self and others.

The Rock Garden

Learning in the Context of Meaningful Relationships

Ryder, John, and Alex are good friends and regularly enjoy each other's company as they play cooperatively together at Crystal's Creative Kids. During the past week, the boys found some rocks around the outdoor bed plants and planters. Intrigued by the rocks, they throw them into the yard. On a few occasions, rocks thrown by Ryder have hit his friends John and Alex.

The teachers gather all the children to discuss the rocks and the issues that have arisen with rock play. They believe that engaging children early in the decision-making process of how to use rocks without hurting each other will help. The teachers' goal is for the children to respect agreed-upon decisions through mutual participation.

Crystal: Teacher Jason and I have seen that the rocks you find in the bed plants are being used quite a lot. We also know that sometimes when the rocks are thrown they hit children.

John: Yes, one rock hit me the other day, and it hurt.

Ryder: I try to throw them low so they don't hit.

John: You did hit me and it hurts, so you don't throw low.

Ryder: I do throw low. I don't want to hit you.

Alex: I got hit the other day also. I don't like it.

Ryder: I did not hit you, Alex. I threw the rock, and it hit you by accident.

Alex: It still hurts. Don't do it again.

Ryder: Okay.

Alina: I like rocks but not being hit.

Sammy: Ryder, Alex, and John are mad when you hit them with rocks. It hurts. They don't like it. Do what I do. I like to use them to make things.

Jason: I hear that Sammy likes to build with the rocks. Does anyone else enjoy using the rocks other than throwing them?

Alex: I like making things with them. Alina and me made soup.

Jd: I like them.

Crystal: It sounds like many of you like using the rocks to play and make things. How are we going to keep each other safe while using the rocks?

John: Not hit people.

Izzy: We can throw the rocks at other rocks.

Jason: If we had a place with more rocks, would you only throw the rocks there?

The children all agree with this proposal. A solution is reached to make a designated rock garden. The teachers think it sounds too simple but decide to give it a try. They plan a rock garden and over the weekend bring in gravel and different size rocks that they place in one corner of the yard. When Sammy arrives, she notices the new rock garden right away and runs to it.

Sammy: More rocks!

She immediately sits and starts playing with the rocks.

Sammy touches the gravel and feels it by moving it in her hands. She takes a large quantity of gravel and tosses it in the air, and laughs as the rocks land next to her.

Sammy: I can't throw them at people.

Sammy uses the rocks for creating houses and buildings. She invites Ryder to join her construction effort. His energy shifts from throwing rocks to building rock sculptures alongside Sammy.

Sammy gets up and walks around the yard, gathering sticks of different sizes. She returns to the rock garden and stands the sticks up in a row by supporting them with the gravel. She works hard at placing the sticks in a line. Other children join the play. Alex gets some larger branches and brings them over to the rock garden. Alina joins them and together they dig holes, place the branches in the holes, and use the gravel to hold the branches in place.

Sammy: Look, it is a rock garden.

Alina: We can make things for the garden.

The teachers notice that Colter, the youngest in the group, has been standing by the four children and quietly watching them play with the gravel and rocks. He then turns and starts gathering the gravel with his hands.

Colter finds a plastic cup nearby and begins to fill it with rocks. When the cup is full of rocks he dumps the rocks into the toy truck that is in front of him. Colter continues to play with the gravel for a long time that day. He returns to the rock garden every day to scoop and dump gravel.

Over time, the children use the rock garden to build, dig, and hide treasures. They bury bones and pretend to find dinosaurs, ideas initiated by reading books about dinosaurs. They use sticks and fabric outside to create forts and places to hide. They argue and negotiate different ideas and things to do in the rock garden. There is no more throwing of rocks and the children's play is intentional and purposeful.

Even though Sammy is social and often involved in collaborative play on other parts of the play yard, she returns to the rock garden every day, after other children have grown tired of it, and plays alone. The teachers notice that her building becomes more complex and sophisticated.

She moves the rocks from one part of the yard to another and she incorporates different natural materials.

After the teachers read the book *Everybody Needs a Rock* by Byrd Baylor aloud to the class, the children begin to bring the rocks inside and set them in special places. They paint the rocks and ask the teachers to write words on them. They give the rocks names, and the teachers see the children talking to the rocks when they are upset, angry, or frustrated about something that happened during the day.

Making Theories Visible in Play

Piaget believes social-emotional knowledge is attained through the processes of equilibrium, assimilation, and accommodation. The story starts with Ryder having specific thought processes about his friendship with John and Alex. They spend time together, engage in play, and talk and laugh with each other. He receives information from John and Alex; however, that does not fit into his concept of friendship as the boys express displeasure about being hit by him with rocks. This information creates a state of disequilibrium for Ryder. This is seen as Ryder hears and reacts to John' and Alex's words about not wanting to be hit with rocks. Ryder gains a new equilibrium as he assimilates the words and body language from John and Alex and adjusts his behavior to find other ways of playing with rocks. Later Ryder responds to Sammy's suggestion of building with the rocks and shifts from throwing rocks.

Sammy demonstrates Piaget's concept of constructing social-emotional knowledge. She has developed the ability to recognize others' feelings, adjust to a new situation, and play with others. She acknowledges that John and Alex get mad when they get hit by rocks. Then, she adjusts to the new rock garden setting by finding new ways to play with the rocks, and she engages in collaborative building in the rock garden with Ryder, Alex, and Alina.

The children in this story have been together at Crystal's Creative Kids for most of their short lives. During this time, their relationships have been nurtured, which is a necessary component to develop social knowledge in Piaget's theory. The social atmosphere at Crystal's is one of acceptance and respect. The children's attitude is positive and reflects a feeling of community. Because of these significant relationships, the children's social knowledge expands during the course of this story. They are able to listen to each other and shift their actions from the antisocial behavior of throwing rocks to collaborative behaviors of using the rocks for building, digging, and hiding treasures.

Finally, Ryder's egocentrism or self-centeredness is demonstrated in this story. Other children argue that he is hitting them with rocks while Ryder insists that he is not. He even adjusts his story to include the fact he is throwing the rocks low so that he does not hit anyone. He then attempts to make sense of his position by saying that he throws low but the rocks hit the children by accident. From his point of view, he is the one who is right: the rocks that he is throwing are not hitting the other children on purpose. Ryder challenges the other children by sticking to his position and defending his point of view. As Ryder's social knowledge develops, he will gain the ability to see things from another's perspective.

TAKE ACTION: The Environment

Designing Environments to Help Children Construct Social-Emotional Knowledge

Piaget was a constructivist who believed people construct their own knowledge of the world through experiencing things and reflecting on those experiences. In a constructivist environment, every member of the community is valued and a feeling of ownership is created. Piaget's theory guides educators in providing environments that promote social-emotional development by supporting children's work, interests, and values. The following are some suggestions for creating a constructivist environment to support children's social-emotional development:

- Support children by displaying their work. Children feel ownership of their classroom when their art, writing, and documentation of their work is displayed.
- Provide attractive, interesting, and appealing materials. Curiosity and wonder are key ingredients to Piaget's theory. Incorporate attractive, interesting, and appealing natural materials into the outdoor environment to stimulate children's natural desire to explore multiple possibilities in collaboration with each other.
- Create spaces both inside and out that promote responsibility. Piaget was an advocate for children doing things for themselves. Organize

materials to be accessible to children so that they can find what they need and return items to their proper place without assistance. When children can independently access tools and materials, they develop responsibility and find a close connection to the classroom community.

■ Include materials to support children's developing interests. Piaget believes that real experiences and free play are essential for learning to happen. Create time and spaces for free play. Children learn when actively engaged in working and interacting with people, objects, and materials that support their curiosity with fantasy, art, and construction.

TAKE ACTION: Your Role as a Teacher

Building Respectful Relationships with Children

Piaget talks about the social process of cognitive, affective, social, and moral development. His research highlights the concept that children have many ideas that have not been taught to them. Instead, they have come to create them through a sustained process of exploration. Here are some ways to promote inquiry, encourage healthy discussions, and support children in resolving arguments:

■ Ask questions that engage children in deep thinking about their thinking, emotions, and interactions with others. Take the time to observe and listen to children's ideas and thinking. Support them by providing opportunities to test and explore these ideas.

■ Promote experiences for children to listen to other points of view. This enhances their ability to accept responsibility for their actions.

■ Support children to make decisions, even while dealing with feelings of frustration.

■ Allow children to argue and have powerful conversations with each other. When children argue they are constructing new knowledge and, with the help of a caring teacher, they can move to a more equilibrated state of development. Understand that children's reasoning is egocentric and that they believe things that happen together influence each other, or are a result of something they did.

■ Conduct group meetings to talk about issues and disagreements and the options for resolution. This is one of the most important things teachers can do to create understanding and a sense of community.

Erik Erikson

Children's Sense of Identity and Social Integration

Erik Erikson on Social-Emotional Development of Young Children

Erikson's theory of psychosocial development reveals how trusting relationships, autonomy, initiative, industry, and identity are crucial to children's social-emotional development. The focal point of his stages is an individual's relationship to the social environment and to identity development.

In Erikson's first stage of development, trust versus mistrust, an infant's basic experience of the world is either a secure place where his basic needs are met consistently or an unpredictable one. Both experiences lead to certain conclusions about the nature of social relationships. If trust develops, an infant believes the world is a safe place to be, his needs will be met, and he can count on adults when he needs help. If mistrust develops, an infant concludes that the world is an unpredictable place and that he has little control to influence what happens to him.

The second stage, autonomy versus shame and doubt, involves a toddler's struggle between the drive for independence and feelings of self-doubt about his own efforts. Successful navigation of this stage develops the emotional characteristics of security and confidence.

Initiative versus guilt is the third stage of development. In this stage, a preschooler's curiosity leads to a need to explore a broader social world or the feeling of guilt when actions result in failure or criticism. Success in this stage helps a child learn about social rules and expectations.

The fourth stage of development is industry versus inferiority. During this time a school-age child focuses on developing skills and trying different activities. Emotionally, he develops a sense of himself as capable or incompetent.

Understanding one's own identity is part of all of Erikson's stages. He views identity development as a dynamic process that happens throughout the life span and as crucial to one's healthy emotional and social development. According to Erikson, identity development is accomplished through the successful negotiation and mastery of a series of challenges that are present at each developmental stage. As children grow and develop, they begin to categorize themselves based on the recognition of their own abilities and characteristics or their roles within their family or community ("I am a sister" or "I am the youngest"). Children also begin to classify themselves in relationship (or comparison) to others. For example: "I have browner skin than Erin," "I am taller than Michael," "I am a girl," and "I can run faster than Stephen." Identity according to Erikson is both a state of "being" and a process of "becoming" (Uprichard 2008). A child is able to see herself as part of a group and connect to people based upon her classifications and how others accept her identity. As a child's identity becomes stronger, her social-emotional development grows along with it.

It's a Jd

Investigating Identity

Jd walks into the program one morning and has tears in his eyes. It is apparent to the teachers that something is wrong. Teacher Crystal approaches Jd and his mom to inquire about his tears. Crystal knows Jd has faced many health challenges in his short life, and she is concerned.

Crystal: Good morning. Jd, you look upset. You're crying.

Jd: I'm sad, Crystal. It's a hard day.

Crystal: It must be a hard day. I can tell that you're sad. How can I help?

Jd: I need to be by myself.

Jd walks over to the library area, takes a book off the shelf, and sits down upon the child-sized recliner. Crystal respects Jd's need to be alone and focuses her attention on Jd's mom.

Jd's mom: He plays with a little boy in our neighborhood, and he wants to look like him.

Crystal: What do you mean he wants to look like him?

Jd's mom: This little boy has light white skin and blond hair, and Jd wants to have the same color skin and blond hair.

Crystal: I am glad you shared this with me. I want to make sure that Jd's identity is respected and that he feels valued.

Jd's mom: He did tell me that there are no dolls here like him.

Crystal: Oh, I guess he is right. I'll have to make sure that we have dolls that look like him.

That afternoon the teachers gather. They walk around together and discuss the books available to the children. They notice that there are some books that show adults and children of color in active and leadership roles. They also see that there are a few photos that accurately reflect diverse families and decide they want to display more photos that show Jd and his family. The teachers plan to invite all families to bring photos and artifacts that can be added to the program. They want Jd's identity to be validated. There are dolls that represent a variety of cultures, yet they want Jd to have a doll that looks like him. That same day, Crystal heads out to find a doll that looks like Jd. After visiting a few places, she finds a doll that reminds her of Jd. The doll has skin color similar to Jd and, most important, the doll's hair is exactly like Jd's hair. The teachers place the doll where Jd will see it the next morning. They also add some more photos of Jd and his family in various areas of the program.

The next morning Jd runs into the center with his more typical happy energy. He *immediately* notices the new doll.

Jd yells: It's a Jd!

He runs to pick up the new doll.

For several days, Jd plays with the new doll. He pretends to be a daddy, feeding and changing his baby. He pretends to be a doctor, checking the doll's heart, ears, and eyes.

The teachers notice that when Jd plays with other children, the doll is close by. Jd and Bella enjoy spending time together, and they share caring for the doll. They often place the doll in a carrier and bring it with them outdoors. They both take turns carrying the carrier.

Bella: I carry Little Jd.

Jd: Let's just be careful. We can go to sit over there and check if he is okay.

They walk to the little bench and sit down. They check the doll and place it back in the carrier and cover it with a blanket.

Jd: He is okay; we have to see if his heart works.

Jd has a heart condition and goes to the hospital often. The teachers have observed that he does reenact his hospital experiences in dramatic play. The doll, "Little Jd," is helping Jd address a number of difficult issues with which he is dealing. Everywhere Jd goes, the doll goes!

Erikson

The teachers know that Jd's identity is developing, and they want him to feel confident about who he is. They know it will take extra effort to build Jd's resiliency and acceptance of himself in relationship to others. They also want the other children in the program to gain their own sense of identity and celebrate people's differences. They understand that when Jd says that he wants to look like his friend who is white, he is expressing his desire to be accepted.

The teachers decide to continue to support Jd in feeling more confident about his own identity. They intentionally read books that involve children of color in leadership roles. They set up opportunities for the children to bathe the dolls so they can notice that skin color stays with them and is not washed away.

The teachers continue to explore the concept of skin color as part of the children's identity by setting up a provocation for the children to investigate.

During group-meeting time, Crystal invites the children to listen as she reads a book and then engages them in further discussion about skin color differences and similarities.

After listening to the book, the children begin to compare their hands.

Crystal invites the children to continue the exploration by mixing paint to make their skin colors.

Jd: Mine is like chocolate! I love chocolate!

Sammy (laughing): Mine is like white chocolate! I like dark chocolate better!

Alex first paints his hand using a peach color. He goes over to the sink and washes off his hand and begins to paint it with dark brown paint.

Alex: I like chocolate too! I want to look like Jd!

This makes Jd smile, and his pride is evident in his interactions with the children.

Bella: It's all smooth! My skin is smooth!

Izzy: Mine is too! My skin is tan, but I like your skin too, Bella!

Spontaneously, the children begin to paint a mural using their handprints.

The children paint their arms, hands, and the paper. The experience is pleasurable, and their interactions continue for a long time.

After a while, they start to wash their hands and they notice that the paint changes the color of the water.

Nate: Look, the water is darker.

Izzy: Oh, oh, it is getting darker, but see, my hand is the same color.

Jd: My paint is off and my color is the same.

Crystal: You notice that the paint washes off and changes the water, but your skin stays the same. That is what makes us special.

Bella: My skin is also smooth.

Kainoa: My dad was in the sun and his skin was red and it hurt. Now it is not red.

Sammy: My brother had the same and was red.

Crystal: When we spend time in the sun, we can get sunburned and our skin gets red and hurts. That is why we wear sunscreen.

Jd: But my skin is dark like Little Jd and I like it. We are the same.

After all of this, Jd's mom let the teachers know that Jd no longer says he wants to be or look like his white peers.

Making Theories Visible in Play

Jd's struggle with his sense of identity is visible in his uncertainty about his skin color. He notices the difference between his darker skin and his friend's lighter tone and expresses sadness in being different. In fact, Jd states that he wants to look like his friend. In this story, the teachers respond to Jd's quest to find his identity. They want him to feel proud and embrace his differences and similarities. They reflect on the environment and realize that there are not enough items that reflect Jd's identity. Teacher Crystal's decision to bring in a doll that looks like Jd reinforces his identity. This is evident when he runs to the doll and exclaims, "It's a Jd!"

Jd has established a strong sense of trust with Crystal. He feels safe with her and comfortable expressing his sadness. As Jd trusts the people in his life, in this case the teachers and children in the classroom, he is able to explore his identity without feeling shame or doubt as to who he is. In turning the children's conversations into an opportunity to support their identity, the teachers focus on building a strong sense of trust among the children so they can feel free to explore their physical characteristics. The teachers promote a sense of trust by being responsive, available, ready to support the children's explorations, showing interest in the children's investigations, talking to the children in a way that helps them feel confident and assured, and responding promptly to their inquiries. When the teachers set in motion the exploration of skin color, they are thoughtful and caring. The books they read to children further enhance the concept of differences and similarities.

Jd's autonomy, mastered as part of Erikson's second stage, is visible as he carries and spends time with the Little Jd doll. Jd engages in many independent activities with the doll, from dressing to feeding it. A sense of autonomy is created when a child can make decisions about what he wants and does not want and is able to use words such as *I*, *me*, and *mine*, as expressed by Jd when he said, "My skin is dark like Little Jd and I like it."

As Jd plays with the doll, his sense of initiative—Erikson's third stage—is apparent. His curiosity leads him to explore and develop a sense of self as he expresses his ideas of being a daddy and a doctor. Jd initiates and tries out a variety of experiences and activities around the adult roles of daddy and doctor. This is seen as he feeds the doll, changes his diaper, and pretends to be a doctor and gives the doll a physical examination. Jd gains confidence and competence as he independently plans and follows through with the task of caring for Little Jd. He takes ownership of who he is as he identifies that the doll is "Jd." His doctor role play of listening to the doll's heart further expresses Jd's identity of having a heart condition. Later while painting, Jd identifies his skin color as "chocolate."

Jd is increasingly becoming aware of himself and others. He is developing a sense of who he is in relation to his peers, and his competence and independence are growing. As he explores his environment and tries out new activities, Jd's healthy sense of initiative will continue to develop during his preschool years, and he will be ready to move successfully to Erikson's fourth stage, industry versus inferiority.

TAKE ACTION: The Environment

Designing Environments That Build Trust, Autonomy, and Initiative

According to Erikson, the socialization process consists of eight specific stages. Each stage requires a resolution to a specific task or "crisis" that has to be completed in a satisfactory way. Success in these stages serves as the foundation for future healthy emotional development and provides social-emotional stability. Suggestions for creating an environment that promotes trust, autonomy, and initiative include the following:

- Create environments that are welcoming to children and families by creating spaces for gathering and offering schedules that smoothly transition children into the program each day. Provide comfortable seating on porches and patios where family members can stay, talk with other adults, and watch their children play.
- Design an environment that is predictable, with materials located in the same place, a consistent adult who knows the children and responds to them individually, and where routines are consistent so children know what to expect throughout the day.
- Construct an environment that is flexible and can adapt to children's growing interests and skills. Offering choices fosters independence and allows children to express their own ideas.
- Provide furniture that is small enough for children to feel comfortable in, which allows them to be more autonomous as they use it.
- Provide open-ended materials such as blocks and sand for children to investigate, explore, experiment with, and use to generate ideas.
- Provide children with opportunities to take initiative. Interesting materials and spaces invite children to plan and carry out their own ideas as they desire.

TAKE ACTION: Your Role as a Teacher

Helping Children Gain Trust, Autonomy, and Initiative

Erikson argues that thoughtful and responsive relationships between children and adults are linked to the gradual and positive maturation of the child. These healthy relationships in turn support children to confront the world and society. Erikson's theory guides educators in understanding that trust is the foundation of all emotional and social healthy growth. His research also encourages teachers to foster children's growing need for independence and their need to express curiosity. The following are some suggestions to support children in developing trust, autonomy, and initiative:

- Welcome children every morning and say good-bye at the end of the day. Meet children's needs for nurturing, sleep, and food with consistency and predictability.
- Provide children with opportunities to securely test new boundaries. Striking a balance between allowing curiosity to blossom while keeping a sense of safety and upholding societal moral values is crucial to ensure optimal development.
- Guide children to express themselves. Help children identify their emotions and find ways to gain control over them. Saying "you feel very strongly" allows children to define and describe their emotional experience without an adult labeling how they feel.
- Respond to children's requests and ideas. Use observation and reflection to identify their interests and needs and then set up the environment to support the identified interests and needs.
- Allow children to be in charge of the learning process. This shows them you are confident in their abilities. Encourage children to use language to express new understandings and ask questions. This will promote their curiosity.

Lev Vygotsky

How Children Communicate Their Understanding of the World

Lev Vygotsky on Social-Emotional Development of Young Children

Vygotsky's theory emphasizes the significance of knowledgeable others, culture, language, and play in children's social-emotional development. In his view, social-emotional development focuses on the connections between children and other people and the sociocultural context in which the children live. The transmission of social values, skills, and expectations comes from adults and more experienced peers, particularly through language.

Role of the more knowledgeable other: Knowledge is coconstructed and always involves more than one person. Vygotsky emphasizes how more knowledgeable individuals pass on social information within the ZPD (that is, occurring within the guidance of an adult or more competent peer). Children can perform at a higher level when supported by a peer, teacher, or caring adult. For instance, an older peer may model collaboration skills by initiating play, helping, negotiating, or settling a conflict.

Culture and social interactions: Vygotsky (1978) argues that culture and social interactions have a profound influence on a child's development and are the main influences that children use for constructing knowledge. He believes development cannot be separated from its social context and that social interactions determine both the content and process of children's thinking. Social context consists of everything in a child's environment that has been impacted by culture. This may include people such as family members, friends, and teachers, and materials such as toys and books. For Vygotsky, culture influences our beliefs and attitudes as well as how and what we think. These beliefs shape how we learn as we interact with others and follow the abilities, skills, and rules shaped by our culture. For example, children learn that it is either appropriate or disrespectful to look an adult in the eyes or that they are to sleep alone or with other family members. Through experiences with family members, teachers, and classmates, children develop social understanding about how to respond and behave in social situations.

Social development and language: Social development is always joined with cognition and language. In his sociocultural theory, Vygotsky (1978) states that humans develop tools and strategies while they interact with their social environment. Vygotsky asserts that language develops from social interactions for the purpose of communication. It is through social and language interactions that more knowledgeable people teach less knowledgeable people the information, values, and skills that are required to be a part of the community. Language is also the main tool that supports children in expressing their feelings, needs, and ideas as they navigate their social environment. As children use language, they gain mastery, self-control, and independence, as well as the ability to communicate with others. Young children use social speech to talk with others and language to assist them in navigating social-emotional situations. What Vygotsky refers to as "private speech" is commonly used by preschool children as they talk out loud to themselves while playing. This type of speech performs an important

Vygotsky

function, as it is what preschoolers use to guide their behavior and thought. Such speech serves the purpose of self-regulating behavior, or the ability to control one's impulses, which is an emotional and cognitive competency.

Play: Vygotsky's theory reveals the importance of play in gaining social-emotional competence. The play of preschoolers shifts from being object oriented at age three to being socially oriented at age four. Younger children may say they are playing house, but their focus is on the objects they are playing with and what they can do with the objects. As children get older, there is a context for the social roles they are enacting. They create imaginary situations as well as negotiate and act out roles. For Vygotsky, make-believe play promotes social and intellectual abilities in children.

They Took My Room Away
Transitioning Relationships

It is time for Lorenzo to start kindergarten. He will no longer be attending Crystal's Creative Kids. It is a time of transition for Lorenzo's family, including his younger brother, Kainoa, who is four. Kainoa is now the "big boy" at the program and he is quite proud that it is "his school" that he no longer has to share with Lorenzo. Kainoa is outgoing and interacts with all the children; he takes a leadership role in different activities and thrives in this new role.

While four-year-old Kainoa assumes his new role at the program, things are different at home. Kainoa and Lorenzo have a new baby sister. This means that Kainoa is no longer the youngest. He has to give up his bedroom and his former nursery furniture to his little sister, and he is not happy about it. The following conversation occurred one morning at the program upon Kainoa's arrival.

Kainoa (in a loud voice): They took my room away, and they painted it pink.

Crystal: I am sorry, Kai. I know that there are things here that are yours; let's go find them.

Kainoa: I want my room back and I don't want it pink.

Crystal: You know this is now your "big school," so let's have an area that is Kai's area. Where do you want to set that space?

Kainoa: Right here with a blanket and a pillow so that I can rest.

Kainoa selects a space, and the teachers proceed to use a blanket to cover a table, creating a space underneath the table that gives him some privacy. It looks like a quiet room for him to rest. Kainoa naps in that space throughout the week.

The teachers want to support Kainoa in this transition, so they encourage his family to send photos of the new baby to display for all the children to see. The family makes sure to also include photos of Lorenzo and Kainoa holding the baby so Kainoa can see himself as an important member of the family. The teachers also want to offer opportunities for Kainoa to express his feelings, so they create a space with a changing table, a crib, and a shelf with a variety of items that the children can use with the baby dolls. This new space is a similar model to the changing table used to change the diapers of the infants who attend the program. The teachers want to engage the children, especially Kainoa, in re-creating through dramatic play their experiences of having a new baby in the family. The teachers place the family photos on the wall above the changing table and model caregiving routines on the infants and toddlers in the program.

The children pretend to take care of the baby dolls. They change the dolls' diapers, bathe them, and get them ready for naps. Both boys and girls participate in this type of play.

To further support Kainoa, the teachers set out the books *Peter's Chair* by Ezra Jack Keats and *On Mother's Lap* by Ann Herbert Scott and encourage his family to spend more individual time with Kainoa.

Around this same time, Ryder experiences some of the same issues. He also has a new baby in the family. The teachers notice that Ryder watches intently as they feed, comfort, and change the babies. He is spending more time caring for the younger babies that come to the program and is also actively playing with the dolls in the dramatic play area the teachers created.

Ryder: Uh-oh, I have to change my baby's diaper. He is stinky.

Ryder proceeds to take a diaper from the table and changes a doll's diaper.

Ryder: First I take off the diaper. Then wipe the baby's bottom. Throw away diaper. Here's the new one. These tabs are tricky. Hold the diaper. There, I got them.

Vygotsky

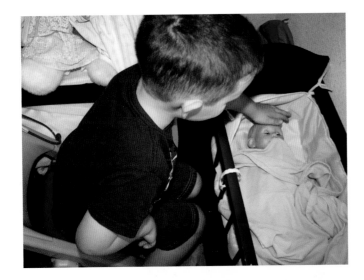

He then gently places the doll in the crib and comes near her. He touches the doll's forehead.

Ryder (singing): Go to sleep, my little baby.

As the children continue to play with the dolls, the teachers read a variety of books about babies and families from around the world, including *Global Babies* by Global Fund for Children. The children enjoy the beautiful photos and ask many questions about the way families from different countries care for their babies.

Olivia: Do babies have cribs in other countries?

Sammy: Do they go to a program?

Nate: Who takes care of the babies?

Crystal: Babies in different countries are just like babies in this country. They have people that love them and care for them. They may sleep in different types of cribs and use different cloth, but they are just like our babies.

Kainoa: Babies sleep like my sister and eat like my sister. There are also big brothers that take care of them.

Ryder: I take care of my new baby.

Teacher Jason: You both help take care of the new babies and everyone here also helps. You watch me as I feed and change the babies.

The doll play continues indoors, and one day the teachers notice it being incorporated outdoors as well. The teachers notice Olivia and Kainoa start to tie some scarves around tree branches that they have stuck into the gravel.

Olivia: Let's get the branches standing next to each other.

Kainoa: I will put more gravel to hold them.

Olivia: Let's tie the big pink scarf here.

She proceeds to tie the scarf around the first branch.

Kainoa (pointing to another branch): I want one here, lower, but I can't do it.

Olivia: I will use the yellow scarf as shade and show you how.

Kainoa: Let's bring the baby.

Olivia: Yes, the baby is in the "ammock."

Kainoa: She can sleep in the shade.

Olivia: Shhh, she is sleeping.

The children build the hammock that they saw in the book about babies from around the world.

Kainoa's baby sister, Kaleia, starts coming to the program and at first this is a difficult transition for Kainoa, who is now used to being alone in his "big school." However, the teachers constantly remind him that he is loved and valued, and invite him to help care for Kaleia. Within a couple of weeks, Kainoa adjusts to Kaleia being at his school and his new role of big brother. He checks on Kaleia throughout each day, watches out for her, and brings her toys that he thinks will interest her.

Making Theories Visible in Play

This story demonstrates several aspects of Vygotsky's theory on social-emotional learning. The teachers and parents are the experienced others, as they are knowledgeable about caring for infants. They model how to care for the infants in the program by feeding, comforting, responding to, and changing diapers while Kainoa and Ryder watch on. The boys later imitate infant caregiving behaviors through play. They pretend to take care of the baby dolls by changing their diapers, bathing them, and getting them ready for naps. Pretending to be a dad, Ryder gently places the doll in the crib and sings the doll to sleep. Ryder's actions show that he understands the role of a father and demonstrates evidence of Vygotsky's theory that children obtain cognitive skills through social interactions. The teachers understand Vygotsky's belief that children take on roles through play and that Kainoa and Ryder use play to reenact the role of being a parent. Play helps the children to take ownership of the situation (arrival of a new sibling in their family) and act out various sequences and things they have observed.

Olivia, who is experienced with tying, assists Kainoa in tying scarves onto the tree branches. Securing the scarf to the tree is too difficult a task for Kainoa to do on his own, but it is possible with Olivia's help.

Once Kainoa's baby sister, Kaleia, starts attending Crystal's Creative Kids, Kainoa takes initiative in helping her. He comforts her when she cries and watches out for her safety with peers and the environment. These are all skills that he learned through knowledgeable others.

The role of cultural or social context also influences Kainoa's experience in this story. Social context consists of everything in a child's environment that has been impacted by culture. In this story, Kainoa has been influenced by the birth of his sister, particularly through the loss of his room. The birth of Kaleia is part of Kainoa's family culture and has influenced Kainoa's social interactions as he adapts to the new family addition. Teacher Crystal acknowledges Kainoa's loss of his room by providing private space and giving him opportunities to reenact caretaking of babies. The teachers respond to the children's transition of a new baby in their families by giving them recognizable caregiving tools from their own culture to play with and re-create their experiences. They introduce tools such as books about babies, family photos, dolls, and baby items. These familiar cultural materials allow the children to master the behaviors of caregiving. Kainoa learns to use these tools first in cooperation with others and later independently, both of which reinforce his social development.

A third aspect of Vygotsky's developmental theory is shown in the children's use of language. The children in this story use what Vygotsky calls "social speech" to communicate with each other. They have multiple conversations about the needs and care of babies that add to their understanding of their social world. Through language, Crystal helps Kainoa process his conflict about the arrival of his sister and loss of his room. She acknowledges his feelings and identifies ways to help him work through the challenge. Kainoa uses Vygotsky's "cultural tool" of language to express his feelings. As Vygotsky articulates, Kainoa uses language to gain mastery and self-control over his situation. He expresses how he feels about Kaleia's arrival and talks about things babies do and the role of a big brother. Kainoa also uses language in his social play with Olivia as he talks about how he is going to solve the problem of keeping the tree branches upright when he states, "I will put more gravel to hold them." While the children use social speech to communicate with others, Ryder engages in private speech as he changes the doll's diaper. He speaks out loud to himself the steps he must follow. This self-talk helps him master the new task of diaper changing. In this story, Vygotsky's theory emphasizes how children's social-emotional development is supported through more experienced others, their own families' culture, and social interactions and communication with others.

TAKE ACTION: The Environment

Creating Environments that Support Social-Emotional Competence

According to Vygotsky, children thrive in an environment that promotes interactions with other adults and peers, where they acquire specific cultural tools that are handed to them by more experienced members of their community. Vygotsky sees play as the central element to support the acquisition of social and emotional competence in young children. Play allows children to control their inner impulses, gain self-regulation, and develop a deeper understanding of social norms, values, and expectations. Environments that provide props and spaces for play encourage the interactions Vygotsky deems so critical for learning. Suggestions for creating an environment that supports social play include the following:

- Offer children opportunities to engage in collaborative art and sensory exploration. These experiences invite children to share materials and space while they create. Collaborative art allows for rich conversations with others who are near.

- Set up water tables both outdoors and indoors for small groups of children to work together. Items can be rotated through to maintain interest and allow children to build each other's thinking. Consider adding rocks to wash or pebbles and sand to create water scenes. Include washable dolls to promote discussion about babies and families, and cultural differences and similarities.

- Plan the environment to promote adult-child and child-child interactions. Designate outdoor and indoor areas for gathering in small and large groups where discussions and social interactions can be facilitated.

- Design outdoor and indoor spaces surrounded with light and natural materials to help children engage in activities with others that promote deeper thinking and more powerful social interactions.

- Put together play areas that represent the specific experiences of the children.

- Foster spaces that have an aesthetic ambiance that includes cultural tools and artifacts.

Vygotsky

TAKE ACTION: Your Role as a Teacher

Supporting Self-Regulation and Cooperation through Play

According to Vygotsky's theory, teachers support social-emotional development by fostering interactions among children and scaffolding social-emotional learning within the ZPD. When children play with each other they start to develop social skills of collaboration. A teacher can assist growth in these areas by encouraging children to use language to express feelings or solve conflicts, helping a child "read" another child's behavior, or providing suggestions on ways to enter ongoing play. Vygotsky believes the teacher's role is to value each child's culture and welcome family members as part of the classroom community. The following are some suggestions based on Vygotsky's views:

- Engage children in conversations that promote communication and allow them to express their ideas, feelings, and emotions.
- Invite families to be an integral part of the classroom community. This is crucial to support the social development of children. When children see their family members participating in everyday classroom activities, they know that the classroom is a place they can trust.
- Display artifacts around the classroom that represent children's family culture. Invite families to share important traditions and family stories.
- Make an effort to touch base with each family as they drop off and pick up their children. These opportunities to exchange information create bonds and resources to promote permanent relationships among all the members of the classroom. Children then experience continuity of care, and their self-concept and sense of belonging increases.
- Promote opportunities for fantasy and dramatic play that allow children to collaborate and develop new ways of thinking. In this way, children can create new ideas and solutions to problems.

Abraham Maslow

Promoting Self-Regulation and Emotional Stability

Abraham Maslow on Social-Emotional Development of Young Children

Maslow's hierarchy of needs addresses social and emotional needs specifically in the safety, love and belonging, and esteem and self-actualization levels of his hierarchy. After the basic physiological needs of food, water, and shelter are satisfied in the first level of his pyramid, children seek to meet higher-level needs. Maslow believes that when individuals are fulfilling only their basic physiological needs, they are at the survival level and trying to cope with life.

- *Safety needs*: The emotional needs of safety and security include being able to trust the environment, adults, and peers, along with a need for protection, stability, and order.

- *Love and belonging needs*: Social-emotional characteristics of this stage include the need to communicate with others, give and receive affection, and have a place in a group. This level is sometimes called the "social stage." The main need of this level is for emotional connections with friends and family. Children have a desire for love and belonging through family affection, acceptance, and friendships with peers. They crave the connection and belonging that comes from being part of a family. Children also develop meaningful relationships with friends and teachers at school. A child learns socially acceptable behavior from his caregivers and often imitates their behaviors. According to Maslow, the social stage is very important, as interactions with others help children maintain emotional stability. In his view, a core desire of all human beings is to feel loved, valued, and accepted by others.

- *Esteem needs*: At Maslow's fourth level, children search for feelings of self-worth. Maslow recognizes two different types of esteem: a lower level that includes respect for others and a higher level that involves the need to respect ourselves. Respect for others includes such things as an awareness of status, fame, and a person's need for recognition. Respect for self involves feeling confident, competent, responsible, skilled, and independent. Maslow says the need for self-respect is more important than respect for others.

- *Self-actualization needs*: Maslow believes children are motivated to fulfill their potential. He writes, "Healthy children enjoy growing and moving forward, gaining new skills, capacities and powers" (Maslow 1999, 30). And, "In the normal development of the healthy child, it is now believed that, much of the time, if he is given a really free choice, he will choose what is good for his growth" (Maslow 1999, 219). Children enjoy gaining new skills, abilities, and power, and being creative, engaged, and autonomous; all of which are self-actualizing and social-emotional characteristics. Children mature into emotionally healthy adults when they grow up with a sense of belonging, feeling loved, and feeling respected. If a child grows up being well nourished, safe, adored, and valued, self-actualization becomes more possible.

Hey, Water on You, Not on Me

Pursuit to Fulfill Hierarchical Needs

The children tire in the late afternoons before their parents arrive. Teacher Crystal has found that water play on these hot days soothes the children. They relax while they connect with each other and build a strong bond around the outdoor water table. Today, Crystal adds plastic containers, funnels, and soap to make bubbles in the water to surprise the children. She waits with eager anticipation to see their reaction. When the children see the bubbles, they quickly place their hands

in the warm, soapy water. Sammy slaps the water and swishes it around. She rubs her hands back and forth in a scrubbing manner, simulating hand washing. Sammy brings her bubble-covered hand close to her face for examination.

Jd grasps the handle of a water toy shaped like a duck and glides the toy through the water. His hand movements create more bubbles. His attention shifts to emptying water from a container.

Kainoa pours water from the watering can onto the wooden deck. He gazes as the water splashes against the wood and changes the wood's color to a deep brown. He moves the container over the water table and watches in silence as the water cascades down into the water table. He seems fascinated with the water's movement. The children repetitively fill and empty containers. Crystal encourages this play, which increases the children's joy and confidence.

Eventually, Kainoa and Jd immerse their whole bodies into the soapy water table. They laugh as they splash in the water with their hands and kick their feet. Nate laughs with pleasure at the two younger children. He seems to take delight in their exploration.

Water play becomes a favorite activity for the children. Each day, the children race outside to continue their explorations. Quietly enjoying the water, Bella concentrates on pouring water from container to container. She securely grasps a cup in her right hand and a bottle in her left. She uses the cup to fill the bottle with water. At one point, she experiments with raising the cup high above her head. A water pouring game begins.

Bella turns around and pours water on Jd's shoulder. Jd spins about.

Jd (in a surprised voice): You got me wet!

Bella stares at Jd, giggles, and then refills her bottle. This time she thrusts water towards Lorenzo's face.

Lorenzo: Hey, watcha doin'?

Bella looks cautiously at Lorenzo. She seems uncertain if he is pleased or annoyed by her actions.

Maslow

Jd and Lorenzo both fill their cups and take aim at Bella. Simultaneously they throw water on her.

Bella (screaming): Not on me! Only on you!

It seems that Bella is happy with the game as long as she is the one pouring.

Lorenzo takes time to replenish his water as Bella moves over to the other water table. He comes up behind Bella and pours more water over her head.

Bella (laughing): You really are my friend!

Making Theories Visible in Play

The children in this story have satisfied Maslow's basic physiological needs as there is no evidence of them seeking food to eat, water to drink, clothing to wear, or shelter for protection from the elements. This fulfillment of these physiological needs allows the children to achieve higher levels of needs.

The children exhibit fulfillment of the next level, safety, because their behavior indicates they feel emotionally protected and safe. At first the children freely play with the soapy water. They laugh, delight, and explore—all behaviors that indicate a sense of safety. Kainoa and Jd even feel secure enough to immerse their whole bodies in the water, and Nate enjoys watching them get wet. As Bella pours water on others, she, too, giggles. While initially she is not pleased with water being poured on her, she later declares that Lorenzo really is her friend when he does so. Such interactions demonstrate a trust in each other, satisfying the children's safety needs.

At the next level, affection, relationships, and friendship are what Maslow labels "love and belonging needs." In this story, the children crave interaction with each other, as evidenced by their social behaviors. Even though Kainoa and Jd have limited language as toddlers, they engage in reciprocal behavior as they splash sudsy water and kick their feet. The children's body language of smiles, eye contact, and imitation of actions such as slapping water shows they like to be near each other. When Bella pours water on Jd and Lorenzo, she indicates her interest in engaging with other children. Her behavior creates attention and interaction, both signs of a desire to play.

In meeting their need for esteem, which is Maslow's fourth level, the children exhibit confidence, achievement, mastery, and independence in their use of water play materials. They are independent in their exploration, following what seems to be of interest to them—such as Sammy's attraction to making bubbles and Kainoa's fascination with the water's movement. Overall, the children show respect for each other while engaged in water play through sharing materials and space. Bella's pouring water on others indicates her sense of esteem, rather than lack of respect for others, as she demonstrates confidence with her interactions with Jd. Bella also thrusts water confidently in Lorenzo's face, acts uncertain in her actions after Lorenzo's initial response, and then exhibits a playfulness and desire to connect with the other children.

The fifth level, self-actualization, is a person's ability to achieve full potential as a human being. Even though the children at Crystal's Creative Kids are young, they are expressing their need for self-actualization through their creativity and spontaneity with water play. They are enjoying themselves fully and find satisfaction in their free exploration. Enjoyment and contentment are signs of healthy social-emotional growth and development. The children's self-actualization needs will continue to emerge as they receive satisfaction of their physiological, safety, love and belonging, and esteem needs.

Maslow

TAKE ACTION: The Environment

Designing Inclusive Environments That Promote a Sense of Belonging

Children who have their developmental needs met, have their strengths supported, and feel a sense of belonging and inclusion are progressing along Maslow's steps towards self-actualization. According to Maslow, people who have achieved self-actualization are autonomous and independent. Relationships with family and community are healthy. Self-actualized people accept themselves, are empathic and creative, and often express joyful feelings of excitement, insight, and happiness. The following are some suggestions to support children's growing self-actualization:

■ Create spaces that integrate natural elements such as light, air, and water. Make shelter and food available throughout the day. Create spaces for refuge where children can find a moment of quiet.

- Design spaces that communicate to children a sense of safety. Children thrive in environments that are predictable and provide consistency. When materials are displayed clearly and in the same location, children are more capable of accessing them independently.

- Develop environments that are responsive to individual children and their families and create a sense that it feels good to be here. Include spaces for gathering to share stories and family traditions.

- Make settings that allow children to explore and strengthen their own abilities and skills. Thoughtful, well-provisioned, and aesthetically pleasing spaces encourage children to care and actively participate as members of the learning community.

- Form environments that promote respect, creativity, and spontaneous play. The environment should invite children to explore who they are, what they like, and how they feel, which increases their sense of self and promotes respect for self and others.

TAKE ACTION: Your Role as a Teacher

Beyond Praise to Building Strong Relationships with Children

Children are constantly searching for a sense of identity that is embraced by interactive relationships with caregivers and peers. Maslow's hierarchy of needs serves as a model that teachers can use to effectively support every child's growing self- and social-emotional identity. Creating early childhood classrooms that offer love, stability, and a sense of independence and belonging, and that focus on self-actualization will develop the child's capacity to conquer the world beyond the conventional way of thinking, learning, being, living, and feeling. Some suggestions to support self-actualization include the following:

- Respect the children's needs for quiet spaces to reflect, rest, and relax. Respond to children's physical needs for resting, eating, and toileting on an individual basis.

- Develop strong connections with children and families to better promote children's growth and development. Respect children's need for transitional objects, such as a blanket or stuffed animal, that help them soothe themselves. Display photos of families around the classroom to support transitions and increase bonding to a new environment.

- Create the foundations that build community and support the essential connections with children and families. Have spaces that belong to children. Respect their work and allow them to extend their ideas as long as needed to satisfy their thinking.

- Listen and support children's ideas and thinking and offer them opportunities and experiences to test and explore their ideas further. Trust that children are capable, competent, curious, and joyful.

- Encourage children to accept themselves and others, listen, express their ideas, and explore freely in their quest to make sense of their surroundings. Celebrate children's creative pursuits.

John Dewey

Collaboration, Community, and Negotiation

John Dewey on Social-Emotional Development of Young Children

Concerning social-emotional development, Dewey believes learning is a social and interactive process that involves real-life experiences. He also believes that education needs to address social inequities.

Learning as a social and interactive process: In his book *Experience and Nature* (1997), Dewey argues that the human individual is a social being from the start and that individual satisfaction and achievement can be realized only within the context of social habits and institutions that promote them. He says learning happens best when children work together with other people. Social skills develop when children have the opportunity to engage in meaningful work through planning, collaborating, discovering, comparing, and negotiating alongside others. Interactions with adults and peers saturate children's consciousness, forming their habits, training their ideas, and arousing their feelings and emotions. Children's perceptions of and reactions to social situations are influenced by their attitudes, beliefs, habits, prior knowledge, and emotions gained through interactions with others.

Learning involves real-life experiences: One of Dewey's democratic ideals is that authentic educational experiences increase personal and social growth. This means that active, interesting, and meaningful experiences promote

Dewey

individual and social competence. Gardening in a communal yard, for example, enhances emotional development of increased confidence and self-esteem and improved social development as children develop a sense of responsibility, community ownership, and identity and work on a common goal. Activities are meaningful when there is a sense of personal purpose. Dewey points out that people invest more attention and effort in what interests them (1975).

Education addresses social inequities: Dewey's emphasis on democracy includes a charge for schools to address social inequities. He believes schools should be a place where social reform occurs. By reform he refers to a change in education as far as what and how children are taught. According to Dewey, the role of education should be to create socially responsible people. Children should have an opportunity to learn about leadership, shared purpose, and communication. Children should play an active role in shared classroom decision making and be taught conflict resolution skills and techniques for getting along with others. Conversations and interactions in a democratic environment are an integral part of learning.

The Tipping Tree

Social Collaboration

One of the trees in the play yard is dead. It had been losing its leaves for a few months. It is just a sapling, only about eight feet tall and not very wide. The children notice that it is tipping to the side and they talk about what they want to do to save the tree.

John: We can feed the tree.

Nick: We can use more dirt.

Ryder: Can we add mulch?

The teachers give the children the opportunity to feed the tree and add more soil and mulch. After a few weeks, the children realize the tree will not survive. John, Nick, and Ryder walk over to the tree and try to move it.

Nick: It is moving.

John: It is tipping.

Ryder: We can make it fall.

John: We need to move it so that we can plant another tree.

Teacher Crystal: The tree is heavy. It is going to need a lot of pushing.

John, Ryder, and Nick push the tree a few times.

John: It's hard!

Sammy (joining the group): I can help push.

John: This is hard work for boys.

Sammy: Remember, girls are also strong.

Ryder: We need help. She can help.

Sammy starts pushing with the boys. As the children begin to push the tree back and forth, it begins to tip a little more.

Nick: Hey it's moving. Sammy is helping; keep pushing.

John: Let's do it together; one, two, three, go!

They continue to push the tree back and forth.

Ryder (stops): Wait. Let's see if it is moving from the dirt.

They stop and the tree returns to a standing position.

Ryder: I can't see if it moved.

John (beginning to kick the dirt around the tree): Let's move some dirt and see what happens.

Nick: Ryder, help me hold the tree this way and see if John and Sammy can tell if it is moving.

Ryder places both hands on the tree and moves backward using strength to push the tree.

Ryder: It's moving a little bit. We have to keep pushing.

John: I can see the roots!

Sammy: We need to keep going. I can see the roots too.

They again begin to move the tree back and forth. Each time the tree tips more.

Sammy: Let's do it hard.

Ryder: One, two, three, push hard.

Nick: I *am* pushing really hard!

Their faces show the effort they are putting into moving the tree.

Sammy: This is hard. We need to keep going.

John: I am going to use my foot.

Ryder: Hey, I hear it make noise.

Nick: We are almost there. Let's keep going.

John: Let's stop and see how many roots we can see.

Dewey

Nick: It's moving, but not enough to take out.

Sammy: We need to do something else.

John: We can dig around the tree and make a big hole.

Ryder: I am tired and that is too much work.

Nick: Let's push it the other way and see what happens.

John: Good idea, ready? One, two, three.

Ryder: Look, it's moving more and more.

Sammy: I will push with my body.

Nick: Keep going.

John: I will start pulling from the roots.

Sammy, Ryder, and Nick join John in digging and lifting the tree out. Finally, after a lot of hard work, the tree comes out and falls straight down.

Other children gather around to see what just happened.

Crystal: Wow, you worked hard and moved the tree.

John: What are we going to do with it now?

Sammy: Let's save it.

Nick: We can cut it and make wood.

Teacher Jason: I have an idea. Let's move it inside and we can hang it near the window.

The children (at the same time): Yeah!

Sammy runs inside and brings back a tape measure.

Sammy: We have to measure it and make sure it fits inside.

Sammy, Ryder, John, and Bella begin to measure the tree.

Sammy: Ryder, hold the tape to the other side.

Bella: I hold in the middle.

Sammy: It's eight and three. It's too big.

Jason: It's eight feet and three inches. I think it will fit.

Nick (holding some magnifying glasses): Look, there are bugs, and we can see what they are.

Ryder: Maybe that is why the tree died.

Sammy: Some bugs are good and others eat the roots. I remember from the book.

Nick: Look, you can see them up close.

Jason: There are many bugs in there, so we have to wait before we can bring the tree inside.

Sammy: We don't want the bugs inside.

Jason: That is for sure. We don't want to have any of the bugs inside.

John: Let's wait and leave the tree here for a few days so that the bugs find other homes.

Jason: I think that is a good idea.

The children continue to visit the tree every day to see if the bugs are still there. They start a chart to see how many days it will take for the bugs to go away so they can bring the tree inside.

Making Theories Visible in Play

Learning is a social and interactive process. This story provides a window into the play sequence between children who have a common goal of removing a dead tree. In their interactions, there is a strong sense of collaboration, which is described by Dewey as the core for learning and educational democracy. John, Nick, Ryder, and Sammy engage in what Dewey calls a social and interactive process that supports their learning. The children collaboratively work to first save, and later remove, the dead tree. Their social skills are enhanced through multiple conversations and the long, arduous work of removing the tree. The social-emotional points of Dewey's theory are seen as the foursome makes plans, negotiates strategies, and works in partnership to remove the tree. Teachers Crystal and Jason support the children in their investigation by encouraging their collaboration and allowing them to test their ideas and hypotheses. They challenge the children to find alternatives to their ideas and multiple solutions to their problem. The teachers' actions embrace Dewey's support for cooperation and problem solving, learning through doing, and projects with active exploration at their core.

Real-life experiences that unfold in the everyday lives of children promote Dewey's belief that curriculum must be meaningful. The children's encounter with a dead tree in the yard is relevant and has immense value. They are fascinated by something of such significance in their environment—a dead tree, roots, dirt, and bugs. The children are providing further

Dewey

evidence in alignment with Dewey's theory as they invest their attention and energy in work that interests them. In this case, the children are occupied with their quest to conquer the task of getting the tree out of the ground. They gain personal purpose and social competence with the challenge of tipping the tree.

This story also demonstrates how education can address social inequities. Through the experience of removing the tree, the children gained skill in leadership, shared purpose, and communication. Dewey says each of these skills is needed in a democratic society to assist in addressing social inequities. At first the children demonstrated concern for the dying tree and worked together to save it. They discussed possibilities as a group to preserve nature and later talked about how to use the tree's wood. While these actions may not relate directly to social inequity, they certainly show the children's awareness of sustainability and saving the resources on our planet, which is a form of social advocacy. The children shared their ideas for removing the tree and then negotiated the best plan. Negotiation and articulating one's thoughts are also abilities necessary for addressing social inequities.

As Ryder, John, Nick, and Sammy engaged in their purposeful work, they learned about their roles in a community of people that supports and helps each other achieve a common goal. This is what Dewey refers to as "democracy": the idea that all are valued and their individual contributions are important to the development of a strong community (2008). Meaningful play, such as the kind in this story, helps children develop their full potential and prepares them to be citizens in a democratic society. As the children in the story work hard together to develop a system that works to move a heavy tree and find other uses for it, they are also making sense of a larger process that takes place in society: that of collaborative work to remove obstacles that are present in everyday life.

TAKE ACTION: The Environment

Creating Democratic Classrooms

Dewey believes children are social beings who actively influence their environment and are influenced by the environment. To support social-emotional development, he suggests the inclusion in the classroom environment of meaningful materials that are familiar to children from their households and community. Interaction with such materials involves social collaboration. Some ideas to create community-minded, democratic environments include the following:

- Design environments that represent real life and encompass representations of the home, playground, school, neighborhood, and community in which the children live.

- Include familiar materials and equipment that provide opportunities for meaningful play. Children gravitate toward real tools and will use them in their social-dramatic and active play. Adult clothing and real, working tools help children make strong connections to their familiar experiences, which increases learning.

- Display photos around the classroom that are representative of the neighborhood and community. Photos of local bridges and architecture can be mounted in the block area to stimulate construction. Incorporate photos of local work, such as harvesting crops or fishing, or community events—for instance, a kite-flying festival or cultural gatherings—in the dramatic play area.

- Create environments that support children's ideas and interests. For example, when children see and are excited about construction going on around the community, add hard hats, tape measures, and other construction tools to their play areas.

- Provide materials in the environment that allow children to take measured social risks, such as trying new things that are unfamiliar to them. Offer familiar objects that children can take apart and put back together, such as pipes and fittings, or fort-building materials. Allow children time to make sense of meaningful items.

TAKE ACTION: Your Role as a Teacher

Supporting Community

Dewey says the teacher's role is to observe and reflect in order to identify what kinds of experiences children are interested in and ready for. When a teacher knows children well, he can plan thoughtful experiences that build on their past learning. Children need support in making sense of their social and emotional world. They need opportunity for disagreements as a means to understand varying perspectives and resolve conflicts. Go beyond any specific academic requirements to promote a community of inquiry in which there is not a simple answer to one question, but instead are multiple possibilities to resolve a single problem or situation. To create a supportive, democratic community, consider the following:

Dewey

- Ensure that every voice is valued as part of the collective process. Engage children in conversations about rules and responsibilities and invite them to share their ideas.
- Foster empathy by having children actively participate in their community both inside and outside the classroom. Encourage children to develop a view of life that goes beyond them in order to consider the lives of others.
- Reflect on your role as teachers; become a researcher along with the children and engage them in meaningful investigations.
- Invite all children to complete meaningful tasks, such as setting the table for lunch. Children are proud of their space and want to maintain it. They value the well-being of others. When they complete meaningful tasks, they also gain a stronger sense of their own value.

Howard Gardner

Multiple Intelligences as a Tool to Develop Self-Esteem

Howard Gardner on Social-Emotional Development of Young Children

Gardner argues in his MI theory that children demonstrate a range of aptitudes, skills, and cognitive strengths. These intelligences can function independently, but they are all also closely linked and interact together. Every child possesses each intelligence to some extent, but the strength of each intelligence and how they are combined varies. Children have the potential to develop multiple intelligences when provided with a supportive and nurturing environment.

Gardner also emphasizes that intelligence is the result of the complex interactions between children's heredity and their social experiences. A child may be born with natural skill for certain intelligences, such as spatial thinking or musical aptitude, but those skills can also be strengthened or hindered depending on that child's environment. A child's social-emotional development has a significant impact on her development of various intelligences, and the opposite is also true: a child's ability to use his multiple intelligences can aid his personal and relational growth. Intrapersonal and interpersonal are two specific intelligences that are seen in people with high social-emotional skills.

Intrapersonal intelligence, in Gardner's view, is concerned with the ability to understand oneself, and to appreciate one's feelings, emotions, and motivations. Individuals use their understanding of inner self to guide their own behavior. A child can be said to be strong in intrapersonal intelligence because he knows who he is, what he can do, what he wants to do, how he reacts to things, and which things to avoid or focus on.

Interpersonal intelligence entails the ability to understand the desires, intentions, and motivations of other people. It builds on a fundamental capacity to notice differences among others in their temperaments, moods, intentions, and motivations. Children with high interpersonal intelligence have the social ability to understand others and work effectively with them.

Walk in My Shoes

Exploring Strengths

Inspired by an idea from Bev Bos and Michael Leeman from Roseville Community Preschool, Teacher Monéa, who is a practicum student, decides to introduce a labyrinth of shoes to the children.

As the children arrive, they notice that the labyrinth waits for them outside on the deck. Their delight is obvious in their smiles, laughter, and comments, such as, "Wow, look at all the shoes," and "I want to try them on." Teacher Monéa invites the children to walk around and follow the trail created by the shoes. The children begin to walk and try to find their way to the end of the labyrinth. They spend a considerable amount of time walking back and forth. As they are doing this, they comment on the differences in the shoes.

Alex: Look. Those are high.

Nick: I like the red boots.

Sammy: Those are for working, like my dad's.

The children walk around the shoes for a while.

Kainoa: I have to try some shoes on.

Other children (chiming in): Yeah, let's see if they fit.

The children begin to take shoes and try them on their feet. They exchange them back and forth and they compare sizes.

Kainoa wears a different shoe on each foot.

Kainoa: Look, this one is bigger and this one fits better, but I like the big one.

Alina (picking up a pair of high heels and speaking to Izzy): Here, put this on.

Izzy puts on the shoes and walks around, attempting to keep her balance.

Izzy: These are like the ones my mom wears when she goes out. She says that her feet get tired.

Bella (standing next to Izzy): My mom wears those too. Why do they wear them if their feet get tired?

Kainoa and Jd start putting on the boots.

Kainoa: It is hard to put these on.

They continue to work on getting the boots on. Finally Kainoa manages to get both boots on his feet and attempts to walk around.

Kainoa: This is hard. I want my shoes back.

Jd walks over to a pair of high heels and puts them on. He walks around and exclaims.

Jd: Look, I am tall!

Jd is one of the smallest children in the program, and he is constantly talking about being taller and measuring himself against other children.

Even Teacher Jason joins in and begins to try some shoes on. The children laugh and bring different shoes for him to try.

Jason: So, do you think these are too big for me?

Sammy: No, silly, they are too small, but they are red like the boots I am wearing.

The children model the shoes for Crystal, who is sitting on a bench watching and taking care of a new baby. They pretend to be shoe models and go from one tree stump in the play yard to the next exchanging shoes. Sammy continues to test her shoes by walking on different surfaces. She wears them throughout the day.

The play continues, and the children begin to sort and classify the shoes both by size and color. They argue about which shoes do and do not make a pair. Nick takes off his shoes and looks inside.

Nick: Look, I see numbers. There's a three.

This engages the children in a new quest to find sizes. They start lining up the shoes in a row, and they work together to put them in order.

Alex: I have an idea. We have many shoes, like a store.

Sammy: Yes, we can sell them and make money.

Nick: We need to make some money. Let's get the markers and paper.

Some of the children start creating paper money while another group of children takes the shoes inside and lines them against the wall in the dramatic play area. Teacher Monéa helps these children organize and decorate their store so it will be ready to open the next day.

~~~~~~

Making Theories Visible in Play

Gardner's theory illuminates several ways that social-emotional intelligence is happening in this story. When Sammy tests her red shoes on the different surfaces around the yard, she carefully analyzes how they feel. She is able to reflect and remark on her strengths and her interest. When the teachers allow her to work alone and independently, Sammy shows a well-developed intrapersonal intelligence. She is able to make connections between her past and present knowledge, such as comparing Nick's boots to her dad's work boots. She explores her own skills and limits by wearing different shoes in different environments. By investigating her own responses to the various shoes, Sammy is continuing to develop her understanding of her needs, ideas, and emotions, leading to stronger intrapersonal intelligence.

The children also develop their interpersonal intelligence in this story. When the children test different ways to model their shoes for Crystal, they are practicing the ability to understand another's point of view. The relationship between the children and Teacher Jason shows that the children are comfortable engaging in interaction and expressing themselves, as they laugh at him and allow him to try on shoes too. As with all of their relationships with adults and each other, the children's interactions allow them to practice communicating and understanding others, thus developing more social-emotional skills.

As the children make a decision to start a shoe store, they develop social-emotional skills through several interactions involving Gardner's intelligences. The children use their interpersonal skills to listen to each other's ideas, talk, and negotiate while collaborating in the store design. The children's sorting and classifying skills develops visual-spatial and logical-mathematical intelligences, as does their focus on money and decorating the space. They use and grow their linguistic intelligence to collaborate on opening a store. Each of these intelligences—which develop with more opportunities to practice—also gives the children chances to expand their relationships and social skills.

TAKE ACTION: The Environment

Creating Spaces to Support Interpersonal and Intrapersonal Intelligences

MI theory can guide teachers in designing spaces that nurture and support children's social-emotional development. In order for children to develop a strong emotional and social self, they need to be able to practice their multiple intelligences in an environment that is safe and nurturing. Below are ideas to create environments that focus on intrapersonal and interpersonal development:

- Create places for children to reflect and examine their ideas in quiet contemplation to support their growing intrapersonal intelligence. Start by considering places where you personally feel comfortable or introspective, and identify the qualities of the place that drew you to it.
- Set aside a cozy corner for thinking and pondering. Benches, tree stumps, comfortable chairs, canopies, and tables can be set up indoors and outdoors to give children places to think. Natural ele-

ments, such as plants and the sound of water, are soothing and can be used to delineate spaces of seclusion and peace.

■ Include books of poetry and prose in the classroom library. Write the children's spoken words to support them in expressing who they are. Depending on the children's needs, consider providing a selection of books that address feelings or touch upon thorny moments, such as death and dying, to help children answer difficult questions.

■ Design spaces for interpersonal development that encourage children to work together, make friends, socialize, be leaders, and resolve peer conflicts. Children can practice social skills in all areas of the classroom as they play with each other.

TAKE ACTION: Your Role as a Teacher

Guiding Interactions alongside MI Theory

Understanding intelligence to include multiple avenues for knowledge allows the image of the child to be one of a person who is competent, curious, and capable. The role of the teacher is to support children's use of multiple intelligences to develop a deeper understanding of themselves and the world—in this case, to develop socially and emotionally. The following are ideas to create experiences that focus on intrapersonal and interpersonal development:

■ Offer activities that promote opportunities for children to work together, make friends, be leaders, and solve conflicts. Experiences such as building and constructing, putting together large floor puzzles, and working together on a collective art project or in a small-group investigation can encourage children who are leaders to guide children who are still developing leadership skills.

■ Encourage children to serve as resources for each other while working together. If a child is struggling with writing her name, the teacher can suggest asking for help from another child who is an accomplished writer.

■ Promote multiple group gatherings throughout the day for children to discuss their ideas, express their feelings, and share their thinking with each other.

■ Respect children's desire to be alone and reflect. Creating a cozy corner for thinking and pondering will provide children time and space to reflect and make sense of a new idea or thought process.

Gardner

- Record children's language and document their ideas using photographs, anecdotes, charts, and newsprint paper. Capture their ideas in writing. During group-meeting time, invite children to review the documentation in order to promote powerful conversations to help them identify ways other children feel and behave.
- Provide opportunities for children to share their thinking, feelings, and emotions by discussing family events that are meaningful, exciting, or unsettling.

Louise Derman-Sparks

It's Not Fair! Children as Social Activists

Louise Derman-Sparks's Anti-Bias Education on the Social-Emotional Development of Young Children

In the book *Anti-Bias Education*, Derman-Sparks and Olsen Edwards (2010) introduce four core goals (identified in part 1). Each goal interacts with the others, and together they serve as a foundation to build safe, supportive, and inclusive communities for every child.

Derman-Sparks discusses healthy self-awareness and positive social identities as two ways that children develop healthy social-emotional development.

Healthy self-awareness: According to Derman-Sparks, "Children cannot construct a strong self-concept or develop respect for others if they do not know how to identify and resist hurtful, stereotypical, and inaccurate messages or actions directed toward them or others" (Derman-Sparks and Olsen Edwards 2010, 5). Self-concept is a key component of a child's social-emotional development. A child's perceptions and feelings about himself are usually based on how the significant people in his world respond to him. A growing sense of self-awareness helps children become more competent in their relationships with others. As children gain self-awareness, they recognize what is right and wrong and gain the ability to speak up against injustices. When children stand up against injustice, their own identities are also validated, and they acquire a strong sense of self and gain power and freedom. As adults, we have the responsibility to help children develop positive feelings about their own identities and gain respect for others' identities.

Positive social identities: Social identities include characteristics of a group of people defined by society rather than an individual. Such definitions contain societal advantaged or disadvantaged messages about a person's gender, abilities, racial identity, age, religion, or socioeconomic class. According to Derman-Sparks and Olsen Edwards, children learn about their own and others' social identities through both overt and covert messages (2010, 13).

These messages influence a child's social-emotional development. An anti-bias approach encourages children to learn and celebrate how they are different and similar to each other. This increases a sense of emotional safety and well-being. A respectful environment invites children to express comfort with human diversity and develop respectful and deep social connections. When early childhood settings nurture children's individual and social identities, children's social and cognitive development is strengthened.

Cheerful Letters

Everyday Empathy

Group gathering is a special and important ritual at Crystal's Creative Kids. In addition to music, morning greetings, and special stories, group gathering is a time for the children and teachers to engage in meaningful discussion about a wide variety of topics that are of interest and meaning to the children, both individually and as a group.

One of these discussions began a wonderful experience for the children, families, and teachers of the program. Because a few of the children had been ill during the prior week, the teachers felt it was necessary to talk with the children during group gathering about the importance of covering their mouths when sneezing or coughing and washing hands to prevent the spread of germs. Three days before this, Bella, who had been ill, visited the doctor. The doctor ordered an X-ray of her lungs to ensure she was not developing pneumonia.

During a discussion, Bella begins talking about her experience having an X-ray taken of her chest.

Bella: I had a ray of my lungs. It was scary; my mommy was not with me.

Derman-Sparks

This leads to an intense discussion between the children about their many experiences with doctors and hospitals.

Jd: I was scared when I was in the hospital. They had to fix my heart.

Kainoa (lifting his shirt): See, I have a scar from when I was little.

Alex: They take my blood from here (he points to his arm) and it hurts.

Sammy: They put tubes in my ears, and I was in the hospital too.

The children talk about having to get shots, getting their ears checked because of ear infections, and many other experiences that happen while visiting the doctor. All of the children express their feelings about these visits.

Nate: It is scary.

Cruz: It makes me mad.

Bella: I don't like it.

Alina: It's scary to go to the doctor. I like stickers.

Sammy: It's happy. The doctor makes you feel better!

The teachers listen to the children sharing their stories for a while.

Crystal: You know, sometimes when children are very sick, they have to stay at the hospital for a lot of days. How do you think children feel when they have to stay in the hospital?

The children immediately begin to shout out their thoughts: Angry! Very scared! Not happy! Crying! Bored! Lonely! Mad!

Crystal: If you ever had to stay in the hospital for many days, what would you like to have or do while you were there? What would be important to you and help you feel happy?

As the children express their ideas, Teacher Jason writes them down on a large piece of paper to revisit later.

Alex: Blankie.

John: Puzzles.

Jd: Books.

Nick: Carrots to help me get better.

Cruz: Ice cream.

Ryder: Paint and stuff for drawing.

Kainoa: Games and playdough.

Alina: My teddy bear and toys.

Bella: I know! How about we take stuff to the kids who have to stay at the hospital? Maybe they will feel better!

Sammy: And we can make them cards and paintings!

Crystal and the other children all agree that these are wonderful ideas. They decide to write a letter to the children's families asking for help in purchasing items for children at the hospital. Crystal calls the Child Life Department at a nearby hospital to find out proper procedure for donating items to the children in the Pediatric Critical Care Unit. That day, as families arrive to pick up their children, each receives a copy of a letter asking for their participation. The response is fabulous, and over the next two weeks the families contribute very generously to the cause.

The teachers set out a variety of materials for the children to create cards, drawings, and books. They listen to the children as they make cards and artwork. Over and over they hear the children expressing their intention to "cheer the sick kids up."

Each day at group gathering the discussion continues, with the children sharing their excitement about their progress, as well as empathy and compassion for other children who are battling illness.

Sammy: We have a lot of things for them, but those things will all be gone because they will use them. How will they remember us?

Nate: Hey, we can make a big painting for them to hang up. They won't use that up!

Again, the teachers and other children agree that this is a great idea and decide that they will create a group painting to be hung in the hospital playroom. The teachers purchase canvas and oil paints and set them out for the children to paint as they chose.

As the children work on the painting, the teachers again observe and listen closely to the children's conversations. As they listen, the teachers become quite aware of the children's sense of empathy and caring and their desire to engage in acts of social justice. The children not only discuss the current project, but also begin to discuss issues in their community.

Kainoa: I saw a homeless man on the street, and my mom and dad gave him some

Derman-Sparks

money. My dad said that some people don't have a home and have to sleep outside. That is very sad.

Izzy: I rescued my cat, Brown-Brown, from the animal shelter, and there were a lot of animals there that don't have a family. I think they were lonely.

The teachers and children agree that those are important topics and that when they finish with the current project they will further discuss ways to help other people and animals in need.

At the end of two weeks of collecting contributions and making gifts for the children at the hospital, Crystal delivers the "cheerful letters" and items to the hospital. Although the children are disappointed that they cannot help deliver their gifts, they understand that it is important, as Bella said, "to not bring germs to the children in the hospital because they could get sicker."

In the end, the children are very proud with their work, and they have performed a memorable act of giving.

Making Theories Visible in Play

Young children are observers. They notice differences and classify them from their egocentric point of view. Since their experience is limited, when faced with a new experience, children will attempt to explain it in terms of a previous occurrence. Given the frame of reference young children have about children in the hospital, it is common that they struggle to make sense of what they observe and what they know.

As each child in the story gains an individual sense of self-awareness, they are able to engage in conversations about others. The children share with each other their own experiences of going to the doctor and having medical procedures that have been scary and discomforting. As the children ask questions to attempt to satisfy their curiosity about what they see and hear, the teachers respond with accurate yet developmentally appropriate answers that satisfy the children's curiosity. The children are developing their capacities for fairness and empathy as they talk about hospitalized children. The goals of anti-bias education are used to create a community where everyone's voice is heard and respected.

Derman-Sparks and Olsen Edwards (2010) discuss the importance of recognizing that injustice hurts and to speak up against it. Creating environments that give children a sense of activism promotes cognitive and social development. The children in the program have gained knowledge and respect for children who are in the hospital. They have taken action to comfort someone else who needs care. The children gain a stronger sense of self as they spend time creating cards and a special gift that can be given to children who need their comfort. More important is the fact the children have learned that giving to others leaves them with a sense of pride and joy.

When the children decide what to get for the children in the hospital, they first think about what would make themselves feel better. They recognize that it is not fair that the children are hospitalized and that "unfairness hurts," as Derman-Sparks points out (Derman-Sparks and Olsen Edwards 2010, 5). When the donated toys start coming in and the children want to play with them, they remind each other that they are for children in the hospital. They are gaining a strong ability for self-regulation and have learned to turn a frustrating moment into a sharing experience that builds community for all the children involved. As they make their cards and paint the canvas together, the children learn that everyone is a valued member in the community whose contributions deserve to be supported.

The children also gain a powerful message about fairness as they learn about sick children in the hospital. They are developing empathy and an understanding of differences between themselves and sick children. Crystal assists the children in taking action to make a difference in the world. The children make life better for sick children through their cheerful letters and other gifts. As each child's identity is supported, each child will continue to acquire a stronger sense of self.

TAKE ACTION: The Environment

Environments That Promote Self-Awareness, Family Pride, and Positive Social Identities

Children notice differences at a very young age, and they discriminate based on what they perceive from society values. The concept of cultural identity is real for young children. They need concrete experiences in every interaction and activity they have in the classroom environment (Derman-Sparks and Olsen Edwards 2010). Children learn to internalize the overt and covert messages they receive from the people in their lives and other messages in their environment. Environments that encourage children to actively explore their identity in a variety of positive ways can enhance their success and ability to access important social resources. The following are some suggestions to enhance environments in order to promote social identity:

- Include photos of families, children, and teachers working together so every member of the community is represented in the classroom environment. Photos of the children in the classroom can be adhered to blocks or made into puzzles. This allows children to further recognize their physical characteristics and abilities.
- Make mirrors available in various spaces to allow children an opportunity to see themselves and value their own physical characteristics.
- Provide art materials that represent the skin colors of all racial and ethnic groups.
- Invite families to participate in meaningful ways during everyday activities. Develop gathering places that encourage families to interact and know each other to promote a sense of community and develop trust.
- Respect family home languages by incorporating books, welcome signs, and labels in all languages that families with children in your program speak. Learn how to greet children and families in their home language.
- Create family photo books for the library area so children can see each other's families and find differences and similarities. Make a family shelf for families to take turns bringing in artifacts they use daily or on special occasions.
- Plan the environment carefully to avoid stereotypes and token symbols.

TAKE ACTION: Your Role as a Teacher

Supporting Children's Cultural and Social Identity

Derman-Sparks proposes that anti-bias education helps teachers support each child's identity. Healthy self-identity develops through gaining awareness and eliminating social limitations and stereotypes that hinder emotional development. An anti-bias approach is designed to help children become responsible for their own learning. It also enhances children's sense of identity and confidence in their own abilities. Following are some suggestions to support children's cultural and social identity in the classroom and community:

- Develop the skill of self-reflection and deepen your thinking about the role diversity plays in learning and development. In an ever-changing demographic composition of early childhood programs, teachers can find both opportunities and challenges in being more responsive to children from different backgrounds.

- Help children gain the ability to explore differences and similarities and celebrate each other's strengths. Promote children's self-exploration and self-reflection through meaningful collaborative experiences, such as creating a classroom mural to celebrate their diversity.

- Provide opportunities for children to talk about personal conflicts, concepts of fairness, and injustices. These opportunities can help children gain a deeper understanding of situations that happen in the classroom and in their community.

- Design experiences that help children think critically about their social world and to take action against injustices. Finding a meaningful cause and creating an action plan helps children build empathy for others.

- Take the time to learn about each family's traditions and cultural beliefs and invite families to share them with the children and other families.

In Conclusion: Social-Emotional Theories

The theorists guide educators in knowing that social-emotional development is a social and interactive process that happens within the context of meaningful relationships. Social-emotional development is promoted with the assistance of more knowledgeable others. It is guided by culture and language. Conditions for healthy social-emotional development include trust, safety, security, and the social needs of love, belonging, and connections. Healthy social-emotional development involves real-life experiences along with developing healthy self-awareness and positive identities in young children. Social-emotional development is the foundation for all other development. In an environment that promotes social-emotional well-being, children learn to give and accept love, to be confident and secure, to show empathy, and to be curious and persistent. These are abilities that will allow children to relate to others and lead a healthy and productive life. It is through social-emotional development that children acquire competence and resiliency. They learn to respect differences and find similarities. They are capable of speaking up for equity and becoming activists for themselves and others.

Derman-Sparks

Your Turn

Now it is your turn to identify theory in children's play. The following story is designed for you to apply your analytic skills in relation to children's social-emotional development. As you read the story, identify which theories are visible in the children's play, consider key concepts, and reflect upon how you would support the children's interests and needs based upon the theories.

Squirrel Needs a House

A Survival Investigation

One morning the children discover a squirrel climbing up a tree outside the window. They watch, mesmerized, for a long time. As they observe, the children have many questions and concerns.

> Bella: What do they eat?
>
> John: How do they stay warm?
>
> Izzy: Can they die?
>
> Alina: They need food and a place to be warm.
>
> Sammy: Yes, it is cold and windy now. We need to care and feed them.

The children make important connections to previous knowledge about their own needs for food and shelter. This leads to a deeper investigation of how squirrels survive and what they eat. The teachers recognize the children's concerns and see the opportunity to help build on the children's empathy by caring for the animals that live in their area. The teachers and children begin the process

by researching what squirrels eat and where they sleep. As the children share their ideas, they question each other and offer new possibilities. The older children have responses that are more advanced and challenge the younger children to question their hypotheses. The teachers guide the conversation and offer new resources for the children. Since there is a concern about the cold weather approaching, the children decide to build a cozy place for the squirrels. Influenced by a previous investigation on construction, the children create blueprints for a squirrel house. The teachers add wood, carpentry tools, and other materials to the environment. The older children carefully guide the younger ones to hammer the nails that hold the squirrel house together.

Ryder: Our house is finished because we work hard together.

John: Let's take it outside.

Sammy: It needs a soft cushion for the squirrels to sleep.

The children place the squirrel house outside and include cotton balls as cushion, as well as some food. Every day the children keep watch and wait for the squirrels to come and use their new house. The children rejoice when they see the squirrels coming in and out of the house. The children add new food to the house throughout the winter months.

Alina: We saved the squirrels.

Jd: Now they have food and shelter.

Bella: Yes, we worked hard to save them.

Making Theories Visible in Play

Reflect on how theory informed the decisions used by the teachers. Which theories do you see in the story? What theory would you use to respond to children's interest? How would you use the theories covered in the chapter to create a responsive environment that increases children's knowledge?

Going Deeper: Questions for Your Reflection

Now that you have reflected on the story above, use your knowledge of the theories to think about how you can use theory to expand the learning of the children in your care.

1. Think about a child who you know well. How does Piaget's theory clarify your understanding of this child's relationships and personal growth? What about the other theories?
2. How can you provide multiple opportunities for children to discuss and argue their different points of view? What personal values do you have that may affect the way you view an argument?
3. How does Erikson's theory of how children acquire identity compare to your own experience? What can you do to support the identity of children in your program?

Your Turn

4. How can you support empathy development in children based on Piaget's ideas? Based on Derman-Sparks's ideas?

5. How do you develop appropriate consciousness in children of what is "right" and "wrong" behavior while still supporting their needs, desires, and demands as individuals? What might different theorists say about this?

6. How does Vygotsky's explanation of culture and language help you promote social-emotional development in children?

7. Think of your own intelligences and the ones you prefer to use. How can you use this information to support multiple intelligences in children and their social-emotional growth?

8. How can you expand a sense of fairness and social action into all areas of the environment?

Part 3

Beyond ABCs and 1, 2, 3s: Children as Protagonists of Their Own Knowledge

Cognition is the ability to think and reason. Its development begins in infancy when children use their senses and motor skills to understand how the world around them functions. With the absence of language, infants rely completely on their senses and motor systems to explore and manipulate their environment. During this stage, infants begin to think by using mental as well as physical actions.

As children grow, play becomes their most important vehicle for acquiring new knowledge, and yet there is not an agreed-upon definition of play educators can rely on. Most of us recognize play; however, play is difficult to describe as it is an abstraction such as love or happiness. Characteristics of play include being active, pleasurable, engaging, freely chosen, intrinsically motivated, nonliteral, and process oriented. Play gives older toddlers and preschool-age children the concrete experiences they need to symbolically re-create what they already know using words, letters, numbers, or items to represent their understanding. Children's ability to think symbolically is seen especially in their use of language as they begin to think and talk about objects in play and separate from their actual experience of those objects.

Children also begin to use symbolic representation in play for everyday experiences. For instance, children may use one object to represent another, such as using a block to represent a car. Young children see patterns in objects and events of the world and then attempt to organize those patterns to explain the world around them. As children manipulate their world through play and make sense of the symbols that surround them, they begin to form hypotheses, generate ideas, and evaluate their own points of view, developing their cognitive abilities. In other words, cognition allows children to distinguish between appearances and reality.

Children are remarkably active participants in their own cognitive development. They constantly attempt to understand, explain, organize, manipulate, construct, and predict. The early learning and development theorists offer insights into how a child's thinking progresses as he develops. Children's cognitive skills transition from an infant's use of senses and motor skills, to a preschooler's symbolic thinking, to a school-age child's concrete thinking, to the abstract thinking of an adolescent and adult. The theorists' perspectives help us understand how a child's thought processes affect her behavior.

Jean Piaget

Children as Active Learners

Jean Piaget on Cognitive Development of Young Children

Piaget's theory of cognitive development focuses on how children think. Piaget observes that children make sense of the world through active exploration and direct experience with people and objects. He maintains that children gain understanding through their own discovery and construction of experiences rather than through passive observation. In other words, children create or construct their own knowledge. Through his stages of cognitive development and the concepts of assimilation, accommodation, schemas, and equilibrium, Piaget's theory gives us a way to understand how children think.

Most of Piaget's research focuses on developing a theory of the cognitive stages of children's thinking. Piaget outlines several stages of cognitive development:

- Sensorimotor stage (birth to two years old) occurs as children use their senses and motor skills (for example, sucking and grasping) to explore the environment. Intelligence takes the form of actions. Preoperational stage (three to seven years old) includes the ability to learn through symbols (language and mental representations of thought). Children use interactions with meaningful experiences to acquire knowledge that can be integrated into previous information. The stage begins when children are unable to understand logical thought concepts such as *reversibility*, which is the idea that once something is changed it can be returned to its original state, or *cause and effect*, which is the idea that events are related. During this stage, children demonstrate *egocentrism*, which is seeing and feeling things from only their perspective. Intelligence in this stage is intuitive; thinking is controlled more by perceptions than logic. Concrete operational stage (seven to eleven or twelve years old) is when children understand particular thoughts and apply them to actual situations. Intelligence is based upon specific, concrete experiences.

■ Formal operational stage (eleven or twelve years old through adulthood) involves the ability to think abstractly and reason analytically. Intelligence at this stage is abstract.

As children are exposed to a variety of experiences, they gather, organize, and store knowledge for future use in their interactions with new experiences and information. *Assimilation* is the process children use to take in and process information according to their existing knowledge. *Accommodation* is the process children use when they need to change old ways of thinking to adjust to new situations. Often this adjustment happens through building a new *schema*, which is a model of how things work, and that adjustment results in *equilibrium*.

For example, Taylor has lots of squirrels in his backyard. When he sees squirrels jumping along the ground, through assimilation Taylor can fit that action into his past experiences of the way squirrels move. If he sees a chipmunk for the first time on a family camping trip, Taylor has to adjust or accommodate his understanding to include a new animal that is similar, but different, to a squirrel. He does this by developing a new schema for a chipmunk that includes descriptive characteristics of the animal's appearance and behavior. In order for Taylor to successfully understand this new information, he must regain a mental balance as he reconciles his conflicting perceptions and experiences. As Taylor rearranges his understanding of outdoor animals to include both squirrels and chipmunks, he gains equilibrium.

Piaget's research into how children's logical thinking patterns develop at different ages reveals the way children use various schemas as a framework to rationally understand their world. A child who is exploring a "transporting" schema may be fascinated by picking up, moving, and dumping transportable things. An infant who is exploring a "trajectory" schema may drop a spoon repeatedly to the ground as a way of testing how objects fall. As children test schemas they are mentally and actively involved in learning, which Piaget emphasizes is necessary for young children's intellectual development. As you read the following story, look for examples of how children's active engagement contributes to their learning.

An Eruption of Fun

Building a Schema for Geysers

At Crystal's Creative Kids, the children often engage in new experiments and scientific discoveries. They play with water and often mix different materials to see what happens. One day a group of children are engaged with water play. Ryder picks up clear tubing and gently blows air through the tube and into the water. Air bubbles gurgle in the water as a result. Ryder pulls the tube out of the water, looks at it, and then places it underwater again. He blows through the tube again as he stares at the water. The same result is achieved. He blows a third time, but this time he blows with great force. Water squirts up and sprays all over John.

Ryder (giggling with delight): It's like a geyser!

John: Hey, you got me wet!

Ryder: It wasn't me. It was the geyser. It explodes just like on *Dora the Explorer*!

John lowers his head to the water while Ryder blows through the tube again.

John: Listen, you can hear the bubbles. They make a *glub, glub* sound. Do it again.

And so the children's fascination with geysers emerges. Later, together with Teacher Crystal, the children research geysers on the Internet. They look at photographs of real-life geysers and look for ways to make an artificial geyser. The children listen intently as Crystal reads about what causes geysers to erupt. They ask many questions.

Sammy: Is it smoke that comes up?

Ryder: No, smoke is from fires. Geysers are water, not fire.

The children and Crystal discuss the differences between smoke and steam.

To simulate how a geyser erupts in an explosion of water and steam, Crystal gathers liquid soap, a soda bottle, a tub, and effervescent antacid tablets to conduct an experiment. The children eagerly watch as she fills the bottle with warm tap water, adds a few drops of liquid soap, and then drops in a crushed effervescent antacid tablet. She immediately places her hand firmly over the top of the bottle.

Crystal: What do you think is going to happen?

Sammy: It's going to shoot high like in this picture.

Ryder: Yeah, it's going to blast off like a rocket. Watch out!

When Crystal removes her hand from the top of the bottle, there is a loud *POP!* The children squeal excitedly.

Izzy: It popped! (She refers to seeing the experiment online.) Like what we saw! It makes that sound, like a *real* geyser!

Nate: It's bubbling! Like a soda!

Ryder: It's raining soda!

Liquid spurts out of the bottle and flows over its sides. Sammy, Nate, and Cruz squeeze the bottle, which causes more liquid to cascade over the sides. All the children place their hands in the tub, feeling the fizzing bubbles and warm liquid.

Crystal: Why do you think the bottle erupted?

Nate: 'Cause it exploded.

Ryder: 'Cause it's a geyser.

Crystal: Yes, but what makes geysers explode?

Ryder: It's the soda.

Crystal: I didn't put soda in the bottle. It was water.

Ryder: It's the bottle. I know 'cause it exploded like that at my house when my mom dropped the bottle.

Nate: It's the stuff you put in the bottle.

Crystal: Which stuff?

Crystal does not explain anything about the physical reaction. She wants to see if the children will discover what made the explosion happen on their own.

Crystal: What do you think would happen if I didn't have my hand over the bottle?

Ryder: It would blast off to the sky.

After the experiment, Crystal places pencils, crayons, and clipboards with paper on a large outdoor picnic table. She encourages the children to draw what they know about geysers as a way for the children to develop meaning and understanding. A fascination with the bubbling reaction of substances emerges as children describe their drawings. To provide more opportunity for the children to continue their interest in fizz, Crystal sets out baking soda and vinegar. This allows the children to further investigate chemical reactions. Crystal first introduces this new experiment during a small-group gathering inside.

After a discussion about the substances, the children move outside to conduct their research. Nate and Jd demonstrate how to mix the soda and vinegar together as everyone looks on with eager anticipation. Then, the children begin their own individual explorations. There is contradiction, however, between the children's expectations. Jd is interested in stirring the two substances together. He pours large tablespoons of vinegar on the soda and mixes them together into a muddy paste. He seems focused on the thickness of the mixture. Izzy and Nate slowly pour droplets of vinegar onto the soda. After each splash of vinegar, they pause and observe the fizzing bubbles. When the bubbles subside, they drip on more vinegar. Their concentration is on the physical reaction of the materials. Eventually their concoctions stop bubbling and their attention shifts to the soupy mixture.

The children take their mixtures and pour them into a large tub. Their focus changes to dumping and stirring.

Izzy comments: The bubbles are all gone.

Ryder: Now we can make mud soup.

Making Theories Visible in Play

The geyser story provides us with a glimpse into Piaget's belief that cognition happens through active exploration and direct experience with people and objects. As the children create their own understanding of geysers, they work with each other, Teacher Crystal, and real materials. Each child experiments with baking soda and vinegar individually, allowing each child to actually transform the substances rather than passively watching the teacher. The children learn cognitive ideas such as cause and effect through this hands-on learning.

The children in this story are in Piaget's preoperational stage. Their inability to see another's perspective and understand causality is evidence of their preoperational thought. Ryder demonstrates Piaget's concept of egocentrism when he says it's the "geyser" that gets John wet and not Ryder's own actions. Ryder's words show how he cognitively assumes that others see the situation from his viewpoint as well.

We can also see Piaget's emphasis on the cognitive ability to understand cause and effect relationships as the children observe the effervescent antacid tablet experiment. In this situation, Ryder believes the bottle is what is causing the liquid to erupt. His perception indicates that he hasn't yet made a connection between the eruption and what is actually causing the chemical reaction. He focuses his understanding on his experience of the exploding soda bottle at home. Nate, on the other hand, connects that the "stuff in the bottle" causes the explosion, and when he drops vinegar on baking soda he pauses and watches the chemical reaction. In both instances, Nate's actions indicate that he understands combining substances causes a reaction. In other words, he accurately connects cause and effect, which is an indication that his thought processes are transitioning to concrete operations.

As children are exposed to a variety of experiences, they gather, organize, and store knowledge that they will later use to accommodate and assimilate new concepts and information. In this story, Ryder demonstrates Piaget's concept of assimilation by fitting information into his existing ideas of geysers. Ryder affirms that geysers shoot water high into the air. He had seen a *Dora the Explorer* cartoon episode with a geyser, and he remembered seeing a geyser shoot water up into the air. The fact that Ryder could easily assimilate the shooting water with his knowledge of geysers shows that he still has equilibrium according to his current schema of geysers. The concept of accommodation is seen as Ryder restructures to accommodate the new information that geysers make noise. Ryder's growing cognitive development is also visible as the children explore the difference between steam and smoke. When Ryder says, "Smoke is from fires. Geysers are water, not fire," he is developing schemas for both fire and geysers. Assimilation and accommodation allow him to organize what he understands about geysers, steam, and smoke in a cohesive way. Piaget's theory, as shown in this story, provides major contributions for understanding how children acquire knowledge.

TAKE ACTION: The Environment

Designing Play-Based Environments to Support Cognitive Development

The core belief of Piaget's theory involves children's active engagement in their own learning. Piaget's work points out that children learn as they interact with forces and things in their environment. Play-based environments include spaces and materials that encourage children's inquiry, discovery, and experimentation with physical and earth sciences. Play-based environments allow for multiple play possibilities and provoke problem solving and critical thinking. Below are some ideas to design environments that allow children to construct their own knowledge:

- Incorporate materials into the environment that support spatial relationships. This gives children the opportunity to compare space, movement, distance, and positions of objects in relation to their bodies. Incorporating marbles and cove molding into the environment allows children to experiment with the direction and distance marbles travel based on the molding's position.

- Offer materials with multiple play possibilities to encourage problem solving. When children play with loose parts, they gain an understanding of how objects work, including the functions, properties, and wholes and parts of objects. Loose parts are materials that are open-ended or allow the children to determine what the object is and how it is used. The possibilities are endless.

- Include materials and spaces that promote quantitative reasoning. These types of relationships involve an understanding of such things as number, volume, length, and weight. Number sense, for example, is acquired through knowing that three children fit on the tire swing or two children can paint at the easel, counting shells, or using a lot or a little clay. Materials need to be plentiful, as children need the opportunity to use "too much." Length is experienced with planks or ladders to bridge spaces or stones that can be lined and measured. Children learn about weight as they carry containers of sand and water. They can discover that wet sand weighs more than dry sand, for example.

TAKE ACTION: Your Role as a Teacher

Teacher's Role to Support Cognitive Development

Piaget's theory introduces the idea that children acquire knowledge through the active process of exploration. This is the way children figure out how things work. Children mentally change their environment to adjust to new information as it is presented to them. As children grow, they gain more knowledge and apply these newly learned concepts into existing information as they enter different developmental stages. In his book *To Understand Is to Invent* (1972), Piaget argues that when children engage in meaningful active learning, they are able to retain and apply the knowledge they acquire. Active learning stimulates children's curiosity and promotes deeper reasoning power. Piaget further argues that as children explore and learn, they develop independence and the ability to posses their own ideas freely. The following are some ways to promote cognitive development and the love for learning:

- Foster an experimental attitude among children by showing your interest and delight in their discoveries. You can do this by listening carefully to children's theories and seeking to understand their reasoning.

- Join children in the process of researching meaningful ideas. Ask inquiry questions that provoke divergent thinking. For instance, when attempting to make a specific color by mixing paint, teachers and children can research how to use the color wheel to create a variety of possibilities.

- Ask questions as children represent their understanding of objects through drawing, painting, and collage materials. For example, "How will you make the legs to support your elephant's heavy body?" or "What kind of lines will you use to show the water's movement?" Observe, listen, and reflect on children's ideas. Respond to ideas and encourage children to explore them further.

Erik Erikson

Taking Initiative to Gain Mastery That Supports Learning

Erik Erikson on Cognitive Development of Young Children

Erikson's theory of eight developmental stages, known as psychosocial development theory, presents a set of questions and problems that every person wrestles with at different stages of life. At each of Erikson's developmental stages, there are many implications for cognitive development. In order for children to develop a strong critical-thinking ability and make sense of the world around them, they have to successfully master the different tasks, or "crises," presented in Erikson's theory. Children use cognition to resolve the conflicts presented by each one of Erikson's stages.

In Erikson's first stage, trust versus mistrust (birth to one year old), cognition helps a baby recognize her mother's voice and smell even from birth. This cognitive ability facilitates the familiarity that leads to trust or mistrust. Trust is developed through a caring experience that provides consistency, continuity, and "sameness."

As children enter the autonomy versus shame and doubt stage (two to three years old), their cognitive development strongly influences how they will approach this and future stages. At this stage, children seek to gain autonomy while maintaining the support of caring adults. This requires an understanding of how to approach different tasks; in a nutshell, it requires thinking. Letting children take measured risks facilitates their understanding of everyday situations, which children need in order to be successful during this stage's "crisis." This is also the stage where language, which is strongly linked to cognitive development, develops at a fast pace.

In the next stage of Erikson's theory, children resolve the "crisis" or conflict of initiative versus guilt (four to five years old). At this stage, children become more and more capable of completing tasks on their own and recognizing their own skills. Children are purposeful and are learning at an increased rate during this stage. They are capable of planning and carrying out simple goals. Their sense of self increases, and they begin to intellectually classify themselves and others based on specific physical attributes and skills. Children begin to apply their existing knowledge to resolve more complex social relationships and collaborate with others. They also start to internalize concepts of right and wrong and begin to display rudimentary steps toward perspective taking. However, while they have the initiative to take on projects, children at this stage may overestimate their ability. Trying a task beyond their capability can lead to a sense of guilt.

During Erikson's fourth stage, industry versus inferiority, school-age children are capable of learning, creating, and accomplishing numerous new skills and knowledge, thus developing a sense of industry. According to Erikson, children strive to acquire the cognitive skills valued in their own culture. For some school-age children in the United States this may include learning to read, memorizing multiplication facts or lines in a play, following a cooking recipe, counting money, or playing chess. In another culture, it may include learning to navigate, identifying weather conditions, or bartering. In this stage, children focus on using cognitive skills as they learn to be capable and productive.

How We Build

Stages of Learning and Interest

For several days, the block area has been full of children constructing castle structures using wooden blocks. The teachers decide to support the children's curiosity in building by taking a field trip to see the repair work that is being completed on their block. The teachers want to provoke the children to come up with new ideas about what they can build and explore.

At the work site, the children are particularly interested in the large equipment trucks that are being used to transport gravel. Alex notices that there is an area that is being corded off with orange cones and caution tape.

Alex: Look, it has yellow tape. That means "stay away."

John: Hey, we can do that when we build our castle so no one touches our work.

The next day, the children continue with their building. The teachers add yellow caution tape to the block area, and the children immediately rope off the area.

Ryder: This is like yesterday. Put it here. That way we can keep things safe.

Sammy: No one can break our stuff.

Throughout the week, the teachers continue to set the stage for construction by adding books about buildings, architecture, bridges, and houses. They post blueprints on a wall in the block area to show the work of architects. They also hang the children's drawings and pictures of them building. Over the next few days, the children's attention shifts from equipment to tools.

The children know certain tools are used for specific tasks, and they are beginning to develop an understanding of how to operate various tools. Teacher Crystal notices this developing awareness and organizes a woodworking center with building tools: small wooden blocks, stones, a wrench, hammers and nails, and screwdrivers and screws. She introduces the tools one at a time and intentionally respects the children's capabilities and competency. She gives the children an opportunity to handle each tool. She talks about and demonstrates how to use each tool before the children begin carpentry.

Ryder, Nate, and Alex show interest in hammers. Ryder begins with hammering a nail into a wood block. He holds the hammer at the handle's end and hits the nail with sharp, firm hits. He assumes a leadership role as he directs Nate to move his hand away from the hammer's head.

Ryder: That's too close. This is how you do it, with hard hits. Be careful so you don't hit your finger.

Ryder's confidence grows with each hit of the hammer.

Nate watches closely as Ryder hammers a nail deeper and deeper into the wood. As the children continue to explore the tools, Nate talks to Crystal.

Nate: My dad has hammers at home. He lets me do work at home with him.

Crystal: What other tools does your dad use for building?

Nate: He uses a long thing that he turns over and over. I don't know how you call it.

Crystal: Does is look like this? (She shows Nick a screwdriver.)

Nate: Yes, that's it.

Crystal: It's called a screwdriver.

Nate: Can I use it?

Crystal: Yes, but let me remind you of the trick. Screwdrivers can be dangerous. To use the screwdriver, you first need to start a hole for the screw. It looks like this.

(She shows Nate a screw.) Then place the screwdriver in the straight slot of the screw and for the first few turns hold the screw with your fingers. Press down as you turn.

Crystal shows Nate how to make a hole with a nail and then start the rotations. She knows that Nate has advanced skill and coordination and is capable of using the tool, yet she stays close to supervise.

Nate's self-esteem grows as he gains competence in mastering the use of the screwdriver. He works diligently on turning the screw. His focus is on the movement and rhythm of twisting the screwdriver. He compares the difference between using a nail and a screw.

Izzy comes over, picks up a screwdriver, and manipulates it between her fingers. She explores the thickness and shape of the screwdriver's cold, hard shank and feels its tip.

Izzy (referring to the screws): Which one I use?

Nate (picking up a screw): Use this one. See, this one (he holds up a nail) is for hammers. This one with the line on top is for this.

Izzy takes a piece of wood, screw, and screwdriver over to the floor. She sits down and begins to use the tool.

Brycin, Nate, and Ryder take their turn at the woodworking table. Nate has been hammering with light, fast strokes over the past week. His lack of power keeps the nail from going deep into the wood. Today his increase in skillfulness is seen as he holds the nail and hammers sharp, crisp blows without hitting his finger. He concentrates all his effort on hitting the nail.

Nate: It's going in!

Next Nate tries to use the screwdriver. He is learning function and skill as he places pressure on the driver and turns it in a clockwise direction. He sees progress in making the screw go deeper.

Nate: Look, Teacher Crystal, it's working!

At small-group time, the children share with Crystal their ideas about types of tools and materials used for building. Sammy explains her understanding of

the difference between nails and screws. She describes a nail as "being straight" and a screw as "being rough." Alina talks about her nail bending and the children problem solve about what to do. Throughout their discussion, it is apparent that the children's knowledge about which tool to use in different situations is growing.

As the weeks continue, most of the children still focus on the process of using the tools. Brycin, however, shows interest in moving from process to making a product.

Brycin (referring to *Houses and Homes* from the Around the World Series): I want to make a tepee like in the book.

Teacher Jason: What will you need to make your tepee?

Brycin: I'll need poles and rope.

Teacher Jason: I think that I have some poles in the garage. Let's go see if they will work.

The poles are acceptable to Brycin. He takes on the role of contractor in constructing the tepee. He directs the other children to hold and space the poles like a "triangle" while he focuses his effort on wrapping string to secure the poles. When the pole structure is secure, the children drape a sheet over it and use duct tape to secure the sheet to the poles. Brycin's sense of accomplishment is seen on his face.

The tepee becomes a favorite place for children to hide and get away from the action. The children's interest in tools has evolved into a new direction toward constructing large, outdoor structures.

Making Theories Visible in Play

The children in this story have a strong sense of trust in their environment, their teachers, and each other. They exhibit a sense of trust in their environment because the block area and woodworking center are in the same consistent locations. The children know exactly where to find specific blocks they need for building and the tools they need for carpentry. The trust the children demonstrate show that they have successfully mastered Erikson's foundational stage and are exploring their thoughts and ideas about the next stages.

As the children continue to practice building, the teachers in the program provide them with real tools to explore and test. In providing tools, the teachers demonstrate the relationship between cognitive growth and

Erikson's next stage, autonomy versus shame and doubt. The teachers are willing to let the children take the risk of testing new skills in order to plan and practice their ideas. When the children distinguish between tools and problem solve their bent nails, they develop cognitive autonomy—the ability to choose and explore their interests and to determine solutions for problems. The children are encouraged to work independently, and this sense of autonomy allows them to delve into more complex cognitive tasks as they work at understanding and manipulating the tools.

Throughout their exploration of building, the children demonstrate Erikson's next stage, initiative versus guilt. The children negotiate, exchange, and discuss their ideas and concepts. They support each other in deeper thinking by helping each other learn to use the tools accurately and safely, such as Ryder helping Nate learn to hammer. As the children continue to build, they take initiative in creating new ideas, problem solving, and critically thinking about their ideas. When Brycin approaches the idea of building a tepee, he is taking initiative to move from the process of using tools to actually completing a product. A new task emerges, and the children work together to build the tepee.

Brycin, who is older, guides the children in a group effort to construct the tepee. Brycin's success is significant beyond the tepee. He has gained a deeper understanding of his own building abilities, creativity, and capacity for leadership. Brycin has entered Erikson's next stage, industry versus inferiority (six to twelve years).

Erikson's theory of psychosocial development offers a framework as to how children use their cognitive skills to achieve the tasks of attaining autonomy, initiative, and industry. His theory helps us understand that cognition and social development are linked together and cannot be separated. This knowledge encourages teachers to provide experiences where children can explore their emerging skills.

TAKE ACTION: The Environment

Creating Respectful Environments That Support and Respond to Children's Ideas

Erikson's work supports and cultivates healthy cognitive growth in children. According to Erikson, children's sense of trust, autonomy, initiative, and industry are supported by increased cognitive skills. By intentionally designing consistent, intriguing environments and providing materials, we create ways for children to plan and invent activities with others, both of which are cognitive skills. Here are some ideas to promote cognitive development across Erikson's early childhood stages:

- Design an environment where children can explore and test their ideas for extended periods of time by offering open-ended materials such as blocks, clay, water, and sand. Children need to take time to interact with the materials and experiences in order to test, evaluate, and understand their own thinking.

- Create environments that allow children to take risks and support them in becoming more resilient, creative, and self-confident by incorporating versatile outdoor equipment such as wooden spools, crates, and planks. Taking risks and learning how to maneuver and face various situations and experiences helps children develop higher critical thinking and trust in themselves and others.

- Include a wide variety of open-ended materials in the environment. This offers the opportunity for children to try out new tasks. For example, glass stones added to the light table attract children to use materials in new ways, such as setting them in containers and placing them on top of mirrors. Perhaps in the process, they will discover transparency.

- Add props such as hats and scarves to allow children to be independent and create their own play themes. Children need access to appealing materials and opportunities to experiment with objects. Hands-on experiences provide the necessary foundation for independence and self-confidence.

TAKE ACTION: Your Role as a Teacher

Children's Interests to Promote Trust, Autonomy, and Initiative

Erikson views development as a cycle in which people resolve inner conflicts and emerge from each crisis or conflict with an increased sense of self and what they are capable of achieving. Through each stage, cognition is essential in making sense of the social world around them. It is through cognitive development that children increase their ability to discern moral and ethical dilemmas and acquire a deeper understanding of the cultural and social demands presented by people who are meaningful and significant in their life (Erikson 1963). Erikson considers play a central part of how children make sense of the world around them. The following are some ideas to support children's increased cognition at each stage of development:

- Respond to infants' cues with empathy and care. This helps develop meaningful interactions that create a sense of trust, which is crucial for learning. Create consistent routines that allow children to predict and understand what is happening. All of these actions tell children that the world is a place they can trust.

- Understand that toddlers face two challenges at this time: holding on and letting go, which requires them to use their constantly growing cognitive ability to figure how to overcome the current "crisis" presented by this social dichotomy. Give toddlers space to make small decisions, be patient, and allow them the opportunity to do things on their own and in their own time.

- Encourage and support children's safe exploration of interesting things to investigate. Children's cognitive development is motivated by a continuing curiosity and is either stimulated or hindered by their daily interactions with the environment. Engage children in opportunities to take initiative in planning and exploring their own ideas and interest.

- Foster ways for children to take risks, make decisions, participate in leadership roles, and take initiative in their own learning process.

Vygotsky

Lev Vygotsky

How Children's Play Improves Learning

Lev Vygotsky on Cognitive Development of Young Children

In his sociocultural theory, Vygotsky contends that children's cognition is promoted and guided by older and more skilled people, supported through cultural tools, and developed through play. Cognitive change occurs within what Vygotsky identifies as the ZPD, the skills that a person can do only with help, not yet independently. He suggests children show higher functioning cognitive skills, such as problem solving or symbolic substitution (using an object to represent another), when supported by a "more knowledgeable other." For example, a child who is unable to create a bridge with wooden blocks may, after receiving a suggestion from a peer, be able to solve this problem by scooting blocks closer together. Or a child may imitate an older peer by using a block as a car. When knowledgeable others support children's thinking it is called *scaffolding*. Scaffolding is the help children receive from adults or peers that enables them to learn new tasks they cannot yet complete independently.

According to Vygotsky, cultural tools also support children's cognitive development. Language, for instance, is a cultural tool that is used in many ways to solve problems. Toddlers' problem-solving abilities increase dramatically after they acquire language. Because language allows for the internalization of new concepts, strategies, skills, and ideas, children become more competent thinkers as they learn to talk. This can be seen in two-year-old Colter, who has learned to say, "I'm stuck. Help me!" rather than just squealing in frustration when he is stuck. Children also construct higher mental functioning as they engage with other cultural tools in the environment, such as drawings, written print, numbers, symbols, and traditions. For example, when a child draws a representation of her teacher, Mr. Herman, with exceptionally long legs, she is showing a deeper understanding of her thoughts about his height.

Vygotsky also asserts that play in the preschool years is crucial for the development of cognitive skills. When children play, they use cognitive skills to create imaginary situations, to take on and act out roles, and to determine rules for participating in the play. For example, children playing restaurant take on different roles than children playing pirates. When playing restaurant there are different rules for being a customer, waiter, and chef. When playing pirates, children use different gestures and noises— such as "argh"—as they make a thief walk the plank or fend off bad guys attempting to steal their treasure. When children engage in make-believe play they develop imaginary interpretations of objects they use in play. For example, a colorful block may become a pirate's dinner. Vygotsky considers this process of object substitution through play a higher mental function that increases learning. If Anna uses her imagination to pretend that a large stone is a doll, she is using abstract representation to visualize an image of a real doll.

Let's Make Chow Fun

Scaffolding Children's Learning

At Crystal's Creative Kids, the children pretend to cook each day as part of their dramatic play. The teachers notice that this interest is beginning to extend to the outdoors as children use twigs, rocks, and water to make pretend soup. The teachers start to reflect on the type of tools the children use and how they can slowly enhance this experience for them.

A practicum student comes up with the idea to provoke the children's thinking by introducing real cooking tools into the environment. Their hope is to give children opportunities to learn how to work with tools and recognize the type of tool they need for each cooking task. They also want to support the children's multiple interests and bring the frustration level down by providing authentic tools and materials that actually work. In addition, the children will enhance their knowledge by cooking with real tools.

Vygotsky

Teachers Crystal and Dolores place a variety of tools in different areas of the environment, including wooden spoons, measuring cups of different sizes, spatulas, bowls, and potato mashers. The teachers are delighted with the children's immediate interaction with the tools placed in the dramatic area. Children pretend to cook different dishes. A small-group investigation unfolds based on the children's interest.

Sammy: Let's make chow fun.

Dolores: What do you need to make chow fun?

Sammy: I need a big spoon.

Olivia: No, you need chopsticks.

Dolores: I haven't made or eaten chow fun before. Do chopsticks work better than a spoon?

Olivia: My grandma makes chow fun for me. She stirs meat, vegetables, and noodles. (Olivia pretends to stir ingredients.) The noodles are yummy. You eat them like this. (Olivia imitates holding chopsticks between her fingers, bringing food to her mouth, and making a slurping sound.)

Sammy: I've had chow fun at the restaurant. They give you chopsticks to eat it.

Sammy stirs her imaginary chow fun with a spoon. John pretends to fill measuring cups and pours the make-believe substance into the chow fun. Bella joins in the chow-fun making.

Alina (nearby): I am making fish for my mommy.

During their daily meeting, the teachers reflect on how to enhance the children's interest in pretending to cook familiar food. They marvel at the wide variety of food that is described and the children's thoughts on how to make it. They are

curious about Olivia's understanding that different tools, such as chopsticks, work better for preparing and eating certain foods. They discuss the children's experience with chow fun and restaurants and decide to add relevant items such as chopsticks, place mats, and guest checks for taking dinner orders to extend the children's knowledge of food preparation and restaurant dining.

The next day, Sammy goes to the dramatic play area and notices place mats and yarn "noodles." She puts the noodles in a bowl.

Sammy: I am going to make more chow fun.

She uses a wooden spoon to stir the mixture.

Sammy: I need salt and pepper.

She goes over to the cabinet, gets the salt and pepper shakers, and sprinkles a generous amount on the noodles.

Bella: You need eggs.

Bella hands two plastic eggs to Sammy, who pretends to crack them into the bowl. Bella sets the table with placemats and a plant centerpiece in preparation for dining guests. Ryder and John come to the table.

Ryder: What are you doing, guys? Cooking again?

Bella: We're making chow fun. If you want some you have to sit down. How many you want?

Bella carefully records Ryder's request on her order form and then brings bowls of chow fun back to the table. The boys work on mastering the use of chopsticks as they pretend to eat the noodles. Olivia demonstrates how to use these tools.

This kind of play continues for a number of days. The teachers decide to make real chow fun with the children for lunch. They research the difference between chow fun and chow mein and ask Sammy's mom to make a picture recipe. The children "read" the pictures as they follow the recipe and mix in all the sauces.

John: Our chow fun is going to be good!

Teacher Crystal: John, would you like to take the recipe home so your parents can make it for you?

John nods his head yes.

Crystal: We can also make our own cookbooks so you have the recipe.

During lunch the children taste the chow fun and comment on its salty flavor.

Crystal: We did not add salt to our chow fun. How do you think it got salty?

Sammy: I think that it was the brown stuff we added.

Crystal: You mean the soy sauce or the oyster sauce? Should we try each to see if one is salty? Sauces and spices make our food taste delicious.

Ryder (who has been quietly eating his noodles): These noodles are bigger than psketti. They're softer too. I like psketti, but pizza is best.

An animated conversation follows as children share their experience with pizza and spaghetti.

Dolores decides to enhance the children's interest in spices used to cook as well as their familiarity with pizza. She sets up a variety of dried herbs with grinding rocks and bread dough with tools for pizza making as provocations. She adds cookbooks to the environment and also prepares paper recipe books for the children to record recipes. As children walk into the classroom the next day, they notice there is a different smell in the air.

John walks into the center and runs over to the dramatic area. He picks up a dried basil leaf and smells it.

John: This smells like pizza.

Sammy: No, it smells like spaghetti.

John grasps one of the rocks to use as a pestle for crushing spices. He twists it from side to side hard against the wooden cutting board, grinding basil and oregano. The room begins to fill with a pleasant aroma. Younger Bella comes over to John.

John: You do it like this. (He models to Bella how to crush the herbs.) Be careful, Bella, so you don't hurt your fingers.

Sammy: Mmm, it smells good. What's that? (She points to a table with a ball of dough and cooking utensils.)

Crystal: Go over and see.

Sammy walks over to the dramatic play area.

Sammy: Crystal, look! This smells like pizza. I'm going to make pizza.

Sammy puts on an apron and chef's hat. She grasps a pizza cutter and rolls it over the dough in varying directions, making deep lines. Next she takes a rolling pin from the tool can and begins to roll the soft dough back and forth.

Crystal: Why did you choose that tool, Sammy?

Sammy: Because it makes it flat.

Crystal: But there are other kitchen tools used to make things flat. Even your hand can be a tool to make it flat.

Sammy: No, silly. This is the way you make pizza. Like this. (She demonstrates how to rotate the rolling pin to and fro over the dough.)

Sammy (to John): Hey, I need some of those green things for my pizza.

Crystal: They're called herbs or spices.

Sammy: I need spice.

John brings over a cup of freshly ground herbs.

John: Here you go.

Sammy sprinkles the herbs on her dough.

At this point Bella, John, and Nate start making their own pizzas. John leans close to "read" the instructions in the cookbook.

John: It says use the fork to press down like this.

While John uses a fork, Nate uses a rolling pin, after watching Sammy do so, to flatten his dough. The rolling pin sticks to the dough.

Dolores asks: What do you notice with the dough?

Nate: It's sticky.

Dolores: What could we do to make it less sticky?

John: Add water. See, the recipe says add water.

He goes back and forth from the dough to check the recipe.

Dolores: Do you think that will make the dough smooth? Let's try it.

The children use a measuring cup to add more water to the dough. Nate mixes the water and dough with his hands, creating a slippery mixture.

Bella: Is more water. (Meaning that there is too much water.)

John: Oh, no! This is not going to work.

Dolores: What can you do to make it work?

Nate: More flour.

He adds more flour and kneads the dough on top of the pizza stone. Meanwhile, Sammy gets her recipe book and records the steps.

Sammy: I need to write down how to make pizza so I remember. Crystal, what do you call the smelly things again?

Crystal: They are called herbs.

Sammy: Oh yeah, herbs. She scribbles down the words and reads the process out loud.

Bella notices that there is something missing from Sammy's recipe.

Bella: The recipe wants cheese.

She points to the photo of cheese.

Dolores: We have cheese in the refrigerator. Let me get it out.

The children sprinkle cheese on their pizzas. Nate starts to pick up the pizza stone with his pizza to put it in the oven.

Nate: This is heavy for me.

Dolores: Let me help all of you and put the pizzas in the oven. That is an adult task. The oven is hot.

While the children wait for their pizzas to bake, they gather for a small-group meeting. They talk about the tools and ingredients that they used to make pizza. They revisit the steps for making the pizza and the importance of cookbooks.

Sammy: I wrote the recipe in my book for next time. Remember we need that wheel thing to cut the pizza.

Dolores: That's called a pizza wheel. Is there another tool we can use to cut pizza?

Ryder: My mom uses scissors.

The children repeat "scissors?" together with a giggle.

Crystal: I guess that is another way. I've never tried it before, but I bet it works.

John: Mmm, it smells like pizza pie!

The children scream with delight. The pizza is ready. They all sit to enjoy the delightful meal they made together. As they eat the pizza, Ryder suggests they make cookies to share with their parents.

Crystal: We can do that tomorrow.

Ryder: Yes, because we need to look at the recipe and get the things we need.

That night, Dolores makes a peanut butter cookie recipe for the children to follow.

Making Theories Visible in Play

In "Let's Make Chow Fun" Vygotsky's ZPD is visible as the children's cognitive skills are supported by older and more skilled people. Olivia models how to hold and eat with chopsticks for John and Ryder, John shows Bella how to grind herbs, and Sammy demonstrates for Nate how to roll pizza dough. The children in these situations used the cognitive skill of recalling experiences from their memories to illustrate specific skills for less experienced learners. The children attain higher levels of thinking and knowledge as they receive assistance through their peers' repetition and modeling of actions. The teachers also promote the children's learning, serving as more knowledgeable others as they provide appropriate ingredients, recipes, and materials for the children to make chow fun and pizzas. When Sammy says, "I wrote the recipe in my book for next time. Remember we need that wheel thing to cut the pizza," Dolores gives her the actual name, "pizza wheel," and by asking children what other tools can be used to cut the pizza, she scaffolds their learning to help them expand their repertoire of tools and their functions.

Vygotsky's emphasis on cultural tools for supporting cognitive development is revealed through the children's language, print, and the variety of tools used in making chow fun and pizza. The children use language to tell how to make and eat chow fun, determine why the chow fun was salty, solve the problem of sticky pizza dough, and identify new vocabulary, such as "herbs." The teachers provide cultural tools of print, such as easy-to-follow recipes, and they give children the opportunity to symbolically represent their own ideas and thinking through drawings in their own recipe books. John "reads" the recipe as he makes pizza, and Sammy records how to make pizza in her recipe book. The teachers also support children's understanding of different cultures by introducing foods commonly eaten by the children in the program and by providing cultural materials such as chopsticks, rolling pins, and mortar and pestles used in the children's homes. In the story, when the children talk, draw, and write their ideas, they are able to integrate a deeper understanding of the food they eat. They are also able to infer differences and similarities found in familiar foods. They acquire meaningful cultural values that are a part of the community they interact with on a daily basis.

The development of cognitive skills through play, as described by Vygotsky, is seen in the children's reenactment of cooking scenarios. Their play begins with the stirring of twigs and rocks to make pretend soup. The use of these materials to represent another object is what Vygotsky defines as *symbolic substitution*; in this case the twigs and rocks represent food. A child must have a solid mental representation of an object in order to portray the object with something else. Next, the children take on and act out the role of being cooks who stir, fill, measure, crack eggs, and sprinkle salt and pepper as they make chow fun. Olivia takes on the role of waitress by setting the table, taking food orders, and serving the food. Ryder and John assume the role of restaurant diners as they place food orders and pretend to eat noodles. With the pizza play, Sammy takes on the role of chef by wearing an apron and chef hat, and John grinds the spices. In each one of these roles, the children demonstrate the cognitive ability of retrieving similar experiences and reenacting them from memory. In both cooking scenarios, the children's play has specific rules. Following these rules demonstrates cognitive understanding since children must have an awareness of what is appropriate behavior and what is not in the dramatic play scenario. Olivia, for example, informs the boys that they must sit down in order to eat and use chopsticks to eat the chow fun. Sammy insists that a rolling pin must be used to make pizza dough flat. Vygotsky believes that imaginary situations, such as the children's cooking play, require children to act in a specific way to stay engaged in the play. The cognitive skills required to assume roles and remain actively involved in play increases children's knowledge and capabilities.

The teachers in the program acknowledge Vygotsky's position that children's cognitive competence develops through the support and assistance of more experienced people, cultural tools, and play. They encourage the children to help others achieve tasks independently, they offer cultural tools in the environment such as language, drawing, and written print, and they support play by providing "real tools," such as chopsticks, place mats, and guest checks. This enables the children to reenact cooking scenes and encourages them to take the quality of their play to a higher cognitive level.

Vygotsky's theory offers educators an understanding of play's vital role in children's learning. He stresses the importance of experiences in which children are active explorers, and his theory informs us of the importance of a child's culture for learning. His concept of the ZPD is particularly helpful to educators because it provides a way to support and guide children's cognition.

TAKE ACTION: The Environment

Creating Environments for Acquiring Mental Tools

For Vygotsky, cognitive development is always socially mediated. That means that cognition is influenced by social interactions within the environment. He believes that children learn through active exploration, but that they do so within the context of interacting with others and through the use of mental tools—such as language—that help children remember, attend, and problem solve. Below are some suggestions for designing environments that support the development of mental tools:

- Create an environment that provides children opportunities to engage in productive activities that involve an actual outcome, such as story-telling, drawing, writing, or block building. Productive activities require defined areas and specific materials where children can share a common focus and interest. These are different activities than imaginary play, and they focus on the process rather than the product.
- Design spaces that promote building opportunities by making a large, protected space in the environment with a variety of wooden building blocks. When children build and talk together, cognitive development is promoted as they scaffold each other's learning.
- Use realistic materials for toddlers rather than relying on open-ended materials as toddlers are not yet thinking symbolically. Staging an environment with real props provides a context for play and allows them to make sense of the world around them.
- Incorporate open-ended props or loose parts in the environment for preschoolers. When children use an object to represent something else, they are using a higher level of cognition. This is called *symbolic function*—the ability to use objects, actions, words, and people to stand for something else. It helps children understand and make cognitive connections to their social context.
- Design spaces and materials for children to role-play and act out familiar scenes. Include authentic items, such as real pots and pans, rather than toy replicas.

TAKE ACTION: Your Role as a Teacher

Promoting Play as the Basis for Learning

Vygotsky introduces the idea that cognitive development and learning requires social and cultural interactions. He recognizes the importance of language in the acquisition of higher-level thinking skills. Through culture, children acquire much of the content of their thinking. Through daily interactions with the artifacts in their particular culture, children develop the means for their thinking. Once children obtain new information as they interact with their social environment, they will be able to internalize and use this newly acquired knowledge. As children re-create "real" everyday situations in their play, they begin to acquire a deeper understanding of societal requirements. Below are some suggestions to create play experiences that increase cognition:

- Design opportunities for children that are challenging and inviting. Introducing children to both symbolic and real cultural tools increases their capacity for learning. Engaging children in dramatic play and art experiences promotes deep understanding of cultural and societal expectations and sends the message that their work is valued. Children begin to gain a deeper understanding of who they are and recognize the importance of others as they see the world through the lens of their culture as well as the culture of others.

- Model, explain, and provide suggestions to suit each child's ZPD. For example, support a child in following a pictorial cooking recipe or putting together a jigsaw puzzle.

- Observe and document children's learning to make the process visible and to integrate planning that results in deeper learning. This furthers children's cognitive processing and increases their ability to think and reason. In other words, intentional planning gives children the skills to problem solve and think critically.

Abraham Maslow

Art as a Language That Promotes Thinking and Self-Actualization

Abraham Maslow on Cognitive Development of Young Children

Maslow (1987) divide his hierarchy of needs theory into two distinctive areas: (1) basic (or deficiency) needs, which include the physiological needs to sustain life (water, food, and shelter) and the need for safety; and (2) growth needs, which include love and belonging, esteem, and self-actualization needs. Basic needs are at the lower levels of his hierarchy and growth needs are at the highest level. Maslow also identifies cognitive and aesthetic needs as additional growth needs; however, they are not part of his original hierarchy.

From Maslow's perspective, cognitive development comes from attaining several "higher level" needs (cognitive, aesthetic, and self-actualization), *after* children's basic needs have been met. However, it should be noted that the order in which Maslow's needs are fulfilled does not always follow the "pyramid" progression. For example, children can fulfill self-actualizing needs while still trying to achieve esteem needs. Maslow asserts that cognitive skills develop from cognitive, aesthetic, and self-actualization needs, and he also places a special emphasis on creativity.

Cognitive needs: The inborn desire that individuals have to make sense of the world around them to increase their knowledge and understanding are cognitive needs. Maslow sees this impulse expressed through a person's natural tendency to discover, explore, and learn. Children crave learning as they investigate the properties of materials and how things work. For example, a child fascinated with water (a cognitive need) learns that water added to dirt makes mud, that water takes the shape of the container it is in, and that water can move horizontally and vertically when coming through a hose. According to Maslow, cognitive development happens when the environment offers opportunities to explore and supports children's interests and creative process.

Aesthetic needs: As educators, we also see cognition develop when Maslow's aesthetic and self-actualization needs are met. Maslow's aesthetic needs overlap with cognitive needs because both needs involve symmetry, order, and an appreciation of beauty—all of which require cognitive capacities such as reflective judgment, perception, knowledge, and memory.

Self-actualization needs: According to Maslow, *self-actualization* means using one's intelligence to define oneself (Maslow 1971). A person who is self-actualized has done the intellectual work of understanding who they are, making sense of the world around them, and making the most of their abilities. Such individuals are operating at a high intellectual level.

Creativity: Additionally, self-actualizers display high levels of creativity. It is through the freedom of creativity that children achieve the highest level of self-actualization. Children's thinking is revealed through creative experiences in a wide variety of areas including music, construction, dance, engineering, and art. For example, in making art children use mental abilities to discover and create meaning. Children problem solve as they draw an object on paper, because this task requires cognitive, perceptual, and technical skills. Every child's drawing of, for example, a dog will be different as the representations are based on each child's experiences with dogs of a certain breed, color, size, energy, intensity, friendliness, playfulness, and temperament. One child's interpretation may reveal a dog with large teeth, perhaps because one like it has bitten him, and another child's drawing may emphasize long legs because her family dog is a Great Dane. Children gain aesthetic appreciation and creativity as they increase their cognitive abilities, and as they increase their cognitive ability, they gain aesthetic and creative skills.

~~~~~~

I Want Quiet Music

Finding Creativity Cognition through Art

The teachers notice children gravitate to the art area upon waking from naptime. The children ask for what they call "quiet music" as they paint and draw. The noise level in the room is noticeably quieter as children focus and engage in deep exploration with the art materials. A routine is being established that nourishes children's interests and creative thinking process.

To support their interests and engagement with significant materials and interactions, the teachers discuss how to rearrange the area to create more of an artist's studio. They move a table by the window, allowing the natural light to stream through and enhance paint colors to deeper tones. The teachers organize a variety of diverse art materials on low shelves, arranged and sorted for easy access. The teachers also set out liquid watercolor, a different art medium, on the table for the children to investigate.

Sammy wakes up from naptime and goes over to the art area. She takes a paintbrush and begins to carefully dip it in the vibrant violet watercolor paint. She starts to make a variety of thick strokes on the paper, first at the top, systematically working from top to bottom and then reversing her strokes from bottom to top. Ryder comes to the table and they both paint on the paper. The teachers notice that during this quiet time, children are not arguing over tools and materials as they did earlier in the day. They are sharing different experiences and ideas. Perhaps the open art center stocked with a variety of materials and art media has made a difference in promoting the children's creativity and the way they interact with each other. The teachers begin to reflect on how to expand this stress-free time and meet the children's creative needs even further.

Over a period of days, the younger children begin to join the older ones in the art center, so the teachers offer materials that allow children of varying ages to successfully engage with creating art. The teachers begin by setting out small bottles filled with different colors of tempera paint. Both older and younger children begin to press little dots of paint on the paper. The dots begin to grow larger as the children manage their strength to squeeze the bottles harder.

Alina (laughing): I am making many dots.

Maslow

She applies tiny purple beads of paint on the paint surface.

John: I am making big dots.

Izzy: I can make big dots and little dots.

Izzy squeezes large puddles of orange paint out and then gazes intently as she constricts another bottle and brown paint oozes into the middle of each orange paint blob.

Izzy: Oh, I like how the colors mix. See the orange and brown. They look like cat eyes.

Ryder: Look, I am making lines.

The children continue to look at each other's work and they help each other with ideas of how to get more paint out of the bottles. One of the younger children, Jd, struggles with a bottle. John comes over and helps him by placing his hand over the younger child's and squeezing the bottle together. Later Jd tightly grips the bottle on his own, constricts it, and watches as blue dots of paint splat onto the paper. As the children gain more control, they start moving the bottles up and down, creating lines and squiggles. The helpful interactions between children continue as children work with the new art medium. The teachers want children to have more opportunities to use the paint bottles, so they leave the bottles in the art center for the children to use as they please.

Earlier in the week, the teachers observed children making mud pies with dirt and water outdoors. The children seemed to enjoy the natural elements as they first scoop fistfuls of dirt into a bucket, then pour in water and stir the concoction with a spoon. The children poured the sloppy mixture into pie tins and repeatedly patted and molded the wet "batter" with their hands. Reflecting upon the children's enjoyment with mud pies, the teachers wonder what children will do if clay is introduced into the environment. The next day, while the children sleep during naptime, teachers place slabs of potter's clay on tile work surfaces in the art studio, where a small group of children can focus and concentrate. At first, tools are purposefully absent in order to offer children an opportunity to explore and manipulate the clay itself.

As the children wake from naptime, many of them go over to the table and discover the large hunks of clay. They become familiar with the substance by rubbing the cool, smooth surface with flattened hands and fingers spread wide apart. Sammy and Izzy start to squeeze the clay with open hands and then slowly pinch and poke the clay with their fingers.

Kainoa gazes at his hand, which is stained with the clay's pigment. He brings his hand to his nose.

Kainoa: It smells like dirt.

Kainoa gets more clay and squashes it by pushing down. Again he stares at his clay-coated palm, and then he firmly presses it into the clay, leaving an impression of his hand.

After several days of manipulating the clay, the teachers notice that the children seem ready for clay tools. They add carving utensils to the art area and the children's work changes again as they experiment with the tools and clay.

Izzy: It feels hard.

Izzy grasps a roller's handles on either end and makes short back and forth strokes, which levels the clay. Sammy etches deep slashes across the clay. Bella selects a wooden modeling tool from the jar of clay tools and digs a deep hole in the clay, creating small crumbles. As the children use the clay, the air and their hands cause the clay to dry out. Bella seems aware of the change in the clay's consistency.

Bella: It is like dirt. It is falling.

Teacher Crystal: Bella, the clay is dry and hard. What can we add to make it soft again?

Bella looks up at the sink and back at Crystal.

Bella: Can I have some water?

Crystal: You want to try to add some water to see if it works?

Bella nods her head yes.

Bella: I need the spray bottle.

Crystal solicits Bella's help to fill the spray bottle with water. Then Bella brings the water-filled bottle over to the clay. She begins to spray the clay, carefully at first and then drenching it.

Bella: Look, it's not dirt no more. It's mud pie!

Maslow

Bella gleefully slaps the slippery clay. Izzy and Sammy spray their clay with water as well. The teachers wonder if the children will discover that too much water is not good and creates soggy clay that does not mold. But for now the children are finding pleasure in their sensory play, interacting more with each other and commenting on each other's work.

The ritual continues and after naptime the children look forward to creating art. The teachers notice that the youngest children are also eager to participate in the experience, so they respond to their interest by adding an easel near the art studio. They want to give the youngest children the opportunity to test their painting and emerging drawing skills. Colter experiments with making marks on the easel's whiteboard surface.

As the children continue to draw, paint, and sculpt, their symbolic renditions increase in sophistication. They begin to incorporate items from their own imaginations. The teachers continue to offer different media for them to work with. Since there has been such an interest in working together, the teachers set out a large canvas on the table to encourage the children to create a collective work of art. Bella, Ryder, and Sammy add pictorial representations on the canvas, and Colter and Jd add their signature scribbles.

Art is used now in different areas of the environment, and the teachers observe the children working individually and together. The children use art to capture things they see in the environment or structures they build. By the teachers' displaying the art with respect and in a visually aesthetic way, the children's work is honored. Art has become an important part of the daily routine, and the children integrate it into everything they do.

Making Theories Visible in Play

Because Maslow's basic needs of safety, love, and esteem are satisfied for the children in this story, many examples of higher-level growth needs are also visible as the children fulfill cognitive, aesthetic, and self-actualization needs. As the children engage in art, they demonstrate growth toward increasing their cognitive ability. Their behavior also reveals cognitive needs in what Maslow identifies as their desire to discover, explore, and learn—in this case about using the art tools and materials. Sammy's cognitive needs are revealed as she experiments with paint and learns about color, thickness of brush strokes, directionality, and space. Jd's cognitive needs are shown in his dot making as he problem solves how to manipulate the paint bottles. The children also exhibit an innate propensity to discover, explore, and learn about the clay. They investigate the clay's properties by squeezing, poking, rolling, and smelling it. As they add water to the clay, the children discover that water changes the clay's texture and malleability. The children's work with clay increases their knowledge and understanding of its properties. Maslow believes that this desire to understand how to work with these kinds of materials demonstrates that the children are meeting cognitive needs.

As Izzy makes symmetrical paint puddles, she is meeting her own aesthetic needs. She strategically places dabs of brown paint in the center of each orange paint puddle. Izzy also demonstrates meeting her aesthetic needs as she reflects upon how she likes the way the colors combine and look like cat eyes.

Self-actualization needs are met in this story through the multiple experiences the children have with meaningful art materials and each other. Through art exploration, the children have opportunities to understand their own capabilities as they make sense of their world. The integration of visual arts promotes the children's creative thinking. We see creativity, a key aspect of self-actualization, through the children's pictorial representations of smiling people, thick overlapping lines of controlled crayon scribbles, and wispy meandering lines of uncontrolled scribbles on canvas. It is evident in clay etchings, watercolor brush strokes, and marker lines on whiteboard surfaces. Maslow recognizes the importance of the creative process to promote cognitive development. He argues that creativity is a process and not a product. Notice how this is the case for each child when working with clay. Sammy's interest is in molding, Kainoa's is in making impressions in the clay, and Bella's is with the clay's texture and consistency. For each child, varying cognitive skills are enhanced as they cultivate the skills they will need to move from experiential work with clay to representational uses for clay.

Maslow

TAKE ACTION: The Environment

Environments That Invite Curiosity and Creativity to Promote Cognitive Development

Maslow believes children exhibit their cognitive needs through their instinctive desire to investigate, discover, learn, and create in order to make sense of the world. Children are naturally curious, and as teachers, we can design environments with spaces and materials that allow for this natural exploration. Maslow also addresses the importance of aesthetics and creativity for children. We can create spaces of beauty in our classrooms and ensure that materials and spaces are available to encourage creativity. Below are ideas for designing environments to promote children's imaginations and inventiveness:

- Create places both indoors and outdoors that allow children to engage with water and sand. Give them the opportunity to problem solve and understand concepts as they explore these natural elements. This type of play allows children to use all their senses. It provides them the opportunity to engage in functional play to make sense of the world around them.

- Offer an open art studio provisioned with tools that encourage creativity. Include a variety of markers, crayons, paint, clay, and papers in different shapes and textures to collage and explore. This wide range of tools and materials will support children's creativity and potential.

- Include multiple opportunities to expose children to nature, both outdoors and indoors. Include meandering paths, gardens, and lush greenery of interesting textures and colors. Intimate spaces for children and adults to relax can become protected places, bordered by flourishing vegetation. The aesthetic need is also seen in the desire for beauty, order, and symmetry. Visually pleasing spaces offer aesthetic and natural beauty that inspires and promotes creativity and cognitive development.

TAKE ACTION: Your Role as a Teacher

Teaching for Self-Actualization

Maslow's theory is helpful for teachers in understanding our role to support children's cognitive development. The early years lay a foundation for children to learn and achieve self-actualization. We can use Maslow's understanding of children as naturally curious, fascinated, and absorbed to encourage children's creativity, identity development, and problem-solving efforts. We can model self-actualizing traits of happiness, creativity, and spontaneity as we assist children in discovering their own potential. Below are some suggestions to promote cognitive development and self-actualization:

- Encourage conversations when children encounter disagreements and guide them in finding ways to focus on the means required to get to the end. Teachers have the responsibility to respond to children's behavior with curiosity rather than preconceptions.

- Include multiple opportunities for children to solve problems and find a variety of solutions. Part of achieving self-actualization is acquiring the ability to make decisions. Respect children's intent even when it goes against your objectives or thoughts of what they should do with the materials. For example, when a teacher offers children empty berry baskets with the goal of encouraging the children to make neat paint prints with them and instead one child uses the basket to smear paint, the teacher needs to be flexible and recognize that the child has a particular intent of her own.

- Engage children in long-term investigations of topics that are of interest to them. When doing this, teachers are meeting each child's individual needs to know and to learn what is important to them.

- Recognize and celebrate mistakes as a path for learning. The way people respond and react to mistakes shows their ability to know and use their strengths to make changes. This is one of the indicators of self-actualization. This requires an understanding that self-actualization is not a matter of all or some, but instead, a gradual process of improvement.

Maslow

John Dewey

Democracy in the Making

John Dewey on Cognitive Development of Young Children

During Dewey's time, children in most school classrooms sat quietly in their seats and memorized information. Dewey's theory transformed education in the United States from classrooms dominated by authoritarianism and rote learning to classrooms centered on democratic principles and engaged learners. Dewey's theory proposes that cognitive development is an active process that needs to be related directly to real life and enhanced through reflection. He advocates that cognitive growth is achieved through active learning (an approach supported by other early childhood theorists such as Piaget and Vygotsky). Dewey stresses that learning takes hold through effort, thinking, and motivation. He emphasizes that in order for children to make sense of the world around them, which involves thinking skills, they have to be active participants in the learning process. He contends that children construct meaning from experiences through active engagement and sensory input. The implication is that children acquire cognitive knowledge and understanding through active interaction with the real world.

Active learning: Learning, in Dewey's theory, requires personal interest. He advances the idea that interest in a task is necessary in order to learn effectively, as interest is active, absorbing, and satisfying (Dewey 1975). Once children participate in experiences that are engaging and fascinating, they understand the usefulness of knowledge and they are eager to learn about it. In other words, relevance and practical application of information promotes cognitive growth. According to Dewey, knowledge and thought should be intertwined and directly related to life and the world. For example, Dewey would argue that children develop cognitive skills as they participate in a practical and engaging task such as cooking. While cooking, children develop thinking skills and concepts of comparison, following directions, cause and effect, new vocabulary, and oral communication. They develop mathematical concepts such as sequence, measurement, spatial relationships, classification, counting skills, and one-to-one correspondence. Reading readiness skills increase through cooking as children see written words, interpret recipes, and experience sequence development and left-to-right directionality. The work of Dewey illustrates how cognitive development happens through a child's interest, participation, and interaction with his world. Dewey recognizes that great learning opportunities through everyday experiences, such as cooking, promote cognitive growth. Additionally, rather than seeing teachers as directive and all knowing, Dewey believes teacher should be colearners, engaging in learning with children.

Reflection: Another key component of Dewey's work is the idea of reflection as an integral part of intellectual development. He says critical inquiry is essential to cognitive development. As children draw conclusions from their direct experiences and begin to apply these ideas to other situations in their lives, they practice reflecting. Through reflection children create new meaning out of their experiences, which leads to cognitive growth. Cognitive development occurs through our ability to actively analyze, evaluate, and synthesize information. Dewey says children gain more knowledge from reflecting on their experiences than from the actual experiences themselves.

Why Is It Called Green Waste?

Collaborating toward Knowledge

When Izzy arrives in the morning, she runs up to Teacher Crystal.

Izzy: My mom tells me we need to separate paper from plastic. She gets mad if we put it in the garbage.

Ryder (standing nearby): My daddy has two different cans. One is for cans, and one is where we put bottles. Can we make boxes to separate things like at home?

The teachers gather three large boxes. The children paint each box a different color and attach a photo to indicate the different type of items to go in each box (one for paper, one for cans, and one for plastic). These boxes remain inside the early care and education center for recycling of things.

The week progresses, and the children begin an awareness of which recycling bin and outdoor trash can to throw used items in.

Sammy (after washing her hands): Where does the paper towel go? In the green box? (She looks at Crystal.) Do we have a blue box and a green box?

Crystal: Yes, Sammy, we do have a green box and a blue box.

Sammy: I need to put it in the green, right?

Crystal: Let's go see.

John, Ryder, and Sammy follow Crystal outside to look inside the trash cans.

Ryder: There are four trash cans, not just two.

Sammy: One is for plastic, one is for paper, one is for cans, one is for grass, and one is for trash? That's five!

Crystal: Let's see inside. (She lifts the cover of the first can.) This is all grass and leaves. It is called green waste.

Ryder (looking inside the can): Why is it called "green waste" when the leaves are brown?

Crystal: That is a great question. We will write it down so that we can find out.

Later in the week, the children start re-creating the recycle symbol in their artwork. They practice drawing it with markers and then tempera paint. The teachers notice the symbol appears in backyard chalk drawings as well.

The teachers decide to gather the children to talk about recycling. Their desire is to extend the children's understanding about the importance of recycling and its impact on the world. They also want to give the children the opportunity to learn more about their community. The teachers think it is important for children to contribute and participate in a greater cause. However, the teachers are cognizant of responding to the children's questions in a way that makes sense and furthers their knowledge.

The teachers do some initial research about recycling as they learn along with the children. During group-meeting time, Ryder's question about green waste is addressed. In order to make the experience more concrete, examples of green waste are compiled.

Teacher Ana: Yesterday, Ryder asked why we call "green waste" green when the leaves are brown. Does anyone know the answer?

John: We add only grass and leaves, but they change.

Sammy: To remind us that we only put green things inside.

Ryder: Because it is green.

Ana (pointing to the pile of green waste): This is all green waste. Ryder had a very important question that will help us understand what green waste is.

Ryder: It has cut flowers in it that are not green, so why is it green?

Crystal: "Green waste" is everything that can go back into the dirt without hurting it, because it helps plants grow and become green again. We can also add food waste from our lunches, such as uneaten vegetables and orange peels, to make what is called compost.

Izzy: Oh, vegetables, grass, and the leftover oranges are green waste.

Ana: Yes, these are things that change quickly. We call it "decompose." "Decompose" means that it rots or breaks down back into the dirt. Once things change to soil we can use them to help our garden grow.

Crystal: We also have what is called "brown waste." (She points to another pile.) Brown waste includes things like wood chips, dry leaves, sticks, and newspaper. These are examples of brown waste.

Sammy: We can collect leaves and sticks from the outside and put them in the brown waste can.

John: What happens if they mix by mistake?

Ana: We can actually mix them and start what is called a compost box.

Ryder: We have a lot of green things after lunch. Can we use those?

Crystal: Ryder, what green waste do you see after lunch?

Ryder: The cover from the oranges and sometimes I don't like all the vegetables.

Crystal: I have this large plastic box, and we can put all the orange and banana peels in the box after lunch.

The teachers decide to have a visual menu of green and brown waste to help children remember what goes into the compost box. They set the box close to the outside door and the lunch table and place the visual menu right above so the children can see it.

Children use the chart as a reference as they place green waste in the compost box. The younger children come to see what is inside and begin to add their banana and orange peels. Every day children take turns rotating the pile to make sure that air circulates through it. They have the idea to keep a calendar next to the box to mark how many days it takes before the waste decomposes. While all of this is going on, the children continue to sort and collect recyclables. Families start bringing empty soda cans, paper, and plastic recyclables. The children first use them to build and construct, testing balance and height. Afterwards, they sort

Dewey

them into the different recycling boxes. This play goes on for days, until one of the youngest children, Bella, goes to one of the plastic containers.

Bella: Is full.

The children walk over, and they start to all talk at the same time.

Bella: No more.

Nate: When we leave the garbage and recycling outside, how does the garbage man take all of it? There are a lot of garbage in the world.

John: It is full. We have a lot.

Sammy: We need to give it to the garbage man.

Ryder: Where does it go now?

The children decide together that they will wait for the garbage truck to find out what happens with the garbage. Fortunately, the collection day is the next day. So as the children arrive the next morning, they wait eagerly for the garbage truck to come by. The teachers gather them and sit out in the front yard to wait. The truck finally arrives, and the children get up to watch.

Nate: Look, the truck has arms to pick up the garbage cans.

John: I see a recycle symbol. (He points to the recycle symbol.)

As the younger children play outdoors, the teachers gather the older children and show them a video about recycling as another way respond to their questions.

Izzy: That's the letter "R." (For recycle.)

Ryder: Those machines have to be strong so it can smash all the cans.

John: But how can that machine make paper from the tree?

As usual, more questions emerge. The teachers write them down to follow up on later. The next day, when Sammy comes into the program, she has something to share.

Sammy: My mom and me took bottles to the store and got money.

This captures the children's interest and they immediately want to take the plastic bottles and soda cans they collected to the recycling center. The teachers plan a field trip to the recycling center the following day.

As they walk to the recycle center, the children are excited.

John: Look! I found the recycle symbol!

The children and teachers find the recycle machine in the shopping center parking lot and the children take turns putting in cans and plastic bottles. Once they have no more items left, they press the "finish" button together. The machine gives a receipt.

Kainoa: What is that paper for?

Crystal: It is called a "voucher." It tells us how much money we made by turning in our bottles.

Izzy: We can use the money from the paper to buy something for the other children.

Ryder: We can buy plants for the garden.

Sammy: Yes, so we can use the compost.

The teachers and children drive over to the supermarket where they redeem the recycling voucher. When they arrive back at the program, the children share their story with the younger ones and together they make a list of plants for their new garden.

Nate: We can get plants that have peels so we can make more compost.

Kainoa: Yes, that way we can keep helping the earth.

Ryder: Can we keep collecting plastic bottles so that we can get more money?

Sammy: We can plant many flowers and give them to people to make them happy.

This conversation opens many more questions and provides multiple possibilities to contribute to the community. The children decide to invite their families to help with the garden. A special day is set to share their hard work with their families.

Making Theories Visible in Play

This recycling story shows how Dewey's concept of active learning helps children acquire cognitive skills. During the recycling activity, the children are active in their learning processes. When the children are able to encounter the recycling process step-by-step, they are applying scientific and mathematical thinking to their immediate situation. The children are physically engaged as they participate in creating recycling bins, sorting materials into the correct bins, and rotating the compost. The children experience a conceptual understanding of corners, proportion, shape, size, directionality, and spatial relationships as they paint the bins. Sorting aluminum cans, plastics, and paper involves discrimination, decision making, and classification skills. While rotating waste in the compost pile to circulate air, the children learn science knowledge about decomposition. Marking the days on the calendar contributes to the children's sense of time. These tasks reflect Dewey's concept that learning happens through a child's participation in experiences that interest him. Additionally, the story emphasizes Dewey's idea of teachers as colearners instead of the holders of knowledge. The teachers are partners with the children in learning about recycling.

Dewey also stresses the necessity of interest in order for children to learn, and the children in the recycling story exhibit a curiosity that helps their learning process. Relevant experiences at Crystal's Creative Kids unfold as the children become fascinated with what can be recycled from their lunches, such as leftover banana and orange peels. Families support the children's inquisitiveness about recycling by bringing in aluminum cans and plastic bottles to recycle. This reveals Dewey's relationship between interest and cognitive development: as the children begin to understand the usefulness of recycling, they continue to be eager to learn about it.

The children's recycling process is directly related to Dewey's notion that learning is advanced through effort, thinking, and motivation. In this case, the recycling process takes effort as the children collect all of the cans and bottles and take them to the recycling center. The children practice multiple cognitive skills at the recycling center. They identify the recycle symbol and the word "finish" on a button, showing their understanding that print carries meaning and their awareness of symbols and letters. They follow the recycling instructions, showing that they understand multistep instructions in a new situation. They even learn new vocabulary with the word "voucher." The children's motivation is also encouraged by the idea of receiving money for their efforts. Overall, the children demonstrate comprehension of the meaning of recycling. They are able to practice each of these cognitive skills because of the effort and motivation that the recycling process requires of them.

Throughout the recycling investigation, the children also engage in Dewey's reflective practices as they analyze the purpose of recycling and their role in sustaining the earth, further demonstrating their cognitive growth. Dewey considers reflection to be an intense and rigorous process, one that is central to the acquisition of knowledge. Throughout the story, the children have group conversations about recycling, and they express themselves through language and increasingly complex vocabulary to describe recycling. Ryder questions why it is called green waste when it is brown. The children use language to explain and predict what will happen to items placed in the compost. They question what can be recycled and reflect upon the meaning of the recycle symbol. They consider options for using the money they receive from their recycling efforts and determine how best to use it. They engage in scientific inquiry as they create a hypothesis around the concept of recycling and composting. Each of these steps is a form of reflection, which increases children's understanding of how the world functions around them.

TAKE ACTION: The Environment

Designing Relevant Environments with Children

Dewey insists that education be society centered because children grow up to be members of society. He advocates that four- and five-year-olds engage in the (then-familiar) home and neighborhood activities of carpentry, cooking, and sewing while in school. Children need to be given opportunities for natural explorations of concrete materials to promote cognitive skills such as problem solving, discovering new things, and figuring out how things work. Below are some ideas that can support cognitive development by creating environments that are motivating and interactive and build upon children's interests:

- Define spaces with fabric, light, and screens that can be moved and by bringing outdoor elements such as plants into the environment. Adding textures, color, and opportunities for social work as well as spaces that allow for individual reflection to the environment allows children to feel in control of their learning.

- Offer real machines, such as a corncob sheller, hand water pump, calculator, and typewriter in the environment to promote children's understanding of meaningful tools and work.

- Organize the environment to reflect family life. The child's home environment should be centered in the school. Incorporate carpentry, cooking, folding laundry, and other everyday home activities that include the cognitive precursors for reading, writing, and math.

- Include materials and spaces for sewing and weaving. Introduce children to different weaving looms that can be used several different ways. Consider walls, fences, wooden frames, plastic garden mesh, orange fencing, twigs, and branches. Provide a variety of different textiles for children to weave—ribbon, yarn, fabric strips, string, streamers, and natural materials such as twigs and branches. This is not only enjoyable, but it promotes important cognitive connections to the home environment.

Dewey

TAKE ACTION: Your Role as a Teacher

Assessing Our Roles as Teachers to Promote Cognitive Development

The art of teaching requires more than knowledge of pedagogical practices and subject matter or a love for children. It requires intentionality on the part of the teacher and the ability to reflect and respond to children effectively. Dewey presents the importance of reflective practices to promote highly qualified early childhood professionals. Below are some ideas to promote cognitive development using Dewey's teachings:

- Guide children in the acquisition of knowledge. Children need to experience and question their own ideas in order to acquire specific knowledge. Serve as both a researcher and guide in creating a culture of inquiry and reflection.

- Be a strong observer and identify the child's interests and ideas. Provide the tools to explore and further investigate their thinking. Children need to have the opportunity to test their hypotheses in a variety of ways. This can happen when children play with blocks, sand, and water and as they cook items they can eat.

- Offer children real tools and encourage children to test their cognitive and physical abilities. Children learn that they are capable of safely manipulating tools used by the adults in their lives. Design into their daily lives meaningful rituals and routines that create a sense of community. A ritual such as engaging in daily conversations about important life events promotes a sense of well-being and weaves joy into the classroom community.

- Create opportunities that lead to meaningful long-term investigations, which increase children's learning. Follow children's leads as they explore things that are present in their daily lives, and make the learning visible to children.

- Develop an environment where everyone feels safe and can express what they think and feel. Invite children to be a part of the decision-making process when creating classroom guidelines.

Howard Gardner

Using Multiple Intelligences to Acquire Knowledge

Howard Gardner on Cognitive Development of Young Children

Gardner defines intelligence as a "biopsychological potential to process information that can be activated in a cultural setting to solve problems or create products that are of value in a culture" (1999, 33–34). Gardner believes that every individual has the potential to develop more than one intelligence, and that each intelligence is fluid and varied. All eight of Gardner's intelligences reveal aspects of cognitive development; however, this section focuses on the cognitive nature of the naturalistic, logical-mathematical, and spatial intelligences. These intelligences specifically involve such cognitive skills as reasoning, visualizing, and recognizing and solving problems.

Naturalistic intelligence: This involves an interest in exploring and learning about nature. Gardner contends that children's thinking in relation to naturalistic intelligence is seen in cognitive tasks such as identifying and classifying insects, plants, rocks, or animals. Naturalistic intelligence can include categorizing things by common traits, observing the behavior and movement of animals, and recording details of a plant or an animal in a journal. Individuals with high levels of naturalistic intelligence have the ability to recognize differences in information and can sort information into classifications and hierarchies. This task may be a challenge for a young child who knows, for example, that a parrot is a bird but may not have a higher order of understanding that parrots are animals as well as birds.

Logical-mathematical intelligence: In logical-mathematical intelligence, cognitive development is initially visible through children's manipulation of objects, in ordering and reordering them, and in counting them (Gardner 2011a). As children's intellectual capacity grows, logical, mathematical, and scientific thought can be seen in children's actions. As this intelligence is strengthened, the cognitive skills of reasoning, problem solving, and seeing relationships emerge.

Spatial intelligence: Cognitive development is seen in spatial intelligence through the ability to mentally rotate objects. Gardner asserts that central to spatial intelligence are the cognitive capacities to perceive the visual world accurately and then to re-create objects according to one's visual perceptions (Gardner 2011a). The use of drawing tools or three-dimensional materials to make a representation of an object is an example of spatial intelligence.

Naturalistic, logical-mathematical, and spatial intelligences each demonstrate cognitive development as children grow and develop. Gardner says that children's thinking is supported by their use of these intelligences to understand and act on their world as they use perception, memory, and learning.

~~~~~~

I Don't Want to Eat the Centipede

Investigating Multiple Intelligences

As the children play outside one day, they encounter an unfamiliar insect. Bella screams and runs towards Teacher Crystal. Nate, Alex, John, Izzy, and Sammy gather around the insect. They stare intently but avoid touching it or picking it up. Alex approaches Bella and puts his arms around her shoulders.

Alex: It's okay, Bella. I stay with you.

Bella stops screaming and hesitantly approaches the group of children.

Teacher Jason arrives with an insect-collecting box. He looks at the insect.

Jason: This is a centipede. Do you know why it is called a centipede?

The children offer their different ideas.

Nate: Because it is big.

Sammy: It moves a lot.

Jason: Well, let's think about it. Centipede means "one hundred feet."

Alex: Oh, I know. It means he has one hundred feet.

Sammy: Can we count them?

Jason: Let's bring it inside, and we can look with a magnifying glass.

Jason scoops the centipede up in his hand and brings it inside with the children. He places it on a table, and the children attempt to count the feet, which turns out to be an impossible task. But everyone gets a turn trying.

Nate: Maybe it does not have one hundred feet. Do they all have one hundred feet?

Sammy runs to the bookshelf and finds a book on bugs.

Sammy: Let me see if we find one.

Sammy begins to turn the pages of the book and pauses at every page trying to find a centipede. The children gather around and wait to see if there is a centipede. After going through the entire book, they realize that there is no centipede information in it.

Bella: What happen to it?

Alex: They probably forgot to put him in.

Crystal comes over with a piece of paper in her hand.

Crystal: I found out that a centipede is not a bug. It is more like a shrimp or a crab. That is why we can't find him in the book.

Crystal shows the children the photo she's printed out from the Internet.

Sammy: A shrimp? Yuck, we eat shrimp, but I won't eat that! I don't want to eat a centipede.

The children start laughing

Nate: I won't eat it either.

Bella (shaking her head): Me too.

The children continue to compare the live centipede to the one in the photo.

Crystal: I think we need to bring him back out into his habitat so that he can go home and live.

Alex: What is a habitat?

John: That is their house, outside. If it's like shrimp, then it needs to be in water.

The children follow Jason as he takes the centipede into the garden and gently places it on a tree branch. He values the importance of teaching children to respect nature and be gentle with every creature. He also uses these opportunities to teach children about the cycle of life. Once again, the teachers learn new information and grow along with the children.

The teachers begin to notice that the children are constantly looking for insects. They begin to bring magnifying glasses outdoors so the children can look at insects closely. The teachers decide to support this interest by setting up a provocation with books, photos, and insect nets. The teachers also set out a microscope for closer looks at captured insects.

Children begin to use the tools, and their interest in insects grows. Every day they encounter a new bug that captures their attention. Some children are more daring; they pick the insects up and let them crawl in their hands. Some children watch.

The teachers marvel at how friendships grow. They delight in the care and empathy children show each other and insects they collect. They observe children gently placing insects under the microscope and then carefully releasing them into their natural habitat.

During one of their daily bug hunts, John discovers a cocoon in one of the tree branches. He comes inside.

John: I found something! I found something!

The children and teachers follow John back outside, and he points out the cocoon. Alex runs back inside and gets an insect book.

Alex: Let's find it, let's find it!

He starts to turn the pages.

Sammy: I see it, I see it! What does it say in here?

Crystal: It says it is a chrysalis.

Bella (pointing to a photo of a monarch butterfly): Bottlefy.

Crystal: Yes, Bella, it is a butterfly.

Izzy runs inside and brings out the book *The Very Hungry Caterpillar.*

Izzy: It is like the caterpillar that is then a butterfly. Here it says it's a cocoon not a chrysalis. How can that be?

Crystal: That's a good question. Let's see if we can find out.

After researching the question, they discover that a moth spins a cocoon and a butterfly spins a chrysalis. The children, however, continue to use the familiar word cocoon throughout their investigations rather than the scientific name.

The children's research increases their interest, and they go back to see the cocoon.

Sammy: I wonder if this [cocoon] will hatch a moth or butterfly? Maybe there are more.

They all scatter around the tree branches and bushes looking for more cocoons. The younger children follow, and the teachers notice older children protectively holding their hands or putting their arms around their shoulders.

Sammy: I see one! I see one! I see one!

The children surround her and use their magnifying glasses to see the new cocoons.

All of a sudden Alex and Bella shout from the other end of the yard. They point to another cocoon.

Children continue to look, and they find one cocoon; now they have discovered a total of four different cocoons in the yard. The children run, find their clipboards, and begin to draw the cocoons.

Nate: We can make a chart to see how many days it will take for them to be a butterfly.

Bella: I want bottlefy.

The children draw representations of the cocoons every day. With daily observation the drawings get more and more sophisticated. The drawings have transformed from simple ovals to intricate lines representing the cocoons. The children decide to also take photos every day to document the growth of the cocoons. They visit the sites each day and record their findings. The teachers create a documentation book and a panel to keep track of the children's art, photos, and other observations. They add the children's comments into the documentation and read them during group meeting time. The teachers, with the children, review the photos and drawings every day and note the changes. After a few days, the children notice there is a little movement in one of the cocoons that is hanging on a branch. They gather around and remain very quiet so as not to disturb the process.

Bella: Shhh . . . (She puts her finger to her mouth.)

Sammy: We need to be quiet, because we don't want to scare it.

The children sit for a long time and watch to see if something happens. They finally tire and one by one start to move to play in different areas. Crystal notices that Sammy periodically comes to check the cocoon and carefully observes to see if there is something happening. Finally in the afternoon, something happens.

Sammy: Look, something is coming out! It's happening!

Everyone runs to see what is going on. Anticipation mounts as the butterfly emerges from a chrysalis dangling from a branch. It sits on the tree branch and does not move.

Sammy: Look, it's a butterfly! Why is not moving? I think it broke its wing.

Crystal: Their wings are wet when they hatch from their cocoon.

The children watch in awe and complete silence as the butterfly pumps its wings and eventually flies off. The butterfly lands on Sammy's finger and all the children watch. Crystal puts her hand out and the butterfly lands in her hand. She gently shows it to all the children before it flies away.

The children witness the cycle of life taking place right in front of them. They continue to watch the other cocoons and learn two are chrysalides when they see butterflies emerge. The fourth cocoon does not turn into a butterfly or moth. This causes some deep conversations about the cycle of life and death.

John: That means that the caterpillar was not able to turn into a butterfly. Is it dead?

Sammy: What can we do with it? Can we help it?

Alex: I don't want it to die.

Crystal: You know the caterpillar spins a cocoon and then it turns into a butterfly. That is what we call the "cycle of life." Sometimes the caterpillar can't turn into a butterfly, so it dies.

Sammy: Does it hurt?

Jason: I don't know if it hurts, Sammy, but the caterpillar does not feel anything once it is dead.

Alex: We saw other butterflies, so we have to be happy.

Nate: Let's bury the cocoon and sing to it.

The children dig a small hole in the garden and place the cocoon very gently in the hole. They put dirt on top and add some leaves and a flower.

They sing together:

Good-bye, cocoon, good-bye,

We will miss you a lot.

Good-bye.

As they finish singing they see a butterfly in the bushes. They run to it and start laughing.

Sammy: That is the cocoon's sister.

The teachers once again marvel at children's ability to understand deep issues. The teachers know that answering the children's questions with honesty allows them to make better sense of things that happen on a daily basis. They have buried many bugs and cared for many creatures, always with the hope of teaching children to respect all living creatures, the Earth, and each other.

Making Theories Visible in Play

As the children interact with living organisms in this story, they develop cognitive skills through Gardner's naturalistic, logical-mathematical, and spatial intelligences. Through exploration of the natural world, the children acquire a range of knowledge that supports their thinking and reasoning.

The children develop naturalistic intelligence as they explore the lives of living creatures. When the children investigate the centipede, cocoons, and butterflies, they are developing scientific inquiry skills of noticing, wondering, and questioning. They use magnifying glasses to carefully observe the centipede's legs and cocoons and books to compare and contrast varieties of insects. As the children continue to explore, they observe closely, collect and record their data, and represent their experiences through drawing the cocoon. The teachers support these cognitive skills by encouraging the children to reflect on their experiences, explore patterns and relationships, and construct reasonable explanations. The children draw conclusions and formulate ideas and theories, such as John's belief that centipedes need to be in water since they are like shrimp or Sammy's belief that the butterfly's wing is broken since it cannot fly.

Logical-mathematical intelligence is developed in the story as the children use their problem-solving skills to determine what a centipede is and if a butterfly or moth will emerge from the cocoon. Mathematical skills and sense of time further develop logical-mathematical intelligences when the children chart how many days until the butterflies come out of their cocoons.

The children use and grow their spatial skills by drawing representations of cocoons and butterflies and by reading books about insects and interpreting pictures and photos. Spatial intelligence is also evident in the children's ability to recognize the details of the centipede, cocoons, and butterflies. As the children develop and practice their naturalistic, logical-mathematical, and spatial intelligences, they will also continue to develop their knowledge and thinking skills.

TAKE ACTION: The Environment

Designing Environments That Promote Multiple Intelligences

Gardner asserts that children have different propensities for learning and use a variety of intelligences to solve problems and create items required by their culture.

Gardner

Intelligences work together in complex ways, not in isolation, so each of Gardner's multiple intelligences involve different aspects of cognition, which include logical-mathematical, spatial, musical, interpersonal, intrapersonal, naturalistic, and linguistic intelligences. Below are some suggestions on how to design spaces that promote some of these intelligences:

- Include areas in the environment where children can experiment with cause and effect, solve problems, and ask questions throughout the day. Add materials that allow for classifying, patterning, sequencing, and measuring.

- Design spaces that will excite an artist, architect, or interior decorator. Select an area that is filled with natural light and has linoleum floor and water access for easy cleanup. Organize and attractively display materials in containers that are accessible and easy to put away, such as sculpting, drawing, painting, building, designing, and collaging. Consider the multiple possibilities each material will inspire.

- Allow children areas they can decorate and change together. Having props such as flowers, vases, baskets, place mats, and tablecloths allows children to rearrange the dramatic play area. Include sheets, blankets, mats, boards, boxes, and crates that can be used by children to create forts.

- Create a music garden where children can explore sound and music at their leisure. Have open areas for children to dance, perform, and move to music.

- Set up a nature table for children to explore items such as shells, rocks, bird nests, or plants. Include tools such as magnifiers for careful observation.

TAKE ACTION: Your Role as a Teacher

Supporting Different Intelligences

Gardner considers every intelligence a neutrally based system that is "jump-started" when a child encounters internal or external stimuli or information. Our role as teachers is to help children recognize and use all of their intelligences. We can explore our own intelligences by discovering and learning along with children. Below are some suggestions for experiences that support a wide range of intelligences:

- Offer children opportunities to solve problems in a variety of ways to deepen their knowledge, such as providing different types of loose parts. Children can manipulate these items in a variety of ways that stimulate thinking in any or all of the intelligence domains.

- Invite children to test their hypotheses. The process of problem solving requires children to analyze different variables before accepting or rejecting an idea. Create a culture of inquiry where children's ideas are challenged in respectful ways. Allow them to experiment with different possibilities to find multiple solutions to the same problem.

- Urge children to tell stories and encourage conversations. Ask open-ended questions (questions that have more than one right answer) as children investigate. Offer children time to think and reflect on their work. Rather than pushing children to focus on specific ideas, create schedules that provide them ample time to reflect. Quiet places can allow children to isolate themselves to think and accomplish their personal goals.

- Recognize children's individual talents, abilities, and multiple intelligences. Some children have strong verbal intelligence, while others have a more developed spatial ability. Teachers can strengthen children's existing intelligences while also promoting talents that have yet to emerge. Describe out loud the process a child is following to resolve a problem or to create a new piece of art or invention. This can help children understand their own abilities and recognize their own knowledge.

Louise Derman-Sparks

Engaging Children in Deeper Thinking

Louise Derman-Sparks on Cognitive Development of Young Children

The anti-bias education developed by Derman-Sparks acknowledges that children see differences at an early age and discriminate upon these differences. Derman-Sparks argues that cognition plays a key role in how children acquire knowledge about themselves and others. The process of learning about ourselves begins with the development of a strong identity and self-awareness about differences and similarities.

Derman-Sparks

One sense of awareness that children develop is an understanding of their sexual identity. This includes a child's understanding that he is a boy and also an understanding of the cultural aspects of gender roles. Young children do not understand that their gender stays the same regardless of their dress, behavior, or feelings. For example, Amy is a girl even if she wears a baseball cap and plays baseball, but a child may believe that Amy is a boy because of her dress and sport choice. Derman-Sparks believes gender identity is based on both gender anatomy (physical characteristics) and gender role (environmental influences) and that typically, a child's gender anatomy and gender role align (Derman-Sparks and Olsen Edwards 2010). She encourages teachers to support all children in trying out a wide variety of activities away from gender stereotypical play. This does not mean that children are forced to try out all activities, but rather that activities are made available to them and they are encouraged to try. Derman-Sparks affirms that children's cognitive skills develop as they discover contradictions between their ideas about gender behavior and their experiences. The key is to provide children with many opportunities to expand their ways of thinking and acting (Derman-Sparks and Olsen Edwards 2010).

Boys Don't Play with Dolls and They Don't Cook

Exploring Cognitive Bias

As the children at Crystal's Creative Kids encounter different biases over a series of weeks and months, the teachers help them make sense of differences and similarities by integrating an anti-bias approach into all their practices. One morning, Thomas arrives at the center with his father.

Thomas: Bye, Dad. I have to go check on my baby.

Thomas runs directly to the dramatic play area and picks up a doll and wraps it in a blanket.

Thomas (to the doll): It's okay. Here is your daddy to take care of you.

The teachers observe Thomas's dad's mouth drop and his face turn red. He does not say a word; he just leaves the house very rapidly. This father's reaction is not uncommon. It is one that teachers have seen before with other dads, and moms too. The teachers acknowledge the parents' concerns and support them in understanding that playing with dolls and playing with gender roles is just part of how children make sense of their everyday experiences.

There are new babies in the program, and a few of the children have new siblings, so doll play is a common sight. Boys play with dolls and assume the role of either doctors or fathers nurturing their babies. The teachers respect and support this type of play as they know it supports the development of children's thinking. They make an effort to avoid introducing biases and stereotypes into the environment, but similar to any other early care and education program, there is always a moment that makes teachers pause and reflect on the subtle messages they inadvertently send children.

One day the boys pretend to be superheroes outdoors. They wear scarves to simulate capes and pretend to fly. Izzy and Sammy ask to join the play.

John: Girls can't be superheroes. It's only for boys.

Since the teachers have been talking about boys and girls being equally strong and capable of running and jumping, they opt to approach the subject. Teacher Jason gathers the children in a small group to address their understanding of gender behavior.

Jason: What are some of the things that superheroes do?

Jason is honoring the children's play and respecting their developmental level.

Ryder: They fly high and are not afraid.

Izzy: I can fly high and I am not afraid. I can go that high. (She points to the top of the playhouse where Zachary sits.)

Ryder: They are strong.

Ryder takes a stance with legs spread wide and arms up, flexing his muscles.

John: They take care of people and save people.

Jason: Who else do you know takes care of you?

Alex: My mom takes care of me when I don't feel well.

Izzy: My mom and dad take care of me, and they are both strong.

Jason: Do you think your mom could be a superhero?

John: My mom can, and she is a girl.

Jason: Both boys and girls can be superheroes, just like both moms and dads take care of children.

John: So, I guess girls can be superheroes. Come on, Izzy. Let's go.

The teachers recognize that the boys' actions of wanting to exclude the girls may be a simple example of exerting "power," or it may be that the boys have preconceived ideas of gender behavior. The teachers plan to engage children in more conversations to question their thinking and

remind them that both boys and girls can play with all the toys and tools in the environment. The teachers are also aware of the gender-defined media messages children receive. Once again, Jason will serve as a role model by intentionally engaging in nontraditional male roles. He plans to build the children's skills for critical thinking during lunchtime conversation. As the children talk, another form of bias emerges.

Ryder: We had macaroni and cheese for dinner.

Jason: Was it yummy?

Ryder: My dad makes the best mac and cheese.

John: What? Dads don't cook. Moms cook.

Jason: I cook and like to make spaghetti. Does that mean I am a mom?

The children (looking at Jason and giggling): No!

Jason: Do you know other men that cook?

Izzy: My dad makes yummy chicken with rice for dinner.

Jason: My dad taught me how to make ice cream.

Sammy: When we eat at the restaurant the men make food at our table, and they wear the hat like we do when we make pizza.

Jason: Someone who cooks is called a chef, and they can be either men or women.

These types of conversations continue to challenge the children's thinking skills. Teacher Dolores encourages John to think about what is or is not "fair" with respect to sewing and wearing an apron. Then, when one child says, "boys don't sew, only girls do," John negates the child's comment.

John: No, Teacher Jason wears an apron when he cooks. I am going to make my own apron.

Dolores: My husband also wears an apron. Would you like to make your own apron?

John: Yes, I need paper, scissor, and pencils.

John follows Dolores to the art center, and they begin to work on the apron together.

Dolores: Let's measure you so that we know how big we need to make the apron.

They draw the apron on butcher paper using a ruler that teachers introduced in the environment as a tool.

John: This part has to be round, like the bottom.

He uses the protractor to draw a semicircle on the paper while Dolores holds the paper down.

Once the drawing is complete, John cuts the paper carefully, following the lines. Dolores helps him by holding the paper as he moves it. Finally after working hard at measuring, cutting, and stapling, the apron is finished.

John puts on his apron and smiles.

John: See, I made an apron, and I am a boy. I can wear it and cook like Jason.

After this event, John is seen in the dramatic play area wearing his apron while he cooks. More children follow his lead and begin to wear the aprons and chef hats.

As children discover their gender identity and make sense of how societal rules function, they continue to engage with the multiple materials available. The teachers notice that both boys and girls continue to play with dolls and they engage in well-defined gender role play. The boys are fathers and the girls are mothers. However, there are moments when their conversations and interactions introduce stereotypical thinking. As Ryder is holding a doll and singing a lullaby, Izzy approaches him.

Izzy: Boys can't be mommies and play with dolls.

Ryder: I am a dad and I can sing.

Izzy: Only mommies take care of the babies.

Other children join in the conversation, and it is apparent that there is a division between the boys' and the girls' thinking.

Alina: Mommies hold the babies, not daddies.

Izzy: This is a girl's area. (She points to the dramatic play area.)

Ryder: My dad holds me.

John: Teacher Jason holds the babies.

Ryder: He also changes diapers.

Sammy: Ha-ha, only mommies change diapers.

Hearing differences in the children's thinking about caregiving roles, Jason walks over to the area and gathers the children.

Jason: It sounds like all of you want to hold the babies and take care of them. I do take care of the babies and even change their diapers. Do you know any other men that sing and hold babies?

His question is designed to build the children's critical-thinking skills.

Lorenzo: My dad takes care of my new baby, and he sings and plays with him. I do too.

Ryder: My dad takes care of me.

Izzy: My dad plays with me.

Jason: It sounds to me that both boys and girls can take care of the dolls and feed them and change their diapers.

The teachers know that these conversations will continue to develop the children's intellectual growth. They plan to integrate photos into the environment

depicting both men and women engaged in nontraditional roles. The teachers want to make sure every child's identity is supported and that the children feel comfortable in their individual gender roles. They also notice that when the children play as community helpers, they assume every role equally. The girls are firefighters and police officers. The boys play in the dramatic play area too. During group-meeting time, Sammy shares that she had seen the movie *Annie*, and she talks about the story. The children decide they want to act out *Annie*. They run into the dramatic play area, and both boys and girls proceed to put on dresses, jewelry, and necklaces. They all want to be Annie.

Ryder, Kainoa, and John begin to sing and dance while Teacher Crystal sings the music of *Annie*. The children twirl their dresses and hold hands as they dance in circles. All the other children watch and clap at the song's end. They take turns pretending to be Annie.

It is late afternoon and some parents arrive to pick up the children. One of the moms has a question for Crystal.

Mom: Is it okay for boys to dress in girls' clothing?

Crystal: Both boys and girls role-play multiple roles they see in their own life in order to make sense of them.

Mom: Oh.

Crystal sees hesitation but cannot continue the conversation because other parents are arriving. After some reflection, the teachers decide that it is important to give all the families some information about gender role play. They conduct research on how gender identity is established. They also want to address how children use gender as power and how this creates segregation among the children. The teachers want to engage the families in supporting play that assists the children in achieving comfort with a wide range of activities, regardless of their gender. The teachers put together a comprehensive handout and make it a point to discuss it with every family.

Some of the parents are still uncomfortable about seeing their sons play with dolls. After several conversations among themselves, the teachers decide to send dolls home with the boys who participate in doll play so that their families can witness firsthand the type of play in which the boys are engaging. When the parents begin to understand that the boys are role-playing what they personally experience in everyday social interactions—being a loving father, or being a doctor or paramedic—they better understand the importance of this type of play, and they no longer discourage it.

Making Theories Visible in Play

In this series of stories, we can see how the children develop an understanding of the roles males and females engage in on a daily basis. The children's preconceived knowledge of gender is based on societal messages. When the boys want to play with dolls or wear dresses, the teachers recognize they are doing so to make sense of the world around them. Through dramatic play, children test different roles, including the role of father and mother. They learn to nurture and care for babies. They also assume the role of doctors, teachers, construction workers, and cooks, exploring the value of each role and their contribution to society. As children engage in doll play, superhero play, and sewing, they develop cognitive skills and self-awareness of their own abilities. As they try a variety of gender roles freely, children develop gender consistency and the ability to know that the way they behave does not change their gender.

The teachers follow Derman-Sparks's suggestion to offer children the opportunity to explore a variety of experiences beyond culturally defined gender roles. The teachers know that gender identity begins with children's

Derman-Sparks

perceptions and continues through their acquisition of new knowledge that contradicts or supports their previous perceptions. Children develop their identity and attitudes by participating in a variety of developmentally appropriate experiences that engage them in exploring nontraditional roles (girls building, boys playing with dolls and cooking).

According to Derman-Sparks, when the boys refuse to allow the girls to play superheroes, they are using their gender as a form of power and exclusion. The teachers recognize this fact and instead of just forcing the children to play together, they take the time to support the children in developing the cognitive skills they need to better recognize the diverse roles that both men and women play in society. The teachers want to create an environment where the children work together and each child develops a comfortable, empathetic interaction with people from diverse backgrounds—a key principle of anti-bias education.

As the children continue to explore different societal gender roles, they often find themselves arguing about who is best and who has more power. They question girls' abilities and boys' skills. The teachers follow Derman-Sparks's suggestions and take the time to have discussions during group time that increase the children's critical thinking against biases. This means guiding children's cognitive development skills to help them identify concepts of similarities and differences, fairness and injustice. It helps children analyze their perceptions and distinguish between stereotypes and facts, recognize inappropriate and hurtful comments (teasing, name-calling), and understand discriminatory behaviors directed at one's own or others' identities (based on gender, race, ethnicity, disability, class, age, weight, and so on). Through thoughtful questioning, the teachers support both parents and children in discovering and responding to gender roles and stereotypes. In doing so they help the children practice the cognitive tools to explore their own ideas and learn about different perspectives.

TAKE ACTION: The Environment

Creating Environments That Promote Empowerment

Derman-Sparks believes it is important to look at classroom environments through a critical lens to determine the messages about diversity children may receive. The materials in an environment send messages to children not only about what is there but also by what is not there. If, for example, a child's race, ethnicity, ability, or gender is not represented, the child may feel insignificant, and it is hard for the child to gain understanding of who she is in the world when she is not represented. Thoughtfully designed settings based on the specific cultural backgrounds of the families who are part of the school community help create a strong sense of identity. When the classroom is full of possibilities for exploring cultural diversity, children develop the cognitive abilities to discern and address injustice. Below are some suggestions for creating environments that promote cognition, empowerment, and a strong sense of identity:

- Create an environment that represents each unique cultural value in a sensitive and thoughtful way. It needs to be free of stereotypical images and a "tourist approach" that only showcases food, festivals, and traditional costumes. Learning about the children's families and their cultures can support designing environments that honor who they are and the values they cherish.

- Offer spaces in the environment for families to display objects of meaning. This could be a flower arrangement, pottery, or other form of art. Consider the addition of meaningful visual displays that bring beauty, culture, and aesthetics into the environment.

- Design a dramatic play area with anatomically correct dolls that represent the families in your program, as well as the major ethnicities in the United States (African American, Asian, Hispanic, Middle Eastern, American Indian, and Caucasian).

- Include books about the body that show gender anatomy in the reading area.

- Create a dramatic play area beyond traditional housekeeping props that includes tools for being a mail carrier, repair technician, veterinarian, firefighter, police officer, teacher, architect, or chef.

- Display photographs that illustrate women and men engaged in home and work tasks.

TAKE ACTION: Your Role as a Teacher

Promoting Critical Thinking

When we talk about an anti-bias approach to early childhood education, we refer to an active process, which gives children the knowledge to challenge prejudice, stereotypes, bias, and the institutionalized and societal "isms." Teachers of young children have the responsibility to actively intervene and challenge the personal

Derman-Sparks

and institutional behaviors that perpetuate oppression, exclusion, and injustice (Derman-Sparks and Olsen Edwards 2010). The following are some ways for teachers to encourage cognition and critical thinking:

- Establish democratic practices that help children gain a strong understanding of both self and group identity. Children have to be aware of others' points of view, balance their own needs with those of other members of the group, and negotiate and cooperate with a wide range of other individuals.

- Decrease children's stereotypical thinking by first reflecting on personal biases. Talk openly with children about the strengths of diversity and how prejudice hurts and oppresses. This provides an example of openness and self-awareness. Be prepared to offer children the opportunity to ask questions and to respond to the questions in a way that increases children's critical thinking about issues of biases and stereotypes.

- Support children in developing a strong sense of group identity by connecting the familiar concept of "family." Teachers can encourage children to discover specific characteristics found in their family, such as hair or eye color. Include different family constellations through photos and special family traditions. After children connect with the concept of belonging to a family, they can expand their thinking into belonging to other ethnic, cultural, or racial groups.

- Offer children multiple opportunities to explore gender identity free of gender stereotypes. Support children in finding differences and similarities in gender roles, and make connections to the children's personal experiences.

In Conclusion: Cognitive Theories

The early childhood years are extraordinary for learning and cognitive development. Each theorist provides a different context in which to understand a child's ability to think and acquire knowledge. Children have a natural tendency to discover, explore, learn, and make sense of the world around them. Children develop thought and understanding through their own active discovery, construction of experiences, and meaningful experiences that are related directly to life and the world. Children construct knowledge as they engage with cultural tools in the environment, and language is important to support the internalization of concepts, knowledge, and ideas. Intellectual development is promoted and guided by older and more skilled people, and play is crucial for the development of cognitive skills.

Cognitive development is visible through many types of intelligences, and children's thinking grows and changes according to each child's cognitive strengths. Cognition plays a key role in how children see and acquire knowledge about themselves and others. The combined work of the theorists provides us with a comprehensive understanding of children's cognitive growth and development.

Your Turn

Now it is your turn to identify theory in children's play. Following is a practice story designed for you to apply your analytic skills in relation to children's cognitive development. As you read the story, identify which theories are visible in the children's play, consider key concepts, and reflect upon how you would support the children's interests and needs based upon the theories.

~~~~~~

How Cameras Work

Exploring Images and Function

The children notice that the teachers have been taking many photos. The children begin to ask questions and are curious about how the photos are created.

Izzy: I want to know how they come up. When you take the picture, how does it come up?

John (pointing to the digital camera they have been using): I want to learn about *that* camera.

The teachers allow the children to learn more about the process by letting them take pictures of each other. They bring in different cameras, both old and new, so the children can see the difference between a point-and-shoot digital and a single-lens reflex (SLR) camera. The teachers also bring in old film and photography paper that they have tested in the sun.

On one of the days after the cameras were placed in the environment, a child takes a screwdriver and tries to open a camera to see where the pictures are. This child's interest is in the function of the camera rather than in taking and developing photos. The teachers did not expect the children to focus on this aspect of cameras, but they continue to allow the children to explore the cameras in-depth.

The investigation continues, and photographs the children took are printed and laminated. Sammy has the idea to make a drawing of one of the photographs she took. The children spend time drawing what is in the photographs they have taken.

Sammy: Oh, I get it—a photo is like a drawing of what we see.

Ryder: Yes, that is how a camera works.

~~~~~~

Making Theories Visible in Play

After reading the story, reflect on how theory informed the decisions made by the teachers. What theories would you use to respond to the children's interest? How would you use the theories covered in this chapter to create a responsive environment that increases the children's knowledge?

Going Deeper: Questions for Your Reflection

Now that you have reflected on the story above, using your knowledge of the theories, think about how you can use theory to expand the learning of the children in your care.

1. Think about a child who you know well. How does Piaget's theory clarify your understanding of this child's thinking and reasoning? What about the other theories?
2. Think of a time when you were absorbed in play. What made the experience engaging? How can you incorporate this knowledge to further children's cognitive development?
3. How is Maslow's way of describing children's cognitive development the same or different than Erikson's? What can you do to support children's quest for self-actualization? What can you do to support their quest for initiative?
4. How does Piaget's view on how children acquire knowledge compare to your own personal experience as a learner? What about Vygotsky's view? What role does creativity play in supporting children's cognitive development? What role does it play in supporting their inquiry?

5. Make a list of the ways you learn. How do these reflect your experience of learning in school? What are some of the values you learned that guide a democratic classroom and create a sense of community? If you decided to implement Gardner's MI theory in your classroom, what would the impact be on children's cognitive learning?

6. In what ways have you experienced prejudice in your life? What impact did it have on your view of yourself and others? How can you use this experience to help a child who wants to engage in nontraditional gender play?

Your Turn

Part 4

Physical Development: Beyond Gross-Motor and Fine-Motor Skills

From birth, children use their bodies to explore and learn about the world around them. They are purposeful in their learning and actively engage their bodies in exploring objects, materials, and space. They practice moving their bodies to get closer to a desired object or to move the object closer to them. As children develop this desire and determination to control their bodies throughout childhood, they practice and master movement, balance, and fine-motor skills. As children's ability to coordinate movement increases, they gain more intentional control over their actions. This control offers them the opportunity to bring more meaning and purpose to their work and learning. Children use their senses and their bodies to learn. In other words, physical development supports children in gaining confidence in what they can do and who they are.

Physical development is measured according to specific milestones or developmental changes of a child's physical skills. These developmental milestones include measures such as the development of the brain and increases in body weight and height, as well as the acquisition of gross-motor skills (such as walking, running, or jumping) and fine-motor skills (such as use of the pincer grip, hand-eye coordination, or grasping small objects). The neurological pathways in a child's brain increase through these meaningful experiences and interactions involving their physical bodies.

Child development theories provide us with the foundation to go beyond the physical milestones of childhood. They offer us a deeper perspective of how children think about their actions and how they use their bodies to manipulate their environment and solve problems. Many different child development theories recognize the importance of physical development as an integral process that affects each stage of development. This part addresses how physical development interacts with other areas of learning, thinking, and interaction.

Jean Piaget

Bodies as Tools for Discovery

Jean Piaget on the Physical Development of Young Children

Piaget believes the fundamental basis of learning is discovery—that children learn by doing. Discovery requires physicality, and as children grow and develop more complex motor skills, they deepen their understanding of the world. As children's physical skills become more sophisticated, they are able to move in the environment and manipulate objects to make meaning of what they see, hear, and touch. Piaget (1952) says that just as the body has physical structures (bones, muscles, etc.), the mind builds psychological structures that permit it to adapt to the external world.

Understanding through physical knowledge: Children develop a physical knowledge of how objects move and behave in space (Piaget 1952). Physical knowledge is obtained through physical experiences and sensory information. This means children organize, identify, and interpret sensory information in order to make sense of their environment. This learning lays the foundation for more abstract thinking in the future, such as children understanding how their bodies move in space and how other objects function.

Building physical schemas: Piaget calls the cognitive structures into which children organize concepts and information *schemas*. Children build schemas related to their physical development, about how their bodies move and function. Children change, modify, refine, and organize schemas as new experiences are incorporated into existing knowledge. For example, children adjust their schema of walking to incorporate running, galloping, and skipping as they become more coordinated and have varying experiences.

Piaget's developmental stages are framed in cognitive language, but they involve physical development at every level, especially during the first two stages, sensorimotor and preoperational, as these stages cover development from infancy through age seven.

Physical development in sensorimotor learning: In Piaget's first stage, sensorimotor (birth to two years), infants use their senses and motor skills to gain knowledge about the world around them. Piaget's (1976) research demonstrates how infants construct their worlds from the discoveries they make by using the physical skills of grasping, sucking, looking, pulling, and holding. Through trial and error, they physically engage with their immediate environment and actively use their bodies to learn. Children at this stage have a limited understanding of how things work and react, so they use their bodies to explore. Infants are constantly using their bodies to experiment by throwing things, shaking rattles, moving their hands and feet to knock over objects, or dropping things over and over again. Piaget's theory offers a strong connection between the body and the development of the brain. Broadly speaking, the more the body moves, the more active the brain is. Piaget (1976) asserts that one way children learn is through repetition of a motion—the brain will internalize it and use the motion to solve other problems presented by the environment. As infants grow in their physical abilities to crawl, sit, stand, and walk, Piaget maintains that they start testing more obstacles and objects in the environment. Engagement with a variety of materials allows them to practice and refine their movements while gaining in cognition.

Physical development in preoperational learning: According to Piaget, children develop understanding through their experiences. They make sense of their learning through active exploration and engagement. As children investigate, their ideas or theories are strengthened, challenged, discarded, or changed. Physical skills are a significant part of their investigations as children use motor skills in their play and interactions with objects and people. For example, children learn how a pushing/pulling motion affects a swing or how squeezing affects a sponge filled with water.

When children go across monkey bars, they have to learn about distance and space. As they swing their hands from bar to bar, they need to decide when it is the right moment to move their hands from one bar to the next. They need to know how fast they are willing to go. Conquering monkey bars is hard work and requires a lot of concentration. As children make sense of the distance between each bar and how far they need to stretch their body to reach them, they organize their thinking in ways that allow them to better understand how they use their bodies. The more children move their bodies, the more they make sense of the world.

I Can See My Bones

Healthy Bodies, Learning Minds

Sammy and John are swinging side by side while lying on their tummies, Bella is raking leaves, Ryder is rolling objects down the slide, and Nick and Nate are hiding in the playhouse when a game of chase breaks out in the play yard. The children stop their play and actively pursue Brycin, who runs easily around the yard's perimeter. Squeals of delight can be heard as Brycin twirls and then darts back and forth to avoid capture. He slows and allows Ryder to tag him. Sammy stops running and pauses to catch her breath. She places her hand on her heart as other children stop alongside her.

Sammy (breathlessly): Feel your heart. Mine is going *boom, boom, boom*!

Later during group-meeting time, the teachers and the children engage in a conversation about healthy bodies and strong hearts.

Nate: I wish I could see inside my body.

The rest of the children agree, and they all share different ideas of what their bodies would look like.

Sammy: Bodies are big or small. Brycin is big and runs faster. Colter is small and walks slow. I am in the middle. I can run and walk.

John: We have blood.

Ryder: Our bones are like sticks: hard. (He holds his arm out straight and stiff.)

Izzy: We all have bones and they hold our body. I can move my body like this. Watch me. (She lays flat on her back and then bends her back upward in an arch.)

Teacher Jason: These are all ideas that we need to explore. How do you think we can find out what is inside your body and how your body moves?

John: Remember when Naomi broke her hand she had a "ray" taken?

Nate: Oh, I remember.

Alina: Her arm got an owie.

Bella: I have owie.

The teachers buy a set of body X-rays to share with the children. When the X-rays arrive, the teachers set them up as a provocation to extend the children's interest. They place the X-rays scrambled on the table so that the children can arrange them as they try to figure out what part of the body each X-ray is depicting. The teachers also set out a book on the human body, hoping to support the children's interest and encourage research.

As children arrive in the morning, they run to the table where they see the X-ray provocation. They all start to move the X-rays, and the conversation is exciting. The teachers allow the children to become familiar with the different X-rays. They notice that the children open the book, refer to it as a resource to find the different body parts, and move their own bodies as they talk about each part.

Nate: Look. This is a hand. (He opens and closes his hand as he looks at the X-ray.)

John: This is a head. (He touches Colter's head and presses down.)

Izzy: I think this is this part. (She points to her own ribs and twists from side to side.)

After a couple of days, the teachers bring in an entire skeleton and place it near the X-rays. The children begin taking the bones and attempt to place them on top of the corresponding X-rays.

There are some hit-and-miss attempts, but the children continue to find the parts. The conversation continues.

Lorenzo (holding the femur): Wow. This is long.

Ryder: The hands are big. They are from a grown-up.

Sammy: I found more parts.

Teacher Crystal joins the children and helps them figure out which parts belong with which X-ray by using the book.

Crystal: Let's find the names in the book.

After hard work, the children manage to find the bone that belongs to each body part.

Izzy: Look! Look! We did it.

The children decide to leave their work for their parents to see.

At circle time, Crystal asks the children about the job of bones. There seems to be consensus among the children that bones are strong and help the body move. Crystal challenges the children to move their bodies in different ways to foster their physical development. The focus is on the process that occurs in order to produce specific movements. The children walk on tiptoe and on their heels; take light steps and heavy

ones; walk fast, slow, fast, slow; and walk backwards and in a zigzag. Crystal then encourages the children to use their bones and muscles to move like snakes, bears, giraffes, and frogs. Throughout the week, the children can be seen imitating movements of various animals in their play. Their fascination with movement and X-rays continues to grow.

As the children arrive on Friday, they go to the table with the X-rays and bones. They begin to place the bones on top of their own body.

Lorenzo: Look, here are my bones. (He places the bones on top of his feet.)

Ryder: Zachary and Brycin's bones are bigger because they can balance and run faster.

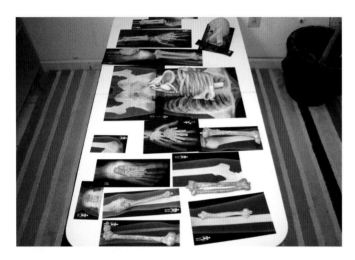

Ryder imitates running in place.

Bella: This is me.

Sammy: Here is my finger.

Izzy: Here is my hand. This is my faimur [femur] and is long.

After a while, the children begin to place the X-rays on top of their own bodies too. They take turns comparing the images of bones on the X-rays to their own bodies.

Lorenzo picks up the X-ray for the hand and places it on top of his own hand.

Lorenzo: This is too big. It's not mine. When I am a grown-up it will fit.

The teachers notice the children are using their observational and small-motor skills to draw their bones. The children refer to the different books and puzzles that have been placed in the environment as they do this. They study the details very carefully.

After seeing the drawings, the teachers decide to offer more opportunities for the children to use art and their small-motor skills to represent their ideas. After some discussion, the teachers agree to set up a table with some of the X-rays along with black paper and white crayons. They wonder how the children will react to the contrast presented by the black paper and white crayons. They want to see if they relate the concept to that of the X-rays.

Lorenzo: This is white like bones.

Izzy: Look, the white is strong on the black paper.

Nate (carefully watching): Oh, I get it. It's like X-ray, black and white.

The teachers continue to offer the children multiple opportunities to explore the bones, move physically, and make connections to their body. They add black paper and different bones to the easels and allow the children to use large-motor skills as they paint using different bones as they would paintbrushes. They provide bones and sketching paper for the children to use small-motor control as they create rubbings of the bones.

Children continue to play hard outside as this work is happening inside. They make connections to their experience with bones as they run.

Ryder: My heart is pounding fast. Can it break my ribs?

John: Can bones break?

Sammy: Yes, like Naomi's arm.

Izzy: What do they do when they break? Is mine going to break?

The teachers want to show the children how strong the bones are and what happens if they do break. Since one of the fathers in the program works as a para-medic, he brings in all the materials used when a cast is placed on a body. The teachers collect different twigs. They make sure that there are some strong twigs and some thinner ones that are easily breakable. They invite the children over for group-meeting time to have a discussion about how bones are strong and don't easily break. The teachers want to make sure the children don't develop any fears about their bodies being fragile. They set a table with the cast materials, twigs, and water and invite the children to explore these items.

The children spend a long time using their motor skills to break the twigs and wrap them in a cast. The teachers help the children place the casts in the sun to dry. The children also attempt to break some of the thicker branches unsuccessfully.

Ryder: This is not going to break.

Izzy: No, it is strong.

Alina: Very strong. Like me. (She jumps up and down multiple times.) See, my legs are strong. They don't break when I jump.

Lorenzo picks up a thin twig that has been wrapped with casting material.

Lorenzo: See, this is strong now.

John: That is how the doctor makes the bones together again.

Crystal: Yes. When someone breaks a bone, the doctor puts a cast on to help it be strong again.

Lorenzo: That is good.

The children continue to play with the X-rays for weeks, and the teachers often hear them talk about how their bodies move and how their bones feel.

~~~~~~

Making Theories Visible in Play

The teachers at Crystal's Creative Kids program encourage the children to discuss the differences they notice. They also help the children deepen their understanding of how their bodies change as they grow and how their physical skills become stronger. Most of the children in the program are in the preoperational stage and are developing new physical abilities. With these new skills comes the curiosity of what is inside their bodies and how their bones work when they run, jump, and twirl.

The children's play shows how they are developing Piaget's concept of understanding through physical knowledge. They are learning how their bodies move and function in space through the physical skills of raking leaves, dumping rocks, and moving tree stumps. Swinging while lying on their tummies and again while sitting on their bottoms allows Sammy and John an opportunity to compare how their bodies swing differently in space according to their body's position. Rolling balls and acorns down the slide adds to the children's physical knowledge of how objects roll differently. Nick and Nate learn about space as their bodies are inside the playhouse. As the children paint with bones, they gain an understanding of how the bones stroke paint on easel paper differently than paintbrushes. All of these physical actions contribute to the children's physical knowledge of how objects move and behave in space.

As the children in the story begin their investigation about bodies, they have what Piaget identifies as a *schema* about bodies: bodies come in different sizes, bodies have blood, and bones are hard. As they look at the X-rays, the children hold them up and match them to respective body parts. They match skeleton bones to X-rays and then skeletal parts to their own bodies. They compare their own body parts to the X-rays by putting a hand under an X-ray or placing X-rays on top of feet. Through these comparisons, the children begin to discriminate between types of bones. These physical processes allow them to confirm a schema of bones that includes bones' appearance, properties, and function. According to Piaget, when Lorenzo compares the skeleton's bones to the X-rays and then to his own hands, he is organizing a series of schemas into a pattern of understanding about how his body works.

Similarly, when the children begin to question how bones break, they connect the possibility of broken bones to their own bodies and fear that it can happen to them. The teachers help the children process this fear by allowing them to break the twigs and put a cast on them. The cast-making experience gives the children the ability to know that bones are very strong and they can also heal. This helps them in gaining a more concrete concept of how their bodies function. The application to Piaget's theory is that the children are developing a schema of how bodies function.

The children in this story are beyond Piaget's sensorimotor stage. They will continue to use their sensory skills along with their motor skills to learn about the world, although now the children are able to use language as they move into Piaget's next stage of development: preoperational.

In the preoperational stage, as in all stages, Piaget views children's learning as an active process. He describes children during the preoperational stage as not being as reliant on their sensorimotor system, but he says children at this stage still use active learning as a significant way to gain understanding. In the preoperational stage, children are capable of connecting simple events to how they use their bodies. The children relate how bones help with movement as they engage in fundamental movement skills such as walking, running, and jumping. Connections are also evident in their motor movements as they mimic various animals. Alina reports that her legs are strong because of their bones and do not break when she jumps. Sammy's and Ryder's statements about their hearts pounding fast demonstrates that they have made a connection between running and the effects on their hearts. Exploring their bodies can strengthen children's understanding of how the body functions and how they have a level of control over their own physical development. As the children explore new physical abilities, they learn that they can be more intentional in using their bodies to learn and that they can manipulate more complex problems presented by the environment.

TAKE ACTION: The Environment

Environments That Engage Multiple Physical Interests

Piaget contended that cognitive and physical development happens simultaneously. Children's cognitive ability develops as a result of responding to physical experiences, and children's thinking is revealed as they use their bodies to relate to, learn from, and explore their world. It is through a child's physical relationship with her environment that she learns to connect and respond in complex ways. Below are some suggestions to design environments that offer multiple physical interests:

- Provide opportunities for children to use physical skills through shadow exploration. Shadow exploration happens naturally as children play outside chasing their shadows or trying to catch them. Create large shadow screens that allow children a full-body experience for exploring shadows.

- Introduce appealing pieces of equipment into the environment to promote motor development and increase spatial awareness. Include large-scale items on the playground, such as nautical rope. Big, heavy nautical ropes take tremendous strength to pull around the play yard. Other large objects or big containers (such as barrels and tires) allow children a chance to crawl in and out or over and under, while large cardboard boxes provide enclosed spaces for children to get their whole bodies inside.

- Design environments that challenge children to interact with a variety of materials, such as baking soda, vinegar, spoons, bubbles, and containers of different sizes. This promotes the use of small-motor skills as children investigate the multiple reactions caused by mixing the different materials.

- Offer children flashlights to create the chance for them to use physical skills as they deftly run and hide from the beaming lights and maneuver the flashlights in different directions.

TAKE ACTION: Your Role as a Teacher

Partnering with Children to Support Their Thinking about Their Physical Abilities

According to Piaget, the teacher's role in promoting physical development is to facilitate opportunities for children to use their bodies as tools for learning. He is a big proponent of "hands-on learning" and active discovery through the senses. In other words, children need to actively and physically interact with the environment in order to learn. As children's physical skills develop, they make meaning of what they see, hear, and touch. They learn through the repetitive behaviors that form what Piaget calls "schema." Below are some ideas teachers can use to promote physical development and learning:

- Offer children opportunities to engage in activities that allow them to use their bodies as learning tools. Encourage children to spend time climbing, jumping, running, and skipping. When children are actively involved, they use their bodies as tools for learning. When they run, they gain a sense of space and time. When they jump, they discover height. Discovering how things move increases children's understanding of how things work.

- Invite children to swing and twirl in a tire swing and to investigate items that rotate, such as wheels and pendulums. Children enjoy twirling, dancing, and moving in circles. This type of play promotes critical-thinking and problem-solving skills as children make sense of how the items rotate and how their own bodies twirl and move.

- Give children the opportunity to explore activities that require repetitive motions. This allows children to reflect on what they have done before. Actions such as conquering the monkey bars require children to learn to swing their bodies and practice coordination. Children can gain practice deciding when is the right moment to move their hands from one bar to the next and knowing how fast they are willing to go. Other repetitive activities might include pedaling a tricycle or balancing on a balance beam.

Erik Erikson

Promoting Physical Mastery

Erik Erikson on the Physical Development
of Young Children

Physical development plays an important role in each of Erikson's psychosocial stages. As children's physical abilities increase and their bodies mature, they are able to successfully master the tasks presented in each of Erikson's proposed stages.

Gaining trust through physical skills: In Erikson's first stage, trust versus mistrust, infants' main task is to develop a sense of trust in themselves and the people around them. They use their physical senses of touch, sight, smell, hearing, and taste to establish connections to familiar smells, textures, and images. For example, infant Kaleia's sense of sight is seen as she looks at Crystal and smiles, and her sense of sound is seen as she turns her head to respond to Crystal's voice. Kaleia uses her physical skills of reaching out to Crystal to be picked up and clinging on to Crystal as a way to stay close to her caregiver. Kaleia also uses her physical abilities to familiarize herself with new objects in her environment. These behaviors illustrate how she is learning to trust herself and others and successfully mastering Erikson's sense of trust through her physical skills.

Gaining autonomy through physical skills: When children enter the next psychosocial stage proposed by Erikson, autonomy versus shame and doubt, they focus their energy on gaining a sense of autonomy and independence. This is the time when toddlers say, "Me do it." Physical growth and development plays an important part in this stage. Children gain what Erikson identifies as a sense of autonomy through newly acquired physical abilities of running, climbing, dressing and feeding themselves, and toileting. As Colter moves around faster and maneuvers more complex terrains, he continuously gets stuck in small spaces. When this happens he will yell, "Help, I stuck," but when the teachers come to help him he says, "Me do it." He wants help, but he also wants to exert his independence. He is mastering physical skills and achieving autonomy as he interacts with the environment.

Gaining initiative through physical skills: When children enter the preschool years, they are in the process of mastering Erikson's stage of initiative versus guilt. In this stage, children increase what Erikson calls a *sense of initiative* as they develop physical skills. As children gain physical control over their bodies, they can jump, gallop, run, pedal, climb, and balance. According to Erikson's theory, children's positive identity is linked to their successful achievement of tasks, such as their physical accomplishments. Children demonstrate pride in their newly acquired skills; their energy levels are high and their ability to focus on tasks that interest them increases. During the preschool years, children take initiative and are ready to take more risks as they engage in physical play. For example, Jd and Bella have just learned to pump their legs in order to make their swings go high. They challenge each other to a game of "I can go higher." This new skill has opened a new door, prompting the children to take the initiative and engage in more complex physical play. It is during this stage when adults' constant concern for safety can get in the way of children accomplishing this task. To support Erikson's third stage, adults need to focus on the children's newly gained skills instead of their mistakes and allow children to practice new skills independently.

Gaining industry through physical skills: When children enter the industry versus inferiority stage, their large-motor and fine-motor skills become more refined and coordinated. A sense of what Erikson defines as *accomplishment or industry* is developed through mastery of new skills that require physical dexterity. For example, children engage in sports and more complex games. They become skilled in drawing, writing, and using a wide variety of tools. Erikson believes children need opportunities to use their physical skills for such activities as athletics, art, and carpentry in order to gain a sense of competence.

As children grow, their physical development demonstrates many of Erikson's stages. Physical strengths developed at each stage allow children to be more successful at future stages. The following story shows how children acquire a sense of trust and autonomy through physical mastery.

Colter and the Tree Stumps

Trust and Autonomy to Support Physical Mastery

From the moment Colter starts crawling, he ventures to explore different areas of the environment. For days, he crawls to the edge of the grass and sits, watching the older preschoolers climb on top of the tree stumps. He places his hands on the ground, gets in a crawling position, and sits up again. Finally one day the teachers see him crawling across the dirt-covered ground toward the tree stumps.

Colter crawls a few feet, sits back, and turns his head to look behind him. He crawls some more and reaches the tree stumps.

Colter grips the stump with his hands and pulls his body into a standing position after a few attempts. Propping himself up, he turns back and smiles. As he balances in that position for a few minutes, he bounces his knees up and down.

The teachers stand back and observe. They do not interrupt what Colter is doing.

They worry about him falling and getting hurt; however, they know that letting him take this risk is an important part of supporting his growing process and accomplishments.

Suddenly Colter attempts to climb on top of the tree stump. First he places both hands farther onto the tree stump's flat, smooth surface and begins to lift his left knee up. He positions his left foot back down on the ground and stops for a few minutes. Then he once again places his left leg up onto the stump and starts to lift his right foot off the ground. Colter repeats this back-and-forth process a few times, stands up again, and places his right hand farther onto the stump. He proceeds to lift one leg and center it on the stump. He cautiously lifts the other foot off the ground and brings it up onto the tree stump.

Some of the older children come over to watch what Colter is doing. Amazingly, none of the children come to help him or interrupt him. They stand around at a safe distance along with the teachers.

Colter now encounters the challenge of turning his body around on the small surface the stump provides without falling off. He begins by moving one hand to the side and brings his leg forward while still keeping the other knee on the stump. He uses his other arm to balance his body. When this gets difficult, he stops and looks around toward Teacher Crystal as if asking for support. Crystal smiles and does not say a word. She wants this moment to belong to Colter. She knows that he has been working hard to get to this point.

Once more, Colter moves the same foot forward, but this time he keeps both hands on the stump. He lifts himself up and pulls one leg and then the other forward.

Colter turns around as he sits down with a big smile that says, "I did this all on my own."

At this point, all the children start clapping and smiling with him. Bella comes over and sits next to Colter on the stump.

Bella: Colter, you did it. You are now a big boy and ready to play with us.

Making Theories Visible in Play

In this story, Colter demonstrates the mastery of several of Erikson's stages. He is showing his foundation and continued ability of trusting adults and himself—trust versus mistrust—and is beginning to develop a sense of autonomy, as shown in Erikson's second stage.

We see Colter exploring the environment with his body and growing his trust in his physical skills. The teachers trust Colter's ability, and from this freedom he learns to investigate the environment and test his limits. Colter knows his surroundings and trusts his own ability to conquer difficult tasks. His trust in the adults that care for him and the environment have led him to develop a strong sense of who he is as well. Colter's strong sense of trust combined with his increased motor skills developed at this stage allow him to move successfully to Erikson's next stage, autonomy versus shame and doubt.

Even though Colter was still young when this story took place, it is evident he was already displaying a strong sense of autonomy. In the story, he begins his journey to conquer the tree stumps by carefully observing other children climb on them. He crawls the distance from the deck to the stump for days, gaining the courage to climb the stump. The teachers watch Colter to keep him safe, but they allow him the time and space to accomplish the task. They recognize the importance of supporting his independence and avoid helping him or putting any pressure on him to hurry and climb the stump. They trust that Colter is capable, and they send him this message by allowing him to complete his journey.

Colter's increased physical abilities and strong sense of trust and autonomy lay the foundation for Erikson's next stage, initiative versus guilt. Although too young to master the tasks of either the initiative versus guilt or the industry versus inferiority stages, Colter is gaining the necessary physical, social-emotional, and cognitive skills to be successful at the next levels. With the support of respectful and caring teachers, he will continue to explore new skills and take more complex risks. At the appropriate point, the teachers will encourage Colter to acquire initiative by taking more physical risks and completing new tasks. In a safe environment, Colter can continue to test his physical skills and try out his ideas to meet the tasks of each of Erikson's developmental stages.

TAKE ACTION: The Environment

Environments That Build Trust, Independence, Initiative, and Physical Skills

Erikson's psychosocial theory supports the idea that our social-emotional and cognitive development is affected by our physical development. Physical activity assists children in being more capable, comfortable, and competent, which in turn leads to confidence, independence, and productiveness. Following are some suggestions to support physical development, particularly throughout the first three stages of trust, autonomy, and initiative:

- Include in the environment materials and equipment that are durable. When children are testing new ideas, it is important that they can trust the tools, materials, and equipment they are using. Items need to be well built to withstand hard use by large numbers of children over a period of many years. Using real items helps with durability. For example, real pots and pans are sturdier than plastic toy cookware.
- Design environments that allow children to trust their bodies at their own pace. Provide varying levels of equipment and materials for children to investigate. For example, each child can use tree stumps in a different way, according to their own ability.
- Plan an environment where children can handle materials without teacher assistance. Materials in open containers on low shelves allow children to exhibit autonomy in getting what they need. Locate items that go together in the same place—for example, buckets and shovels near the sand area or crayons and paper near the drawing area.
- Create a physical environment that shows respect for children's choices. Offer children several toys, materials, and activities to choose from to support their sense of autonomy and develop their physical skills. Making choices helps a child develop a sense of independence, but it is important to keep the choices manageable. Young children need practice at resolving their doubts in manageable amounts. Too many choices can be overwhelming and will be less effective.

TAKE ACTION: Your Role as a Teacher

Gaining Trust, Autonomy, and Initiative through Physical Development

Erikson considers physical play central to the growth and development of children. As they grow, children need to master their bodies and negotiate the rules and guidelines imposed by society while maintaining a strong sense of self. A teacher's role is to provide experiences and support to help children master their physical abilities while they develop a strong sense of trust, autonomy, initiative, and industry. As children's physical abilities increase and their bodies mature, they are able to successfully master the tasks presented at each of Erikson's stages, with the help of a responsive teacher. Following are some suggestions for educators to promote trust, autonomy, and initiative in children through physical activity:

■ Support infants by establishing trust. As infants become more physically adept to moving around, they begin to move away from their original center of trust—the primary adult in their life. You can support infants during the trust versus mistrust stage by encouraging their physical efforts and reassuring them of your presence.

■ Avoid pressuring children to complete a task. When adults place pressure on a toddler to master a task, they may be crossing the line into causing the child shame and doubt. You can encourage a toddler's independence by giving her gentle guidance. This will help her gain the physical self-regulation required to successfully achieve independence and autonomy.

■ Promote autonomy by inviting children to engage in new physical tasks, such as putting on their shoes or using a small spoon to serve themselves. Allow children to do physical tasks such as feeding, washing, dressing, and toileting on their own.

■ Provide ways for children to engage in productive work in order to develop their physical competence, initiative, and industry. Children need to assert power and control over their environment by making play choices, accomplishing tasks, and facing challenges. Encourage children's physical efforts and explorations. Climbing on a variety of play structures supports gross-motor skills, while clay, writing, painting, and manipulating small objects helps develop fine-motor skills.

Lev Vygotsky

Scaffolding and Learning through Physical Development

Lev Vygotsky on the Physical Development of Young Children

Vygotsky (1978) believes physical development is interrelated with cognitive and social-emotional development. He argues that in order to better understand the child's cognitive abilities, it is important to examine the physical transformation the child undertakes during each step of development. In play children develop physical skills that help develop their social and cognitive skills as well. Adults and other children help scaffold children's learning as they enter the ZPD by building further physical and social-emotional skills.

Guiding physical skills through play: Vygotsky establishes a relationship between physical, social, and mental development, which we can see through children's play. As children play, they use large-motor skills that involve movements such as running, jumping, crawling, rolling, and climbing. Children learn to master pedaling a tricycle, throwing a ball, and climbing stairs. Small-motor skills are used to manipulate materials such as clay, dress-up clothes, and puzzles. Children develop small-motor skills as they learn to use an easel paintbrush for painting and build with small blocks. As children play and develop these physical skills, they develop other social and cognitive skills. Social skills grow along with physical skills while children dig in the sand together or play chase. Children expand their mental skills as they negotiate a route to run from one end of the play yard to the other, or they problem solve how to climb down from a climbing structure. The more children's physical skills increase to complex levels, the more they try to do with play. And the more they try to do with play, the more they grow in other developmental areas. In other words, as children master physical tasks, they gain cognitive and social abilities.

As children master more complex physical tasks, they enter the world of organized games and sports. This type of play requires more physical coordination and the more precise abilities that come with physical maturity. It is through physical play and positive interactions with thoughtful adults, peers, and the environment that children are able to acquire new knowledge. According to Vygotsky, "in play, a child always behaves beyond his average age, above his daily behavior; in play it is as though he were a head taller than himself" (1978, 102).

Extending physical skills through the ZPD: At each step of development, children's physical learning is scaffolded by adults and peers through the ZPD, (the gap between what a child can do independently and can do only with help). Children learn to master physical skills through the ZPD. A child can learn large-motor skills such as throwing a ball, pumping his legs to swing, or riding a tricycle with the assistance of another child or adult. Children can learn small-motor skills such as tying their shoelaces or peeling a potato together through the assistance of a more knowledgeable other.

Social and cultural interactions support physical development: Vygotsky believes social and cultural interactions play a significant role in learning. This applies to physical development as well. Children gain physical skills and learn to manipulate tools by interacting with other children in the environment.

My Feet Can't Touch the Ground
Play That Promotes Physical Development

It's Monday morning, and the children arrive at Crystal's Creative Kids after their weekend at home. They dash outdoors to discover large tree stumps scattered around the yard, a product of the efforts of Teachers Crystal and Jason the day before. The two teachers often spend their weekends creating new and interesting provocations for the children. The stumps are a donation from a family. The stumps' play value seems to outweigh the option of splitting the wood for the family's fireplace.

Ryder: Hey, where did these come from? (Ryder jumps on top of a stump.) Look, you guys. I'm king of the hill!

Cruz (following Ryder's lead): Me too! You can't get me!

Sammy, Alex, Kainoa, and Alina climb on top of stumps as well. A gleeful game of jumping from stump to stump is invented. The gaps between each stump are wide, but the children persist in their efforts to successfully leap over the spaces. Different strategies are used to make it from one stump to the next. John springs forward with his left leg and leaps across the space,

landing on the stump first with his left foot, followed by his right. Ryder bends his knees and pushes securely off the stump. His feet leave the stump simultaneously, and he accurately lands on the next stump. Rules seem to be developing.

Cruz: You can only have one person [on a stump] at a time!

Sammy follows behind Brycin, age seven, who just joined the play. Because he is older, Brycin has better physical abilities and easily walks across from stump to stump with his longer legs.

Brycin: Sammy, you've got to balance like this.

Brycin shows Sammy how to place her arms out to the sides of her body to gain stability. She gazes at his body movements, and as she approaches the edge of the stump, she jumps across the gap, placing her arms out to steady herself.

Brycin: Way to go, Sammy!

Bella and Kainoa seem uncertain about jumping from one stump to the next. Cruz, who is older, wraps his arms around their shoulders and provides support.

Cruz: Try it, Bella. Wait for Alex, then it's your turn. You go like this. (Cruz demonstrates how to jump across.) Come on, Bella. You can do it!

Bella: I'm scared.

Cruz: It's okay. I'll catch you.

Bella takes a deep breath and thrusts herself forward. She holds her breath while airborne and lands on the stump. Cruz grabs her.

Cruz: You did it, Bella! You did it!

Bella smiles a wide grin.

Cruz: Now it's your turn, Kai.

Kainoa does a trial jump in place, throws his arms forward and back, then takes off from his stump. He lands on both feet on the next stump.

Cruz: Atta boy, Kai. I knew you could do it.

The jumping continues over the next few days until Ryder intentionally falls onto the dirt and pretends to be hurt.

Ryder: Watch out! Danger! There's lava over here. Help me!

John grasps Ryder's outstretched hand and pulls him to safety.

Ryder: That was close.

The game changes and the children now pretend to jump over flowing hot lava. Jason smiles as he remembers jumping from couch to couch over hot lava in his family's living room as a child. That night Jason adds wooden planks to the tree stump area.

The next day, Sammy adds a new element to their game. She takes a wooden plank and maneuvers it upright. She places one plank end on one tree stump and the other end on another tree stump horizontally. She makes sure the plank is secure and then carefully walks across the beam.

John, Jd, Cruz, and Ryder join Sammy in placing boards from one stump to the next.

Ryder: We've got to connect these [stumps] so our feet don't touch the ground.

John: Like this? Then what do I do?

Ryder: Yeah, that's right. We don't want any space. Remember there's lava there. It will kill us if we fall in.

Once the boards are in place, the children excitedly challenge their bodies as they avoid the dangerous lava. They gain competence in their physical skills by leaping and running. Even Duke the dog joins in the play as a lava monster. The children's sense of power and adventure increases as they take risks and challenge themselves to gain competence.

Making Theories Visible in Play

The children's play in this story exhibits the complexity of learning. Vygotsky believes that physical learning involves cognitive skills and is always socially mediated. As educators, we know that both cognitive and social development happen alongside the development of physical skills.

In this story, the connection Vygotsky highlights between physical, social, and cognitive development is seen through the children's play. The children use their physical skills, jumping from tree stump to tree stump to avoid the dangerous "lava" on the ground. Balance and coordination are used to stand on the stumps and move from stump to stump without their feet touching the ground. The children exercise their physical skills in combination with their social skills as they engage in victim and rescue play. Large muscles are used as they fall off the tree stumps into the pretend lava, and physical strength is used to pull each other up to safety. Physical skills are used in combination with cognitive skills as children estimate the distance to jump from stump to stump and plan how to move around the maze of stumps. As the children's physical skills expand, so does their social and cognitive development. Their play becomes more elaborate. They challenge their bodies to physically move and risk more, a cycle that encourages physical, social, and cognitive development.

Vygotsky's concepts of ZPD and scaffolding are seen in the story as the children attempt the physical skill of jumping from tree stump to tree stump. For Sammy, Bella, and Kainoa, the distance between tree stumps is too far for them to jump across on their own. But all three children are able to make the leap from stump to stump with help from Brycin and Cruz. Vygotsky (1978) identifies the distance between these tasks as ZPD. Not only are Sammy, Bella, and Kainoa practicing physical skills, but their approach to their personal ZPDs also leads them to try physical moves they're barely capable of. Brycin and Cruz provide scaffolding assistance to Sammy, Bella, and Kainoa as they try these new physical tasks. The younger children take on more challenging tasks when they have guidance from these more knowledgeable others.

The children's play in this story is consistent with what Vygotsky describes as the acquisition of cultural and social tools to increase knowledge. As the children engage in the physical play of "my feet can't touch the ground," they are reenacting a familiar cultural play theme. The play theme of escaping danger is a part of the program's culture passed down from older to young children at Crystal's each year. The children's ideas about how to play this specific type of game are passed down through the culture of the program. The children are also able to construct knowledge through the social interaction required of their physical play with the stumps.

Vygotsky's work provides educators with an understanding of the importance of physical play in supporting children's social and cultural development. Children's physical abilities are supported through scaffolding and more knowledgeable others when they work together to solve problems.

TAKE ACTION: The Environment

Promoting Physical Abilities in Real-Life Environments

According to Vygotsky, the child is the active creator of knowledge through play. In other words, learning takes place while children play. Through play, children gain the benefits of self-gratification, use of symbols, and self-regulation. Children are energetic and thrive in environments that allow them to be actively engaged in play. This type of environment promotes healthy physical development and offers children the opportunity to gain control over more complex body movements, materials, and tools. The more they move, the more they engage in learning. Below are some suggestions to design real-life environments that promote physical development:

- Create environments that promote collaborative interactions through physical play. Include large, open spaces to support physical development as children run freely. Such spaces provide a perspective on children's strength and what can be accomplished with their bodies.

- Contemplate how you can change the surroundings to be exciting, exhilarating, exploratory, or risky. Vary the outdoor landscape in physically challenging ways by adding climbing structures, platforms, boulders, logs, and stepping-stones.

- Be deliberate in designing spaces where children can interact together. Lofts, stages, and forts provide designated space to gather and play. Outdoor spaces that allow for choices, taking risks, and activities such as playing with water, digging, moving objects, and mixing concoctions support collaborative play.

- Incorporate double-wide swings or a tire swing to inspire children to sit and work together to make the swing move faster and go higher. Small hammocks and hammock chairs foster togetherness as children snuggle close. The constant movement provides sensory integration and is soothing for children. Hammocks can also provide a place for adults to sit quietly with a child who needs some support in gaining self-regulation.

Vygotsky

TAKE ACTION: Your Role as a Teacher

Culture, Societal Expectations, and Physical Development

Vygotsky's theory helps us understand that educators play a significant role in young children's development by helping them construct meaning of their world. As educators, we interpret Vygotsky's view of the teacher's role to be that of providing play opportunities and experiences where children can use their physical skills to solve problems collaboratively. Children's physical skills are promoted through culturally meaningful experience, scaffolding, and social opportunities. The following are some suggestions to support children's physical development and learning:

- Offer children multiple opportunities to engage in physical play, which is a crucial part of their lives. Physical play helps children gain control of their own physical abilities, fosters their imagination, promotes social connections, and supports their learning.
- Include experiences that promote physical growth and development and are grounded within a cultural context. For example, encourage children to re-create the physical experiences they see at home, such as playing soccer like a family member does on a soccer league or cooking a familiar meal.
- Provide spaces and time for parents to come and engage in physical play with their children. For example, when parents drop off the children in the morning, you could invite them to push their child in the swings or play catch.
- Design schedules that offer ample time for children to play both outdoors and indoors. Time is important for children to develop their physical abilities.

Abraham Maslow

Physical Strength That Supports
Self-Actualization

Abraham Maslow on the Physical Development of Young Children

Maslow proposes that in order for children to obtain their full potential, all their hierarchical needs have to be met. Physical development is important in helping children fulfill their needs. The role that physical development plays can be seen in each level of Maslow's hierarchy.

Physical development through meeting physiological needs: In the lower level of Maslow's hierarchy, he specifically addresses the importance of meeting the physiological needs of children. These are the primary needs of air, food, water, and shelter that are needed in order to survive. When children's physiological needs are not met, their energy and thoughts focus on meeting these needs rather than on learning. A tired or hungry child cannot concentrate. Maslow's theory maintains that until physical needs are met, no other significant growth can occur. The basic physical needs form the foundation for all other needs. As educators, we know that these basic needs are important in developing a healthy body and increasing children's physical abilities. As Maslow affirms, once the physical needs are met, the need for safety and security will emerge.

Physical development through meeting safety needs: According to Maslow, when physiological needs are met, safety becomes the critical need. As children acquire more physical skills, they venture into more complex activities. At this point, physical safety takes precedence. Children often display signs of insecurity and fear and hesitate to take risks. They have a strong need to feel safe and look for adults' help in accomplishing difficult physical tasks. Once caring adults meet their need for safety, children begin to test their own limits in an attempt to understand how their own bodies work in relationship to the objects found in the environment.

Physical development through meeting love and belonging needs: Children learn through physical and social play. When children engage in large-body play alongside other children, they achieve what Maslow defines as a *sense of belonging*. As children use their physical skills for building, climbing, riding, chasing, and creating games in collaboration with their peers, they begin to meet the love and belonging needs of Maslow's hierarchy.

Maslow

Physical development through meeting esteem needs: According to Maslow, esteem needs are developed as children gain self-respect and receive respect. As educators, we know that respect can come through competence, confidence, and mastery of physical skills. For example, as children demonstrate competence in accurately kicking or catching a ball, they feel a sense of achievement and receive acknowledgment for their physical ability from others. This sense of accomplishment, confidence in their physical abilities, and purpose leads to the final need in Maslow's hierarchy, the sense of self-actualization.

Physical development through meeting self-actualization needs: Achieving full human potential, according to Maslow, involves the integration of a child's whole development, including physical development. Creativity in particular is an avenue for achieving self-actualization. Children utilize large- and small-motor skills as they spontaneously express themselves in physical acts of creativity such as painting, sculpting, and dancing.

A Place for Shelter and a Place to Rest
Meeting Needs, Promoting Self-Actualization

Children's curiosity is never ending, and the teachers at Crystal's Creative Kids are constantly observing to see what investigation the children will engage in next. Construction indoors and outdoors is something that constantly interests the children. This always leads to testing new hypotheses and exploring new concepts. Construction is always active and involves the use of multiple physical abilities. As the children build a new idea, the conversations shift to how different people find shelter to keep away from the cold and heat. This particular summer, the weather is hotter than usual. The teachers still encourage outdoor play because they believe in the importance of moving and breathing fresh air. They keep a jug with ice water readily available and offer multiple opportunities for water play to keep the children cool. As the children play, the teachers hear talk about the weather.

Izzy: I like warm, but not too warm.

Brycin: I know. Sometimes when we are outside, the sun is strong and I want to hide.

Ryder: I am hot also, but I am also cold.

Zachary: Sometimes I want a quiet space to hide.

Cruz: A pace [place] for me.

Olivia: It would be nice to have a place to play and be protected.

Crystal: It sounds like we want a quiet and safe place to rest and hide. Does anyone have an idea of what we can do?

The children start talking all at once, and they all seem to have different ideas and suggestions. They finally agree to build a shady structure outdoors. The process begins with the children drawing their ideas on paper. During group time, Brycin shares his idea of building a tepee that he saw in *Houses and Homes*. The children vote on his ideas and generate a list of materials they will need to

create a protective and safe place to rest and relax outdoors.

Jason finds long, plastic pipes for the children to start their project. Zachary starts by drawing a circle in the ground.

Zachary: This is how big the shelter is going to be, that way we all fit.

Brycin starts to place the pipes around the circle.

Brycin: How are we going to have them stand?

The children all give suggestions.

Olivia: Put them together on the top.

Brycin gets a chair and, while the other children hold the pipes at the bottom, he aligns them at the top.

Brycin: Uh-oh, I need tape to hold them together.

Jason: We can use string. Here it is.

Jason hands Brycin a roll of string. The children work hard and use every muscle in their bodies to make the structure stand. Crystal joins in to help them because she sees that the pipes keep falling.

Ryder: Thank you, I want to feel good inside.

Brycin: We have to work fast. I know we can finish and rest.

After some more effort, the children work together and master the task of standing the pipes to create the base for the shelter. Brycin smiles a wide grin as he finishes wrapping the string around the pipes. The other children cheer as he steps down off

Maslow

the chair. The teachers bring over some old sheets to finish the structure. Olivia suggests they make a hole in the middle of the sheet and place it on top. Crystal gets the scissors and makes the hole. Brycin and Zachary place the sheet on the pipes and it falls to the sides, covering the structure all around.

Children (together): It worked, it worked, and we did it!

John: What about wind?

Crystal: Yes, we need to figure out a way to hold the sheet down when there is wind.

Once again the problem solving starts and the children have an opportunity to share their ideas. The teachers want to make sure that every child's idea is valued, so they go around testing each one. After more hard work, the teachers and children decide to make small holes on the bottom of the sheet and tie strings from the sheet to each pipe.

Cruz: Done. Me go inside.

The children bring pillows, snacks, and books, and they gather inside the shelter to rest.

Making Theories Visible in Play

As the children engage in outdoor play during a hot day, we see how their physiological needs of Maslow's hierarchy are met. The teachers make sure that the children's basic needs of air and water are met. This is accomplished by allowing the children to play outdoors in the fresh air and offering the children ice-cold water. We can assume that the children's basic need for food has also been met, since the children are actively engaged and do not show signs of hunger. The physiological need for shelter is achieved by the children themselves as they use their physical skills to build a shelter that can protect them from the hot weather. (And, of course, the program's building is a permanent shelter that the children know as a constant.) Since the children's basic physiological needs have been gratified, the children's next level of needs—safety—will emerge.

The children's physical development is also advanced as they meet their need for safety. The children's actions reveal a sense of security as defined by Maslow (showing a sense of security, protection, and freedom from fear and anxiety). The children are able to experiment with new projects, with the teachers' support. The children's security in their own physical actions and ideas shows that their need for safety—both emotional and physical—has been met.

Since the children's physiological and safety needs are met, a need for love and belonging emerges. The children experience a sense of belonging as they use their physical skills to work in collaboration with each other on constructing the outdoor structure. The children's hard work takes unifying effort as they accomplish the construction task together. Maslow writes about how people "hunger for relations with people in general—for a place in the group or family—and will strive with great intensity to achieve this goal" (1987, 20). In this story, the children achieve what Maslow refers to as a *sense of love and belonging* through their relationships with each other and their teachers. We see that, through the construction project, the children's physical abilities played a role in meeting this need.

This story also demonstrates how meeting esteem needs is influential to physical development. Brycin uses his physical abilities to stand and balance on a chair, align the pipes at the top, and wrap string around the poles to secure them in place. He gains self-respect from his physical abilities he employed to accomplish this task. He receives respect for his physical work from the other children as they cheer when he finishes. All the children express a sense of accomplishment of their physical ability to build the structure as they cheer, "It worked, it worked, and we did it!" Once the shelter is completed and the children enjoy their new space, they have gained a sense of accomplishment and fulfillment. Their needs shift to self-actualization. Maslow states, "The common feature of the needs for self-actualization is that their emergence usually rests upon some prior satisfaction of the physiological, safety, love, and esteem needs" (1987, 22). With this in mind, perhaps the children are at the self-actualization level with all their needs met and feeling content.

TAKE ACTION: The Environment

Designing Play-Based Environments to Support Physical Development

Physiological needs are at the foundation of Maslow's theory. The basic needs of air, water, shelter, and food are survival needs. If they are not met, the human body cannot function properly and will eventually break down. Once these physi-

Maslow

cal requirements are fulfilled, individuals can move toward higher levels of growth and development in order to achieve their individual maximum potential. With this in mind, early childhood educators can ensure that environments provide for children's basic needs by offering areas and materials that support children's safety, love and belonging, esteem, and self-actualization needs. Here are some environment design suggestions for meeting Maslow's hierarchy of needs through physical development:

- Design an environment that recognizes children have individual intake needs and are hungry at different times throughout the day. Having healthy snacks available at all times and not just during snacktime can help children recognize their own internal hunger clock.
- Make outdoor spaces that integrate natural elements such as light, fresh air, trees, sand, and water to support mental and physical health. Spending time in nature reduces stress and depression. Incorporate quiet spaces where children can get away and reflect. It is important to heighten children's self-regulation and self-awareness. Creating nooks both outdoors and indoors can give children much needed time and space to reflect and think.
- Develop well-defined protective spaces that move away from the institutional-style fencing and can add beauty to the environment. Plants are a wonderful way to delineate areas in the outdoor environment. Nesting areas and alcoves serve as spaces for small groups of children to gather and develop strong relationships.
- Construct an environment that gives children the freedom to take physical risks, or create for them the illusion of risk. Risk is an important component of play that facilitates physical and cognitive development. Through risk taking, children learn to know their bodies and their abilities, which is part of the process of self-actualization.

TAKE ACTION: Your Role as a Teacher

Encourage Physical Development by Taking Risks

Maslow discusses the importance of meeting children's individual needs at each level so they can gain progress toward a stronger sense of self. Good health, having basic needs met, and optimal physical development are foundations for a joyful and satisfying childhood. The teacher's role is to set schedules and create environments, routines, and experiences that support children's physical development.

Following are ideas for educators to support children in developing their physical skills through meeting what Maslow identifies as basic needs:

- Help children learn ways to keep safe while still meeting their desires to take risks. By creating opportunities to test limits, take risks, and learn about their environment, teachers give children the chance to experience a place that is safe and caring, which protects them from the unsafe world outside the classroom community.
- Plan to meet children's basic needs. Physical activities for infants can be organized around their sleeping and eating schedules. As they grow and become toddlers who are constantly on the move and busy playing, they may need to be reminded to eat and drink in order to meet their basic needs.
- Teach children about the basic needs. Encourage children to learn about healthy bodies by making water and snack available at all times. Children can then learn to help themselves as their body requires it. This allows them to recognize their own need cycles, and they learn to fulfill their own basic needs.
- Give children multiple opportunities to master physical skills that empower their sense of physical well-being and an emotional sense of achievement and accomplishment. Climbing in complex structures or building a tall block structure helps children gain both fine- and gross-motor skills, as well as self-esteem.

Dewey

John Dewey

Collaborative Play That Promotes Physical Skills

John Dewey on the Physical Development of Young Children

Dewey (1938) says it is impossible to separate freedom of thought from the physical side of development. In his book *How We Think* (1998), Dewey describes the role physical development has on learning. He sees an infant's primary problem as mastery of her body. According to Dewey, mastery of the body is necessary for all later development and "development of physical control is not a physical but an intellectual achievement" (1998, 206). This means that there is a close connection between physical abilities and cognition, and that it is important to consider the whole child when planning curriculum and environments for learning.

Free exploration supports physical development: Dewey's philosophy supports an education that incorporates physical development as a way for children to actively explore the world both indoors and outdoors. He recognizes that maintaining a healthy body is critical to promoting mental health. Dewey proposes that the more opportunities children have to engage in physical activities, the more they will be able to further develop their cognitive and social development. Dewey says, "The joy the child shows in learning to use his limbs, to translate what he sees into what he handles, to connect sounds with sights, sights with taste and touch, and the rapidity with which intelligence grows . . . are sufficient evidence that the development of physical control is not a physical, but an intellectual, achievement" (1998, 206).

Physical, meaningful play increases learning: Dewey's ideas of a democratic process extend to the physical classroom where children engage in meaningful and shared interests. The adults listen, encourage, and support children to explore their ideas through the physical exploration of the environment. Within the context of this democratic environment, children can move freely to engage in physical and meaningful play to increase learning. As children acquire more sophisticated physical skills, they gain more freedom to make meaningful connections with the world and their community. Dewey views this freedom as the way children gain the judgment and the power to carry out deliberately chosen goals and accomplishments. As children gain more control over their physical abilities they can contribute more to the responsibility of maintaining a classroom environment in a democratic way. For example, when they contribute to cleaning and organizing the early childhood space, they are not only using their physical skills, but they are also developing responsibility and a sense of belonging to the community (Dewey 2008).

According to Dewey, "The aim of education is to enable individuals to continue their education . . . and reward of learning is continued capacity for growth" (2008, 91). Children have distinct physical abilities and capacities for learning. By respecting these individual differences, children are encouraged to use their physical abilities to learn. As educators, we know that an environment that promotes physical experiences and meaningful play increases children's learning, curiosity, and the capacity for critical thinking. Dewey's views provide an understanding of why physical development is a necessary component of learning. His work offers educators a perspective on how children's learning is supported as they use physical skills in meaningful experiences and in collaboration with others.

~~~~~~

Emergency 9-1-1

Understanding Democracy through Play

As the children are playing outdoors, they hear a fire truck blaring its siren pass by. Jd runs to the dramatic play area and gets the play phone. He puts it to his ear.

Jd: Emergency 9-1-1, emergency 9-1-1, we need help.

Jd carefully describes that there are children trapped in a fire in the playhouse. The children begin to talk about how firefighters protect people and put out fires. Izzy's dad is a firefighter, and she shares how he helps people and keeps them safe.

Jd's call triggers a sequence of play involving different community helper roles, including being firefighters, police officers, and nurses.

Nate (standing on top of the playhouse): Help! Help! I am in a fire!

The children use a two-by-four to help Nate escape from the fire. Sammy directs the children on where to place the plank so that Nate can safely come out of the playhouse. This type of play goes on for a while as the children re-create different scenarios.

All the children are involved, and they take turns playing the different roles. They save little Colter from a car accident and help Izzy come down from the top of the playhouse.

The children bring their play into group-meeting time, discussing their fears, feelings, and concerns.

Bella (referring to the siren): I don't like to hear the sound. It is scary.

Teacher Crystal: What makes it so scary?

Bella: It is loud.

Jd (gently, coming closer to Bella): They come to help you, so it is good.

Dewey

Izzy: My daddy is a firefighter and he is not scary.

Teacher Jason: Would you like us to invite Izzy's daddy to come and show us his tools?

All the children: Yes.

The teachers and the children write a note to send to Izzy's dad, inviting him to come and show them his tools and equipment. Alex also comes up with the idea of writing a sign that reads, "In case of an emergency call 9-1-1."

Alex: That way we can always get help from Izzy's dad.

The following week, Izzy's dad, Tony, comes to visit the children. He takes the time to show them step-by-step what he has to wear when he is a firefighter.

Tony answers the children's questions and stresses the importance of asking for help from firefighters and police officers. Since he knows the children well, he is able to address their fears and relates his information to the play the children have been involved in. Tony is sensitive to all the children and notices Bella is covering her ears for part of the presentation. He wants to make sure she knows that he cares for her and assures her that firefighters help people.

After he puts on his uniform, including his mask, the children gather around Tony and start touching the uniform and asking more questions. Their curiosity ranges from the feel of the fabric and how heavy the jacket is to how he can breathe with the mask.

Tony very patiently sits on the floor and allows the children to touch and feel the different tools he uses. He gives them the opportunity to put on the mask and breathe through it.

At first the boys seem to be more interested and the girls stand behind, until Tony puts his jacket on Izzy. Then the girls and boys gather and start touching the jacket and laughing. Bella, who had been standing in the background, approaches Izzy.

Bella: Can I wear it too?

The children continue to put on different parts of Tony's uniform and hold the different tools. After many questions, the children seem to have their curiosity satisfied. After saying good-bye to firefighter Tony, they disperse to continue their play.

The next day, Nick and Kainoa use goggles and cans to re-create Tony's mask. They engage in a sequence of play where they use a hose and water to extinguish a fire.

The interest in this type of play continues and the teachers bring it into group-meeting time by reading books and answering many questions.

Making Theories Visible in Play

Dewey's theory of progressive education incorporates activities that promote physical development and play. As children play, they grow and acquire more physical abilities that promote higher thinking.

According to Dewey (1998), children gain mastery over their bodies through intellectual achievement. The children's play in this story demonstrates how children use their physical skills as a means to make sense of the role of firefighters in our community.

The story also demonstrates the importance of Dewey's emphasis on exploration. The activities the children engage in allow them to make connections to how Tony helps people in the community as a firefighter. Dewey's theory is seen when the teachers invite Tony to come and talk to the children. In doing so, the teachers give the children the opportunity to participate in and explore a real topic of interest to them.

This story also shows the significance of physical, meaningful play in the children's development. In the story, as the children play they are not just learning about their own roles in the community they live in, but they are also gaining understanding about their own physical abilities. Their sustained physical and dramatic play—climbing, running, and pretending to be a community helper—allows them to address their fears and test their own abilities to help others. As children in the story engage in dramatic play pretending to be firefighters and police officers, they engage in a deeper understanding of the roles of community helpers and the physical strength each role requires. Physically motivated learning is what Dewey

Dewey

considers a key component of children's education. As the children pretend to be firefighters, they use their physical strength to move a heavy two-by-four plank. They also use their physical skills to model the work of firefighters. Climbing the playhouse ladder and helping each other in and out of the playhouse are examples of the children's physical skills.

Dewey stresses the importance of creating multiple opportunities for children to work together. He further states that physical, social, emotional, and cognitive development only happen in relationships with other children and adults and within the context of a caring and nurturing community. The children's developmental learning is evident in the story when they watch, and later re-create, how Tony uses tools and equipment to protect his body. As they reenact their experience and explore what firefighters do, the children are using physical skills to accomplish higher thinking and are engaging in meaningful experiences that they can apply to their daily lives.

TAKE ACTION: The Environment

Spaces That Promote Risk Taking and a Sense of Empowerment

Dewey is an advocate of hands-on learning and incorporating physical skills. He believes learning to master your body involves thinking. One way that Dewey supports physical mastery is through engaging children in real-life tasks and challenges. That is, children should learn things that come out of actual home, work, and other life circumstances. Dewey believes children need to be taught knowledge and skills that can be integrated fully into their lives as citizens and human beings. With that in mind, here are some ways to encourage physical mastery with real-life tools in your learning environment:

- Design an environment that supports real home experiences of cooking, cleaning, and maintenance. These experiences provide multiple opportunities for young children to practice their physical skills as they become active members of the classroom community.
- Create outdoor community gardens where children can plant, maintain, and harvest. Children can harvest vegetables from the garden and then tear, break, or snap beans and peas, peel carrots, chop celery, and scrub potatoes. Gardening builds community, leads to healthier lives, and gives children a chance to learn an important life skill while promoting fine- and gross-motor skills. Children experience satisfaction as they work in and see their garden grow.

- Integrate tools in the environment that promote responsibility and engage children in the daily household and maintenance tasks. Children use both large- and small-motor skills as they help with tasks to maintain the classroom. Provide sponges for wiping tables at cleanup time and cleaning up spills. Include the provision of real brooms, whisk brooms, dustpans, and brushes for children to sweep up spills.
- Plan a well-provisioned dramatic play space for children to model and reenact tasks they have seen adults do. There are many objects to add to dramatic play spaces that support this role play and assist in the development of fine-motor skills.

TAKE ACTION: Your Role as a Teacher

Encouraging Young Children to Test New Possibilities and Move Their Bodies

According to Dewey (2008), teaching depends in part on our understanding of educational theory. The message to educators from this view is that we need to apply core understandings of how children learn to our practice. One such core understanding from Dewey's work is his belief that children's thought is not separate from their physical side of development. Children use physical skills to learn. With this in mind, our role as educators is to support children's physical development as a means to bolster learning. We need to provide opportunities for children to use their physical skills through meaningful experiences in order to increase their critical-thinking abilities. Learning is linked to physical activity, and periods of silent reflection often occur after children have engaged in hands-on activities that require physical movement. Following are ideas for educators to support children's physical development in order to encourage learning:

- Observe children closely and develop meaningful curriculum that emerges from children's physical experiences and interests. For example, if a child shows interest in jumping, encourage him to estimate how far he can jump, and have him measure and graph the distances he leaps.
- Select appropriate activities based on an understanding of physical development and of the child's readiness for experiences. Teachers can introduce large-muscle curriculum with an activity such as yoga, which addresses flexibility, strength, equilibrium, and coordination, as children are ready.

Dewey

- Engage children in a community garden where they can use muscles to pull weeds, dig holes, plant, rake, and hoe. In the fall, invite children to work together and rake leaves into a pile. This promotes both large- and fine-motor skills and creates a strong sense of community.
- Invite children to cook part of their daily meals. Cooking introduces children to diverse foods and familiarizes them with foods from other cultures. It also encourages social interaction and improves motor skills and coordination.

Howard Gardner

Learning with the Body's Intelligence

Howard Gardner on the Physical Development of Young Children

Gardner argues that every human being has the capacity to develop all different intelligences and integrate them in the way they solve everyday problems. He also recognizes that some people have stronger tendencies to use certain intelligences, and that this is both genetically and socially driven. Physical development plays an important role in the process of developing many kinds of intelligences—for example, physical development helps children develop musical intelligence as they play instruments or move their bodies to music. This chapter, however, concentrates on exploring bodily-kinesthetic and spatial intelligence. Both intelligences encompass the ability to coordinate one's own bodily movements in specific and differentiated ways (Gardner 2006).

Bodily-kinesthetic intelligence: Gardner defines *bodily-kinesthetic intelligence* as the ability to solve problems using the body. It includes physical dexterity, hand-eye coordination, balance, and physical agility. Children use bodily-kinesthetic intelligence to learn. They use both their large- and small-motor abilities to make sense of their world. Children use physical skills while dancing, acting, gardening, building, playing, and cooking. In fact, physical abilities are used in everything a child does. Children with highly developed bodily-kinesthetic intelligence often prefer activities that engage their senses and their entire body to learn. When children are given the opportunity to develop their bodily-kinesthetic intelligence, they have a higher chance of developing the capacity for scientific thinking and creative writing or of becoming artists, performers, musicians, athletes, or dancers. People who have heightened bodily-kinesthetic intelligence can skillfully manipulate their bodies in an expressive way and solve challenges presented in the environment.

Spatial intelligence: This is the ability to solve problems through the understanding of balance and space. It involves using spatial judgment and having the ability to visualize things in one's mind. Children who practice spatial intelligence use their physical skills to create art, build things, and put puzzles together. In creating art, spatial intelligence uses physical skills for sculpting, drawing, modeling, and painting. In block building, spatial intelligence uses physical skills to construct structures. Spatial intelligence comes from a child's action upon the world (Gardner 2011a, 188). This means that children develop spatial intelligence through physical development opportunities. When children are given the opportunity to develop their spatial intelligence, they have a higher chance of developing a capacity for engineering, photography, sculpting, inventing, and designing—all activities that involve physical coordination.

Balancing Bodies

Moving Our Bodies to Learn

While outdoors, the children start testing various ways to balance their bodies, such as walking along the edge of the patio deck and on top of stones that are lined up in the gravel area of the play yard. Alex, John, and Sammy create a balance beam with a two-by-four and logs. They begin by laying two logs sideways in the gravel, a distance of about three feet apart from each other, and then place the two-by-four from log to log as a plank across the open space. The plank creates a bridge but rests upon each log's curved edge rather than extending securely over the top of each log.

As Alex starts walking on the plank, a challenge presents itself. The plank slips off the logs to the ground. The three children attempt to re-create the bridge multiple times, but each time the plank falls. With the help of Teacher Jason, the children begin to solve this problem.

Jason: What do you think is causing the plank to fall?

Sammy: Because it is big.

Gardner

Jason: It is big and also heavy.

Alex: The log is round and the plank can't stay there.

Sammy: Let's move the logs this way. (She moves her hands close together to indicate a narrow span between logs.)

Alex and John try Sammy's idea by repositioning the logs closer together and replacing the plank. This time they place the plank so it extends beyond each log's edge, creating stability. The boys explore different ways to balance on and cross the plank—forward, backward, and sideways. Jason joins them and uses his hands to maintain equilibrium.

Jason: Hey, Sammy, your idea works— the plank is not falling. It's staying balanced.

Sammy flashes a smile as she stands off to the side watching. Alex notices her.

Alex: Come, Sammy, the plank is safe now. I will hold your hand.

Sammy places one foot on the plank and begins to walk as Alex holds her hand. Her opposite hand extends to the side to support her balance.

Sammy: This hand out helps me too.

Sammy, with Alex's help, makes it to the other side and the children's faces show the joy in their accomplishment.

Sammy continues to practice her newly acquired balancing skill with Alex's encouragement while John finds other items in the play yard to test his balance. He takes a large, flat circular disk of plywood that is similar in size to a snow saucer used for sledding. John places the disk on top of a long, dead tree log and attempts to stand astride the wooden disk as if he's on a skateboard. His wobbly legs are spread wide apart. His right hand reaches down and touches the disk for support as he tries to keep the disk balanced on the tree log.

John: Teacher Jason, look at me!

Jason: Wow, John. That takes strength to balance like that.

John: Yeah, but this side keeps going up. I can't keep it down.

Jason: Do you think that your body balances the disk?

John: I think my body moves it up and down but not even.

The children continue to test different ways to balance their bodies. They often encounter challenges of how to place the

planks and disks to support their weight. They revisit a variety of strategies and attempt multiple solutions. The teachers gather together and spend time looking at the photos they have taken of this activity. They want to provide the children with a deeper understanding of how objects balance and what objects can support their weight. After conducting some research, the teachers decide to gather the children to re-create the tree logs and planks on a smaller scale. Jason revisits the children's thinking and introduces the photos and small blocks to them.

Jason: These are the photos we took of all of you balancing your bodies outside. You worked hard to make the plank balance and the disk stay flat, but sometimes they lifted up. What do you think was causing that?

The children have many different hypotheses that range from the need for the disk to be bigger to the need for balance.

Jason offers the children the opportunity to use small pegs and blocks to test their ideas. The children proceed to build different structures. They often pause and look at the photos.

Alex: See, here I am and my hands are to the side. I think that keeps my balance.

Alex starts to build a tall structure, but it keeps falling.

John (watching Alex): You need a longer block at the bottom. That will make it stand. See, like I did. It balances.

The children continue to build.

Alex: I get it—the long blocks are our arms and they help with the balance.

Jason: You built tall structures that fell, and then you added a larger block that helps balance the structure. Your hands help you balance your body when you walk on the planks.

John: 'Cause our body is the center and gives us equilibrium.

Jason: Yes, John, our body does help us with equilibrium.

Gardner

Through this simple experience, the children are able to explore the concept of balance in more detail. Re-creating their ideas on a smaller scale gives them a deeper understanding of how to balance both things and their own bodies.

The children's interest in balancing their bodies continues outside. Zachary and Brycin begin to balance their bodies on the seesaw. They begin by squatting on the seesaw's seat while holding on to the bars. They slowly stand up, but they keep their hands on the bar.

Zachary: Take your hands off.

Brycin: No—wait, do we have to do it at the same time?

Zachary: We have to balance together.

Zachary takes his hands off and then spreads his arms to the side; this causes the seesaw to lift on Brycin's side. Zachary places his hands back on the handle.

Brycin: Wait, wait—we have to be even or I go up.

The children now have to figure how to balance their bodies when the seesaw is moving.

Brycin: We have to make the seesaw be even.

Zachary: But I weigh more than you.

Zachary and Brycin attempt different strategies, such as letting go of one hand at a time. They try to stand up at the same time. Finally they both hold on to the bars and lift their bodies slowly to a standing position, and the seesaw begins to even out. They then count together: "one, two, three," and let go of the bars and open their arms. They are now balancing on the seesaw in full control.

The boys' smiles show their pride in their hard work and accomplishment. They set a goal and worked together to achieve it.

After seeing this interaction between Brycin and Zachary, the teachers know that the children have a rudimentary understanding of how their bodies balance and how they can use their bodies to balance the seesaw. They decide that, once again, they need to give the children the opportunity to explore their concepts on a smaller scale. They present a provocation created from photos of Zachary and Brycin balancing on the seesaw and of small, metal balancing puzzles. These are metal pieces that fit together to create a figure and stay erect when balanced. This new exploration challenges the children to test their ideas in more depth. It also requires them to enhance their coordination in order to make the items balance. This provides them the opportunity to further comprehend how their bodies work.

Nate: Place the bar in the middle or it won't work. (He points to the bottom part of the puzzle.)

Jason: What makes it work when you place it in the middle?

Nate: Because it's not heavy.

Jason: When things are heavy, it moves to one side. So, if Zachary and Brycin have different weights, how did they manage to make the seesaw stay in the middle?

The teachers ask questions to help the children see when there is a discrepancy in their assumptions. They want the children to think critically as they analyze all their ideas.

Alex: Your body makes thing balance, like when you lift your leg up and you have to use only one leg. (He gets up and demonstrates how to do it.) It helps when your hands are out.

Once the children figure that their bodies balance by having a center of gravity, in this case their arms being extended, they explore the concept in more detail by using the metal puzzles.

The children continue to explore balance both outdoors and indoors, and the teachers notice they are getting more skilled in their attempts to balance on the beams, seesaw, and even chairs. The children test their limits and take more risks by placing planks on an incline. As they do this, they gain deeper understanding and confidence in how their bodies work.

Gardner

Making Theories Visible in Play

In this story, the teachers provide the children time to explore how to balance their bodies using a variety of tools and equipment. As they engage in this investigation, the children demonstrate high bodily-kinesthetic intelligence. They spend time figuring out how things work, they have plenty of physical energy, and they use their bodies to learn.

This story shows children learning through bodily-kinesthetic intelligence. Gardner states that children use bodily-kinesthetic intelligence through their senses and motor skills to investigate their surroundings and solve problems. The children in the story begin by testing their ability to use their bodies in multiple situations. They use their large-motor skills to pick up the heavy tree logs and planks to build the balancing bridges. They use their bodily-kinesthetic intelligence to climb on and off the tree logs and balance on top of them. Later the children use balancing skills as they walk across the planks and stand on the wooden disks and seesaw. Children with highly developed bodily-kinesthetic intelligence have a heightened awareness of their bodies and are often seen taking calculated risks with their bodies. This is seen when Brycin and Zachary balance on the seesaw. They challenge each other to remain standing as they gain control of the seesaw. They both learn through movement and by physically doing and engaging with the environment. This demonstration of intelligence challenges the belief that mental and physical activities are unrelated. Instead it confirms how Gardner sees the use of the body as a form of intelligence (Gardner 2011a, 219).

This story also shows children learning through spatial intelligence. In the beginning, the children use spatial intelligence and their large muscles to move from tree stump to tree stump. Next, they use spatial intelligence and their physical abilities as they construct balancing boards with tree logs and planks. Spatial judgment is needed to determine how far apart to place the tree logs that serve as the base. The children physically move the stumps close enough together to support the length of each plank in a bridge-like fashion. Their physical skills are used along with their perception to bridge the space. Spatial intelligence and physical skills are also used as the children balance their bodies to walk across, up, and down the planks. As they walk along the planks, they learn about moving their bodies in space. Later the teachers bring in small, metal balancing puzzles to simulate how the body balances. The children use spatial intelligence and small-motor skills as they determine how to balance the pieces. This experience helps the children begin to learn the laws of physics beyond their own bodies. It also helps them become aware of changes in momentum and balance.

MI theory helps educators understand that children have different strengths when it comes to solving physical problems. Knowing this, teachers can plan a variety of experiences for children to learn concepts and skills and design spaces in the environment to support many problem-solving styles.

TAKE ACTION: The Environment

Environments That Challenge Children's Physical Abilities

We can use Gardner's MI theory to gain insight into how children use their bodies to solve problems they encounter in their environment. Gardner's theory offers a framework for responding to the way different children interact physically in the world. He argues that even though all the intelligences involve in one way or another the use of the body, all children's bodily-kinesthetic and spatial intelligences have a direct impact on how they acquire knowledge and solve problems. Below are some ideas to design environments that challenge physical abilities:

- Design spaces where children can use their bodies to test different ideas such as sense of space, height, and length. This can be done through activities such as climbing trees and mounds of dirt, hiding under or behind things, carrying large or heavy items, or filling large and small containers with water, sand, and other natural items.

- Add porch, tire, rope, or playground swings to the outdoor environment. Swings should be part of every outdoor space because they play an important role in the development and strengthening of perceptual-motor skills.

- Incorporate a variety of textures throughout indoor and outdoor environments so that children can touch them and explore them freely. Providing different types of fabrics children can arrange and reconfigure supports motor and sensory skills. Include the sensory experience of going barefoot as well.

- Create outdoor classrooms that can support large-motor development, dramatic play, science, art, and music, all in a natural setting. Inviting outdoor environments support naturalistic, spatial, and bodily-kinesthetic intelligence when they include plenty of trees, shrubs, flowers, rocks, and dirt. Children need spaces and unstructured time where they can be in nature and physically touch natural items: rocks to pick up and move, sand to dig, hills and trees to climb, and water and dirt to make mud pies.

Gardner

TAKE ACTION: Your Role as a Teacher

Promoting Children's Use of Their Bodies

According to Gardner, children with highly developed bodily-kinesthetic intelligence have a keen sense of how their bodies move and are very skillful in working with objects that involve both small- and large-motor movements. Teachers can support the development of this intelligence by encouraging children to engage in large-body play and by inviting them to explore the environment through dance and movement. Teachers can promote fine-motor development by including opportunities for children to work with small and large loose parts. Here are some ideas of how teachers can continually enhance children's bodily-kinesthetic and spatial intelligences:

- Include ample time outdoors in the daily schedule. Activities such as climbing, running, jumping, pulling, and sand and water play give children the opportunity to develop gross-motor skills. These activities also allow children to relate to different spaces, thus increasing their physical perceptions and abilities.

- Offer children opportunities to control small tools and materials such as clay, carpentry, art, eating/cooking utensils, or Lego blocks to refine their fine-motor skills. When children are fidgeting they need tools and equipment that they can manipulate and explore.

- Involve children in art experiences that involve the use of their entire body. Squirting with spray bottles; painting with toilet plungers, brooms, or mops; or painting on large canvases or collaborative murals offer children the opportunity to express their ideas on a large scale.

- Give children a chance to walk on a variety of surfaces, such as sand, pebbles, tree cookies, mulch, and wood planks. This allows them to balance and feel different textures with their feet. Walking on a flat surface is not the same as walking on a bumpy one. Walking on different surfaces can help children develop their ability to solve complex problems presented by their environment.

Louise Derman-Sparks

Bodies as Identity

Louise Derman-Sparks on the Physical Development of Young Children

The core goals of anti-bias education (ABE) can be applied to the physical development of young children. Physical development is influenced by multiple factors—culture, economic class, and diverse abilities—but this chapter focuses on how physical development is influenced by children's gender identity through Derman-Sparks's view. In *Anti-Bias Education for Young Children and Ourselves*, Derman-Sparks and Olsen Edwards identify additional goals for children that are related to the core ABE goals and, more specifically, to gender identity and fairness (2010, 91). These goals are:

1. "Children, regardless of gender, will participate in a wide range of activities necessary for their full cognitive and social-emotional development." (relates to ABE Goal 1)
2. "Children will demonstrate positive feelings about their gender identity and develop clarity about the relationship between their anatomy and their gender role." (relates to ABE Goal 1)
3. "Children will talk about and show respect for the great diversity in appearance, emotional expressiveness, behavior, and gender roles for both boys and girls." (relates to ABE Goal 2)
4. "Children will recognize unfair or untrue messages (including invisibility) about gender roles." (relates to ABE Goal 3)
5. "Children will practice skills for supporting gender role diversity in their interactions with peers." (relates to ABE Goals 3 and 4)

Below is an overview of how physical development is supported in the first three of the four core anti-bias education goals.

■ Gender Identity and Fairness Goal 1—*Full participation*: First, children's full participation in gender identity exploration helps advance their physical development. At an early age, children begin to recognize differences and similarities in physical characteristics and abilities, particularly relating to gender identity and formation. Children develop a foundation for self-awareness as infants and toddlers. During these two stages, they discover "what is me." Toddlers test their own physical skills and are sensitive to comments and feelings of adults and peers. By age two, children recognize and explore physical differences and mimic the adults around them. By age three, children can describe themselves as a boy or a girl but are still sorting out what that means. They are aware of their own abilities and spend time comparing and contrasting themselves and their abilities to other children. According to Derman-Sparks and Olsen Edwards (2010), as children notice these physical differences, they begin to connect their differences to issues of power and inequities in the environment. For example, when kicking a ball, a boy may say, "Girls can't kick hard." This may be the boy's way of gaining power and control over the role of soccer players as men. Children learn by observing others and absorbing spoken and unspoken societal messages about gender differences. These messages can have a profound impact on their physical and gender identity.

- Gender Identity and Fairness Goal 2—*Development of positive feelings*: Second, children's positive feelings regarding gender identity and fairness also extend to their physical development. According to Derman-Sparks and Olsen Edwards (2010), children may experience emotional conflict over acting differently from societal norms. For example, a girl who wants to play football or a boy who wants to crochet may struggle with society's belief of what is considered acceptable physical behavior for girls and boys. Negative feelings about gender identity can develop when society's view is different from a child's desire to participate in a nontraditional physical activity. When a message says, "boys can't dance," or "girls can't play basketball," it affects children's perception and feelings of their own physical abilities as a boy or a girl. Thus they shift their play to follow the gender rules that they understand to be more acceptable by society. Children develop positive feelings about gender as they feel their physical abilities are accepted by society and their community. A strong sense of self and a positive self-concept emerges about one's gender identity when the child receives acknowledgment and acceptance for her use of her physical skills.

- Gender Identity and Fairness Goal 3—*Respect for gender diversity*: Third, children develop respect for gender diversity, which allows them to express their physical development in new ways. Derman-Sparks supports providing opportunities for girls to test nontraditional female roles and boys to test nontraditional male roles. Participation in large-motor skills that are considered traditionally male roles, such as carpentry and construction, allows girls to feel comfortable in their female gender role. Derman-Sparks believes that girls need opportunities to test physical boundaries and find answers just as boys do. Boys too should have opportunities to participate in nontraditional physical activities, such as small-motor tasks of drawing or stitchery. Participation in a wide variety of physical experiences helps all children develop a strong sense of gender identity while gaining confidence in their physical abilities.

Boys Are Stronger Than Girls—or Are They?

Developing Gender Identity and Respect

Children in the program have gotten to know each other throughout the year, and they have built strong friendships. That is why the teachers are surprised to hear the children talking about each other's physical characteristics in a negative way. The teachers know they have to do something to help the children move back into focusing on each other's strengths and similarities while still valuing their differences.

The teachers begin by setting up mirrors all over the classroom. They want the children to have the opportunity to see themselves and notice the similarities among them. In the afternoon, the children gather around a mirror and start to comment about how they look.

Ryder: I am really strong.

Bella: I am prettiest than all.

Nicholas: No, Ryder, I am strong.

John: I'm strongest.

Izzy: I have purty eyes.

John: Look, we all have eyes.

Later, as the children play outside, the teachers see Bella and Jd on the swings and hear them talking.

Bella: I can go higher.

Jd: No, I am a boy and I can go higher.

Bella: I can stand on the swing.

Jd: I can too.

Bella and Jd continue to pump their legs, making the swings go higher and higher. Their conversation continues for a while and shifts from competitive to more engaging.

Jd: Look, we can climb high together.

Bella: Yes, we can climb up the house and swing high.

The teachers decide not to intervene and allow Bella and Jd time to continue to compare and contrast their attributes. They do notice that the boys often talk about their abilities and the girls usually talk about how they look. The teachers start to reflect with each other on their own biases and on how the children perceive both boys' and girls' attributes and abilities. The teachers want to send a message that is free of biases. They also want to support the boys' sense of self and encourage them to test their abilities, while encouraging the girls to continue to try nontraditional roles.

The teachers continue to observe and listen closely to what the children are saying and doing. They notice the boys gravitate to play with blocks more than the girls. They see Izzy and Alina trying to join play with a group of boys in the blocks area.

Alex (to Izzy and Alina): You can't play here; this is only for boys.

The girls are crestfallen and walk away to find something else to do. Unfortunately, the teachers are too stunned to respond. They know they have to say something, but they do not want to just make the boys let the girls play. They want the children to see that both boys and girls have strengths and that they shouldn't exclude each other from play.

The teachers notice that after this episode, the girls also start to exclude boys as they play "tea party."

The teachers gather the children for group time and talk about how boys are different from girls and how they are the same. They want to send the message that both boys and girls have the ability to engage in challenging tasks and to also defuse any stereotypes the children have about gender.

Teacher Crystal: What do boys and girls often like to do?

Ryder: Boys like to run.

Alex: We like to jump.

Sammy: I like to run and jump.

Alina: Me too.

Bella: I run.

Cruz: Boys are strong.

Sammy: I pick up the big plank. (Referring to a two-by-four the children use to create a pathway between various tree stumps.)

Crystal: It sounds like both boys and girls like to run and jump, and I have seen you do this together all the time. I have also seen Bella, Alina, and Izzy pick up heavy sticks and planks and move them around the yard.

Teacher Jason: So, I hear that both boys and girls are strong and they can pick up heavy sticks.

Alex: We can all jump and run.

Nate: We can work together to move things.

Izzy: Yes, we are all strong.

Jason: What else can boys and girls do that is the same?

Alex: We can both play with blocks and have tea parties.

Crystal: That is true. Both boys and girls can play with blocks, swing high, run, and have tea parties together. The other day I heard two boys say to the girls, "You can't play in the block area." How do you think the girls felt?

Nate: Sad.

Alina: I did not like it.

Jason: When we work together, we can do more things that are fun. Boys can be strong and do many things, and girls are also strong and do many things as well. We also don't want to exclude others.

Nate: I will play blocks with the girls.

Alex: No 'sclude the girls. We will all build with blocks.

The teachers finish the conversation and the children return to their play. This episode makes the teachers rethink how they teach. They want a bias-free environment and want both girls and boys to be empowered. They begin to incorporate some changes to make the classroom more inclusive of both genders.

The teachers add more tools and materials to the block area to invite the children to play together. Both boys and girls begin to play more frequently in the block area. The girls also spend more time in the block area, testing different concepts and ideas.

Another change the teachers implement is to invite the girls to roughhouse. Jason often spends time playfully roughhousing with the boys. The teachers believe this is a great way to allow the boys to express their emotions and energy. Roughhousing is free of rules and full of joy. It releases creativity and teaches children to physically engage without hurting each other. The teachers want to make sure the girls know they can participate in the activity as well.

Jason starts inviting the girls to participate in roughhousing. The girls enter the play with exuberance. The teachers begin to notice that the girls feel more comfortable sharing the spaces that they had previously considered "a boy place." These areas usually involve tossing a ball or some sort of sport-related activity.

Throughout the play areas, the teachers introduce tools that both boys and girls can use. The dramatic play area changes from being a simple kitchen area to a more inviting space for both boys and girls. For example, gender-neutral chef aprons and hats are added, and photos that show males and females doing the same home chores are displayed.

The teachers begin to notice the children playing together regardless of gender. They overhear a conversation between Nate and Alex as they are playing outside one day.

Nate: I can jump higher than girls.

Alex (looking at Nate): Nate, girls and boys can jump high, and we can do many things together.

Nate: Oops, I forgot we do like to jump and run together.

Making Theories Visible in Play

Anti-bias education discusses how young children compare and contrast their physical characteristics and abilities to each other. The children's play in the story demonstrates the need for several of Derman-Sparks's goals for gender identity and fairness.

First, the children's full participation shows their physical development along with their understanding of gender. The environment at Crystal's program offers opportunities for both boys and girls to develop their physical skills. There are swings, a digging area, blocks, an art area, and a playhouse. In the story, Crystal and Jason follow the advice of Derman-Sparks (Derman-Sparks and Olsen Edwards 2010) by observing the children's physical play and noting the way their choices divide along gender lines. The teachers discover that the boys are playing with blocks more than the girls and that the girls are engaged more with dramatic play, such as tea parties, than the boys. Following recommendations of Derman-Sparks (Derman-Sparks and Olsen Edwards 2010), Crystal and Jason make changes in the environment to include tools that both girls and boys can use in the block and dramatic play areas. Teacher Jason encourages the girls to participate in roughhousing with him. The teachers' changes to the environment and their own behavior support the children in using their physical skills to fully participate in the program, regardless of their gender.

Second, the children develop positive feelings regarding gender identity. In this story, the children's play illustrates their understanding of gender-expected roles in relation to physical development. Jd says that, as a boy, he can swing higher than Bella, who is a girl. Alex tells the girls that block play is only for boys. Girls exclude boys from playing tea party. Such behaviors indicate that the boys have internalized the societal messages that assign boys the more powerful skills. The girls have also classified themselves by their physical characteristics, such as "I am pretty." Following the advice of Derman-Sparks, Crystal and Jason address the messages that the children have internalized about physical skills and appearance in an effort to support positive feelings about their gender identity. During their interactions with the children, the teachers change their language to eliminate biased messages that they may be giving. For example, Crystal says that she has seen both boys and girls jump and run. Jason says that both girls and boys are strong. Using Derman-Sparks's approach allows the teachers to nurture positive feelings about gender identity and expand the children's physical development, unrestricted by gender roles.

Third, the children in the story develop a respect for gender diversity regarding their physical development. In the beginning of the story, the children argue about the physical skills of boys and girls. They challenge whether boys or girls are stronger and whether boys or girls can swing higher and faster. Derman-Sparks discusses how "children are influenced by others' attitudes about gender behavior" (Derman-Sparks and Olsen Edwards 2010, 92). She believes the key to changing attitudes is to offer experiences for new ways of acting and thinking. Teachers Crystal and Jason

Derman-Sparks

follow her advice and take opportunities to validate every child's abilities. For example, Crystal tells Bella, Alina, and Izzy that she has seen them pick up heavy sticks and planks and carry them around the yard. The teachers' actions model respectful behavior for the children to imitate in their social and physical interactions with each other.

The work of Derman-Sparks shows how teachers can support children's physical development through anti-bias education. She stresses the importance of helping all children develop confidence in their physical abilities while creating a strong gender identity.

TAKE ACTION: The Environment

Recognizing Differences and Similarities in Our Bodies and Physical Abilities

All children enhance a classroom's culture through the diversity of their many origins, values, beliefs, and languages. When teachers and children investigate together, they discover shared understandings and similarities among cultures as well as ways to celebrate differences between cultures. Derman-Sparks confirms that young children can develop prejudices—which are attitudes, opinions, or feelings without prior knowledge or reason—at an early age. Children make assumptions about gender, physical characteristics, and physical abilities based on societal stereotypes. Following are some suggestions to design environments that challenge these stereotypes and support children in developing a strong sense of self and progressing their physical development:

- Design inclusive environments that support all physical ability levels and promote creativity. All children are creative and need diverse possibilities to express their creativity. There are different ways to adjust tools so that every child can actively participate in artistic endeavors. For children who are unable to manipulate certain tools, such as paintbrushes, there are adaptive brushes that are easier to grasp that could be provided. For a child who cannot sit without support, there are adaptive chairs to help them sit securely so that they can participate in table activities.
- Change the space in which children do art. For example, art can be done on the floor or on a fence. Offer clay and materials such as ooblick (cornstarch and water) at different heights for all children to reach.

- Create an environment that supports children's choices regardless of gender role. How you design the learning environment influences how children play. For example, in the dramatic play area, include both male and female work and play clothes or provide books in the library that reflect diversity of gender roles. We may think girls prefer small-motor activities while boys favor active outdoor play, but in reality both girls and boys engage in—and may prefer—both fine- and gross-motor activities. Both sexes benefit from opportunities to explore all activities.

TAKE ACTION: Your Role as a Teacher

Supporting Children's Awareness of Ability and Physical Characteristics

As children gain more awareness of their own bodies and physical abilities, they begin to differentiate and classify themselves and others. At this stage, they count on an adult's perspective to learn not only what they are capable of doing, but also how to relate to others who are different from them. Children constantly recognize and explore physical differences and make decisions based on their own perceptions. Following are some ways that educators can help children expand gender behavior through physical activity:

- Encourage girls to engage in nontraditional physical activities and encourage boys to engage in nontraditional small-motor activities such as cooking, art, and sewing. This can be done by creating an environment where children can climb, run, dig, take risks, or jump, regardless of their gender.
- Show the children photographs and books of girls in active roles such as playing soccer, working in construction, or fighting fires, and show them books and photographs of men in nontraditional roles such as cooking and caregiving.
- Offer a variety of experiences for children to work collaboratively. Include opportunities for group art murals where children collaboratively create a large piece of artwork or provide large quantities of wooden blocks for children to build elaborate structures together. Such activities encourage both genders to work together and avoid separation and competition. Incorporate experiences that encourage both boys and girls to take leadership roles.

Derman-Sparks

- Organize visits to community places where children can see both genders practicing a variety of roles: men as nurses, women as police officers, or both male and female construction workers. This helps children move away from stereotypical thinking and develop a more global acceptance of differences.
- Use gender-neutral language, such as "firefighter" instead of "fireman." Change traditional children's songs, rhymes, and fingerplays to include both genders. For example, invite the children to add their own name in the song "Mary Had a Little Lamb."

In Conclusion: Physical Development Theories

Children's physical development increases dramatically during their first years of life. Children test their own physical limits to understand how their bodies work. As they acquire physical skills, children gain a strong sense of self. The theories affirm that there is a strong correlation between physical growth, cognition, and social development. Children gain confidence and use their bodies in more sophisticated ways in order to learn. Physical and meaningful play is crucial in order to increase learning. As children recognize their new physical abilities, they take more risks. Physical development assists children in gaining a sense of trust, autonomy, independence, industry, and initiative. Children's physical growth is seen as they practice any and all of the intelligences. As children gain more physical skills and cognition increases, they begin to make connections of their own abilities and characteristics with those of other people. At the same time, children begin to make connections to their gender-expected roles. The theorists featured in this book provide a framework to help us understand and encourage children's physical learning and development.

Your Turn

Now it is your turn to identify theory in children's play. Following is a practice story designed for you to apply your analytic skills in relation to children's physical development. As you read the story, identify which theories are visible in the children's play, consider key concepts, and reflect upon how you would support the children's interests and needs based upon the theories.

Building Ramps and Pathways

Promoting Physical Play

During a walk to observe the construction that is going on in the neighborhood, the children notice the different trucks and cranes in the construction zone and are fascinated by them. After their walk, the children begin to build ramps and series of complex pathways both indoors and outdoors.

The next morning, the teachers notice that the children have started to use the toy cars and trucks outdoors to re-create the construction site. The children first start by gathering containers for holding gravel. Little by little, they begin to test how to move gravel from one end of the construction site to the other. They use different cars and trucks and begin to incorporate other materials and containers, such as rocks and buckets.

The teachers want to encourage the children to explore how ramps and pathways work. With this in mind, they incorporate plywood planks and two-by-fours in the environment. The addition of these materials encourages the children to build some larger ramps. Ryder, Jd, and Alina work together to lean one end of a plank against a tree stump. They then proceed to fill one of the large toy trucks with gravel and push it up the ramp. As they do this, the truck topples over.

Jd: This is really hard!

The children turn the truck over and fill it again. They keep pushing it up the ramp until they manage to get it to the top. They are excited and tired from their hard work but can't wait to test the ramp. Alina pushes the truck, and the three of them watch as it rolls down the ramp.

Ryder (excited): The gravel did not spill!

Alina: No, it stayed in the truck! Let's do it again.

The teachers know that this hard work will continue, so they plan to research different possibilities to build ramps both indoors and outdoors. They realize that through this play, the children will acquire a large amount of information on the effects of gravity, inertia, and speed.

Your Turn

Making Theories Visible in Play

After reading the story, reflect on how theory informed the decisions the teachers made. Which theories do you see in the story? What theory would you use to respond to the children's interest? How would you use the theories covered in this section to create a responsive environment that increases children's knowledge?

Going Deeper: Questions for Your Reflection

Now that you have reflected on the story above, use your knowledge of the theories to think about how you can use theory to expand the learning of the children in your care.

1. Think about a child who you know well. How does Piaget's theory clarify your understanding of this child's physical growth? What about the other theories?

2. How do you cultivate children's physical development while supporting their cognitive and social development? What might Piaget say about this? What about Vygotsky or Dewey?

3. Reflect on your own tolerance for risk taking. How might your personal comfort level with risk taking and your concern for children's safety affect the way you encourage risk taking in children?

4. Consider how Maslow's hierarchy of needs and Erikson's psychosocial stages address children's physical development. How are the theories similar? How are they different?

5. Reflect upon the physical activities that you participate in within your community. What can you do to promote physical development as a way for children and families to connect with their community?

6. Think of your own intelligences and the ones that you prefer to use. How can you use this information to support intelligences in children and their physical development?

7. How were you influenced by others' attitudes about gender behavior growing up? What messages did you receive about gender behavior? What can you do to encourage both boys and girls to participate in non-gendered physical play?

Part 5

Changing the Assumptions of Early Care and Education: How the Theories Give Us a Voice to Initiate Change

The journey of learning about child development theories starts by gaining an overall understanding of each theorist and his or her beliefs. This specialized body of knowledge provides a foundational framework that informs teaching. Your ability to see theory in action is strengthened when you have a solid foundation of child development, as you know what behaviors to look for. It is exciting and inspiring to actually see children develop, reflect upon their behavior, decide how to support their learning, and prepare intriguing environments that engage them in learning.

Each theory provides us with insight into how children grow and learn. Piaget's research offers us an understanding of how children's thinking abilities emerge as they construct and adapt their understanding of the world around them. From Erikson we learn how development proceeds in terms of psychosocial stages where children master specific tasks in order to achieve success at later stages of development. Vygotsky's theory tells us about the significance of social-mediated context on children's development. We learn from Maslow's hierarchy of needs that the potential for human growth exists throughout life and is guided by important physiological, safety, love and belonging, esteem, and self-actualization needs. Dewey's educational philosophy helps us recognize that children acquire knowledge through direct practical experience in a meaningful, reflective environment and community. Gardner's MI theory helps us understand that individuals have different ways of perceiving and understanding the world that allow them to identify and resolve problems. From Derman-Sparks we glean that children's knowledge and understanding are best constructed through bias-free social interactions with adults and peers. We encourage educators to use the key components of each theory's different perspective as a way to guide their work with children and support children's whole development.

We want to encourage you as an early care and education professional to better understand children. We hope that this text ignites your eagerness, enthusiasm, and interest to learn about children and develop a commitment to establish positive interactions with them. We want you to be an enthusiastic learner and willing to add to your own knowledge as you learn along with the children. We want you to be a reflective practitioner and transform your teaching into a more holistic approach of creating meaning. In other words, children learn content as they engage in exploration of a well-provisioned environment and under the support of caring and thoughtful adults.

Making Theories Visible for Yourself

The challenges that early childhood educators encounter can be combated by having a solid understanding of child development theory and putting early learning theories into practice, particularly when it comes to designing early childhood environments and responding to children. As educators, we can respond in ways that will strengthen children's learning and understanding.

Understanding Theories

Knowing how children develop and learn is the first step in supporting children. We encourage you to continue to learn about child development through reading, attending conferences, taking courses, observing children, and participating in discussions. Child development journals, textbooks, and newspaper and research articles are all excellent resources. Your learning will be further extended by asking questions about aspects of children's development that interest you and then researching the answers. Taking college courses and attending conferences, lectures, and in-service trainings can be a challenging and inspiring way to grow professionally. Watching children at play is key to learning: observing and listening to children helps identify what they are thinking, learning, and feeling. Engaging in discussions with classmates, educators, mentors, and professors will help you gain a better understanding of children and deepen your knowledge. As you do all of these things, you will gain a rich, solid understanding of early learning theory.

Watch, Look, and Listen

As you develop a strong understanding of these theories, practice identifying development in children based on theory. As your knowledge of child development grows, so will your ability to identify children's behavior, needs, and interests. Competence in this area develops through careful observation, building relationships with children, and engaging with mentors. Watching a child's body language and facial expressions and listening to his language offers valuable information. As you listen with genuine interest to children and respond with respect to their ideas, you build relationships that will allow you to learn more about each child. Have and build conversations with children's family members as well. You will increase your awareness of behavior by making observation an essential part of your teaching. A mentor can also be an extremely helpful observer and guide. Mentors can point out specific theories in action, explain behavior, and discuss questions and difficulties. This sets the stage for the next step of practical application.

Putting It into Practice

You've moved from learning theory to observing theory. Now it's time to begin applying theory. The final step on the learning continuum involves responding to children in a way that thoughtfully scaffolds their learning and development based on theory. This is the hardest step in many ways. As an educator, you must continually question what, why, and how you do things. With experience you will begin to recognize children's behavior and know how best to take action. This may mean listening and responding, changing the environment, helping with negotiation, or just observing and waiting. Know that at first, a lot of trial and error is necessary as you acquire competence. You may assess a situation incorrectly or respond in a way that is not helpful. The important thing is to reflect upon the child's behavior and your response. Reflective thinking is a vital component of this stage and includes your ability to reflect, evaluate, analyze, and question. A mentor can be particularly helpful during this stage in listening to your feelings of inadequacy or uncertainty as well as your positive feelings and reflections. A mentor will offer guidance and continuing support in understanding children. Remember that your understanding of child development theory will deepen as you learn to observe children, be more in tune with their needs, and reflect—a continuous cycle of learning and growth.

Making Theories Visible in the Classroom

Making Learning Meaningful

As you grow in your understanding of the theories, use your knowledge to interpret and support children's play. Provide learning experiences and environments that engage children and are responsive to their needs and development. Experiences that value play are developmentally appropriate—they are active, satisfying, worthwhile, meaningful, and imaginative and involve a learning-centered educational philosophy. Use your solid understanding of child development theory to articulate to administrators and policy makers how children learn and develop and why preset curriculum is harmful to children's future success. Advocate for learning that is best for children. Standards do not dictate how outcomes must be met, so identify play-based ways for children to construct knowledge based on the work of the theorists.

Designing Your Environment

The theories examined in this book offer a model to teachers for designing learning environments and helping them provision spaces and materials. Your classroom learning environment should have an abundance of materials and experiences for children to explore. Materials that can be transformed or transported, or ones used for pretending, creating, or constructing will promote a child's ability to problem solve, think critically, and use his imagination. Use the theories as a framework to design environments that promote the social-emotional well-being of children and that let children know they belong and are valued. Set up provocative indoor and outdoor spaces to help children develop important cognitive skills and conduct investigations based on their interests rather than imposing a teacher-directed curriculum. Design environments that include materials, equipment, and spaces that support large- and small-motor skills, risk taking, body awareness, and healthy bodies.

Teaching Methodology

Incorporate teaching methods that are based on early learning theory and allow children to actively engage in meaningful investigations. Facilitate learning that is active, engaging, and builds on children's existing knowledge. This type of learning allows children to achieve optimum development in every developmental domain. Use your knowledge of child development theory as a crucial ingredient in building safe, trusting, and responsive interactions with young children. Apply early learning theory to meet children's basic needs, encourage their autonomy and initiative, support their culture, and empower them to take action against unfair behavior and stand up for what is right.

Crystal's Story: An Educator's Journey

This book includes many stories about the children who attend Crystal's Creative Kids early care and education program. As educators and professors of early childhood education, we have seen Crystal's growth in acquiring a deeper knowledge of the child development theories. We asked Crystal to share her story to inspire you to further your understanding of early learning theories and see how such knowledge can impact your teaching. More importantly, Crystal's story demonstrates how knowing ECE theories has helped her move from a teacher-directed pedagogical approach to creating a responsive environment where children can happily explore, grow, and learn. Her deep understanding of child development theories has also impacted who she is, both professionally and as a mentor.

~~~~~~

In My Own Voice:
A Story of Learning and Growth

How the Child Development Theories Helped Me Grow as an Early Care and Education Professional

by Crystal Devlin, MA

My journey with early childhood education theories started when I was unable to find safe, quality child care for my children. When I returned to work after having my second child, I needed child care. I had no family nearby that could assist me in the care of my children and few friends, as I had only lived in my new community for a short time. Without prior experience in seeking care and no knowledge of what indicated a quality program, I placed my children in the first program I toured, a family child care home.

At first, things seemed okay. My children were happy and clean when I came to pick them up, and they were happy when I dropped them off in the mornings. As time went on, I began to notice odd occurrences. I would arrive to drop them off and would have to bang on the windows to wake the provider. Once, I arrived to pick them up and discovered a five-year-old changing my infant daughter's diaper. The final straw was when I arrived to pick up my children and someone I did not know was there instead of the provider. She informed me that the provider's twelve-year-old daughter had taken the children to the park. I drove to the park and they were not there. I returned to the child care home and a grandparent was there to pick up her grandchild who was also not there. The grandparent mentioned that a few days prior, the provider's daughter had taken the fourteen children to Baskin Robbins, over a mile away. I quickly drove there and found the police, along with the children and the provider's daughter. My son's Head Start teacher had happened to be there and had called the police. She had stayed with the children while waiting for the police to arrive.

Naturally, this was cause for me to immediately remove my children from this person's care. This experience affected me in every way imaginable. I was heart-broken and angry with myself. I felt I had let my children down. The lack of quality child care I found in the home child care my children attended was alarming. It affected me emotionally, as I felt guilty and worried that my children had been neglected, and who knew what else had happened when no one was looking? The next day, I quit my job and began the process of opening my own child care program. It affected me financially for a while, as it was a time-consuming process to become licensed and then enroll families, during which time I had no income. Fortunately, my husband's income was enough for us to barely survive financially.

After I received my child care license, things began looking up. I was able to build a successful business while providing the much-needed service that families and children deserve. Not having any background in the field, I thought that quality was associated with teaching the "ABCs and 1, 2, 3s." I bought different types of curriculum to teach math, reading, and writing to the children. I plastered the wall with the alphabet and focused my attention on children completing "worksheets" and predesigned and precut crafts. I began to attend workshops through our county's Resource and Referral agency in an effort to learn as much as possible that would guide me towards offering a high-quality program. Because of what I had experienced with child care with my own children, I vowed to always do my best, to always seek guidance and support when needed, and to build relationships with families that were based on mutual trust, respect, and appreciation.

One year after opening my program, my husband quit his job in corporate America, took his 401K, and joined me as we expanded the business. This had a profound effect on our family, as we now had the ability for both of us to be at home with our own children. We were more financially stable as our income increased dramatically. I no longer worked alone, so there was a lesser feeling of isolation, and I now had someone to bounce ideas off of and to support me as needed.

I continued to offer what I considered developmental activities that were mostly teacher directed. I expected the children to listen and stay on task. My schedule was rigid, and children moved from one learning activity to the next as directed. The children were happy and the families trusted me and liked the program. I knew there was more I could be doing and that I needed to acquire some knowledge of how children grow and develop. I decided to further my education and training in the early care and education field and began to attend classes at the local community college to earn a degree in early childhood education.

I started college for the first time in 2005 while working full-time. I completed my homework during naptimes and my reading in the evenings after work. Although my studies were challenging and kept me very busy, I took pleasure in all that I was doing and learning. I began to implement my newfound knowledge about the science of child development, theories, and developmentally appropriate practice into my program.

This experience affected me and my work with children. Prior to beginning college, and unbeknownst to me, my program was lacking quality. Because my program was highly successful in terms of enrollment and profit, I thought I was doing very well. Where I thought I had been providing children with a solid foundation, I had actually been teaching children in ways that were not developmentally appropriate or based on the scientific research of child development theorists. My new knowledge of early learning theories and education led me to make significant changes to my program, both in how I worked with children and in the physical environment that I created. I no longer expected children to complete worksheets and stopped using the math and language curriculum I had purchased. Instead I engaged them in exploring experiences that I intentionally developed and implemented in response to the children's interests. My vision of the child had changed completely and my vision as a teacher had gone from the "holder of the knowledge" to colearner along with the children.

I learned that when I think I know all I need to know, it is time to seek new knowledge. I learned that it is important to have a strong philosophical and

theoretical foundation, to always reflect on my work and professional growth, and to be intentional in the way I set environments and respond to children.

The theories inform the way I design my environment and support children's learning. I am now intentional in the materials and tools I select. I have come to recognize the importance of trusting myself, my colleagues, and, most importantly, the children. I closely follow Derman-Sparks's anti-bias education. I am thoughtful not to introduce stereotypes and biases and spend time integrating the values and principles into every aspect of the program. For example, I removed commercial pictures of stereotypical families that were on the classroom walls and replaced them with real photos of the children and their families who attend my program. I also took away books from my library that contained biased messages and added books that address diversity in families, gender roles, and disabilities. I've done similar work in my program based on other theorists. Piaget's theory of active learning is evident in my program as I eliminated teacher-directed worksheets and replaced them with open-ended loose parts of rocks and wood scraps for the children to explore. I created an art studio that includes open-ended materials such as clay, goop, and watercolors, inspired by Maslow's emphasis on children's creativity and sense of belonging through art. Art has become a central part of our daily routines and experiences. Along with that, based on Erikson's concept of initiative, I switched the way I do art with children. There are no longer precut shapes, and the children express their initiative through the many languages that visual arts offer them by independently selecting their own art materials off the shelves and creating as they desire.

Because of what I've learned, I respond to children differently: I now know that behind every behavior there is a motivation and that children don't act out just to challenge adults. I am able to guide children more appropriately because I understand who they are and the theory behind their behavior. For example, one day Colter took a toy car off a nearby toy shelf, dipped it into paint, made paint-covered car tracks on the table, and then expressed displeasure that there was paint on the car. In the past, I would have identified this act as misbehavior and rebuked his actions, as the children were painting with brushes. Now I understand that he was asserting his autonomy (as Erikson says) and learning how objects work (as Piaget believes). To support Colter, I simply placed a tub of warm soapy water and a washcloth on the table for him to clean the car and the table.

I have learned to allow children to explore and manipulate their environment and only intervene when safety issues arise or when needed to facilitate play. Risk taking is now an important part of our program since we believe that children get to know who they are and recognize their own abilities when they engage in boisterous and large physical play. The children in my program usually get along and are caring and helpful to each other. However, there was a moment one day when several children started arguing about everything and were screaming the typical "I am not your friend!" My first instinct was to stop the behavior and separate the children; but in this particular instance, I offered the children rolled paper swords and allowed them time to sword fence with each other. After a while, they ended up lying on the floor, tired from the physical work. After the sword fencing, the children went back to spending more time together and caring and supporting each other.

Jason and I have become keen observers of child development theory and regularly involve practicum students in reflection and conversations to identify how early learning theories support children's growth and development. Through this reflective practice, I have seen the practicum students who are placed in my program grow in understanding and knowledge about the theories and how they inform our practices. During my journey, I learned that continuous growth and development are very important. I have now completed my master's program and I am looking forward to continuing to mentor students and making the theories visible to them and others in the field.

~~~~~~

Final Words

You are on your way to a deep, rich understanding of child development theory. As you grow, perhaps recognizing theory in children's play will begin to happen automatically. This foundational framework provides new insight of children as capable, competent, curious, creative, and protagonists of their own knowledge. You have seen how watching learning unfold is intrinsically motivating, as is reflecting upon how to support children's interests and needs. It's exciting to witness children's enthusiasm and delight as they make discoveries.

We challenge you to persist in your conviction of how children learn through play, and advocate and stand firm for what is right for children. Start by changing your own classroom environment to reflect theory and commit to providing relevant and meaningful interactions and experiences for children based upon your newfound knowledge. Help educate families, policy makers, administrators, and colleagues about how children learn and grow, and speak up if you are faced with decisions that are not in the best interest of children. Our vision for you is one of hope and promise as you use the theories to make changes in your and your children's world.

References

Bodrova, Elena, and Deborah J. Leong. 2007. *Tools of the Mind: The Vygotskian Approach to Early Childhood Education*. Upper Saddle River, NJ: Pearson.

Derman-Sparks, Louise, and Julie Olsen Edwards. 2010. *Anti-Bias Education for Young Children and Ourselves*. Washington, DC: National Association for the Education of Young Children.

Dewey, John. 1938. *Experience and Education*. New York: Kappa Delta Pi.

———. 1975. *Interest and Effort in Education*. Edwardsville: Southern Illinois Press.

———. 1990. *The School and Society and the Child and the Curriculum*. Chicago: Centennial Publication of the University of Chicago Press.

———. 1997. *Experience and Nature*. Peru, IL: Open Court Publishing.

———. 1998. *How We Think: A Restatement of the Relation of Reflective Thinking to the Education Process*. Boston: Houghton Mifflin. First published 1933 John Dewey.

———. 2008. *Democracy and Education*. Redford, VA: Wilder Publications.

Erikson, Erik H. 1963. *Childhood and Society*. 2nd ed. New York: Norton.

Gardner, Howard. 1999. *Intelligence Reframed: Multiple Intelligences for the 21st Century*. New York: Basic Books.

———. 2006. *Multiple Intelligences: New Horizons in Theory and Practice*. New York: Basic Books.

———. 2011 a. *Frames of Mind: The Theory of Multiple Intelligences*. New York: Basic Books.

———. 2011 b. *The Unschooled Mind*. New York: Basic Books.

Maslow, Abraham H. 1971. *The Farther Reaches of Human Nature*. New York: Viking Press.

———. 1987. *Motivation and Personality*. New York: Addison-Wesley Educational Publishers Inc.

———. 1999. *Toward a Psychology of Being*. 3rd ed. New York: Wiley and Sons.

Piaget, Jean. 1952. *The Origin of Intelligence in the Child*. Translated by Margaret Cook. London: Routledge.

———. 1965. *The Moral Judgment of the Child*. London: Free Press.

———. 1972. *To Understand Is to Invent: The Future of Education*. New York: Viking Press.

———. 1976. *The Child & Reality*. New York: Penguin Books.

———. 1981. *Intelligence and Affectivity: Their Relation during Child Development*. Palo Alto, CA: Annual Reviews.

Uprichard, Emma. 2008. "Children as 'Being and Becomings': Children, Childhood and Temporality." *Children and Society* 22 (4): 303–313. University of New York, York, UK. Department of Sociology.

Vygotsky, L. S. 1978. *Mind in Society: The Development of Higher Psychological Processes*. Eds. V. John-Steiner Cole, S. Scribner, and E. Souberman. Cambridge, MA: Harvard University Press.

Index

225